MATH SKILLS BY OBJECTIVES

BOOK ONE

This book is derived from an instructional program created by the
American Preparatory Institute
Central Texas College, Killeen

CAMBRIDGE Adult Education
Prentice Hall Regents, Englewood Cliffs, NJ 07632

Cambridge gratefully acknowledges the advice and contributions of the following adult educators who reviewed the draft version of this book.

Donna Amstutz, Chicago Urban Skills Institute, Chicago, Illinois.

Janet Moore, Coordinator, A.B.E. Section, Birmingham City Schools, Birmingham, Alabama.

Nancy Sullivan, Jersey City Learning Center, Jersey City, New Jersey.

Editor: E. Mildred Speiser
New York City Board of Education
E.C.I.A. Chapter I–Corrective Mathematics
Production Manager: Arthur Michalez
Managing Editor: Eileen Guerrin

Acknowledgements: Diana Jacobs and Robert Geno

Published by Prentice-Hall, Inc.
A Division of Simon & Schuster
Englewood Cliffs, New Jersey 07632

Printed in the United States of America

10 9 8 7 6 5

ISBN 0-8428-0200-2

Prentice-Hall International (UK) Limited, *London*
Prentice-Hall of Australia Pty. Limited, *Sydney*
Prentice-Hall Canada Inc., *Toronto*
Prentice-Hall Hispanoamericana, S.A., *Mexico*
Prentice-Hall of India Private Limited, *New Delhi*
Prentice-Hall of Japan, Inc., *Tokyo*
Simon & Schuster Asia Pte. Ltd., *Singapore*
Editora Prentice-Hall do Brasil, Ltda., *Rio de Janeiro*

CONTENTS

TO THE STUDENT

MATH SKILLS BY OBJECTIVES, BOOK ONE teaches you the basics of math. Since nothing is assumed in this book, you get a review that is as thorough and effective as possible. You begin by *reading* and *writing numbers,* and then step by step, work through the *basic operations* (ADDING, SUBTRACTING, MULTIPLYING, DIVIDING) *with whole numbers, fractions,* and *decimals*. Completing this text will also enable you to find *ratios* and *proportions* and to work with *percents*.

The title of this book, MATH SKILLS BY OBJECTIVES, BOOK ONE, means that this is the first book in a three-book, specially designed program. What is special about this program? Here, unlike some math books you may have used in the past, the material to be learned is broken into smaller "objectives" or goals for you to accomplish. The program in Book One consists of a Pretest, 13 Skill Units, and a Posttest.

Here's how the program works:

Pretest—Take the Pretest to find out what math skills you need to work on. Don't worry about the problems you don't know how to solve. This book will help you learn how to do them. Check your answers in the separate Answer Key for Book One and then turn to the Chart on pages xiv–xv in the text. The following example will show you how to use the Correlation Chart.

	IF YOU MISSED ↓		STUDY ↓	FOUND ON ↓
	QUESTION NUMBER	SUBSKILL NUMBER	SUBSKILL NAME	PAGE NUMBERS
Skill Unit One Reading and Writing Numbers	1	1A	Writing Whole Numbers	pages 1–11
	2	1A	Writing Whole Numbers	pages 1–11
	3	1B	Comparing Numbers	pages 11–15
	4	1C	Rounding Numbers Off	pages 15–19

Skill Units—Each chapter of the book, or Skill Unit is divided into smaller units of learning called "Subskills." Since each Subskill focuses on a specific part of a math problem, it allows you to learn one bit of information at a time. You will always know what you are to learn and how you will learn it. Each Subskill begins with an objective explaining what activity you will be able to perform after you finish the Subskill. This is followed by a lesson that contains <u>Examples</u> to show you exactly what happens at every stage of working out a problem. Then there is an <u>Exercise</u> for you to complete to see how well you understand the subskill.

If you need additional practice, you may then complete the optional Supplemental Exercise. You can use these exercises for review at any time. At the end of each Skill Unit is a Self-Check, showing you all that you have learned in the chapter.

Posttest—Take the Posttest to review your performance in all the skills in MATH SKILLS BY OBJECTIVES, BOOK ONE. Then use the Chart on pages 282–283, which is similar to the Correlation Chart for the Pretest, to help you assess your achievement in this book.

With this approach, you can build strong math skills. Take the time to work through this book. You will make progress and the proof will be in your mastery of essential math.

MATH SKILLS BY OBJECTIVES

BOOK ONE

PRETEST

This test is designed to identify your mathematical strengths and weaknesses. It will help you find out which parts of this book you should study. Each section of this test covers a Skill Unit in this book. You should try to answer all questions. If you don't know how to work a problem, skip it and come back to it later. When you have finished, check your answers in the separate Answer Key for Book One.

Skill Unit 1

1. Write this number in numerals:
two hundred three thousand, eight hundred ninety

2. Write 1,004,219 in words.

3. Which number is larger: 360 or 306?

4. Round 4,363 to the nearest hundred.

Skill Unit 2

5. 4 + 9 =

6. 11 + 72 =

7.
$$\begin{array}{r} 12 \\ 52 \\ +23 \\ \hline \end{array}$$

8.
$$\begin{array}{r} 1{,}296 \\ +\ \ 834 \\ \hline \end{array}$$

Skill Unit 3

9. Marie bought a pair of shoes for $63, a scarf for $18, and a pair of pants for $80. How much did she spend altogether?

10. 14 − 9 =

11. $\begin{array}{r} 964 \\ -\ 151 \\ \hline \end{array}$ **12.** $\begin{array}{r} 1{,}029 \\ -\ \ 633 \\ \hline \end{array}$

13. A science-fiction novel has 156 pages. Henry has already read 75 pages. How many more does he have to read?

Skill Unit 4

14. $7 \times 8 =$

15. $\begin{array}{r} 23 \\ \times\ 3 \\ \hline \end{array}$ **16.** $\begin{array}{r} 84 \\ \times 12 \\ \hline \end{array}$ **17.** $\begin{array}{r} 143 \\ \times 243 \\ \hline \end{array}$

18. Louise has four boxes of light bulbs. Each box contains 24 bulbs. How many light bulbs does she have?

Skill Unit 5

19. $48 \div 8 =$

20. $6\overline{)\,456}$

21. $25\overline{)\,7550}$

22. $112\overline{)\,3696}$

23. A farmer has 172 chickens divided evenly into 13 pens. How many chickens are in each pen?

Skill Unit 6

24. $\frac{5}{6} = \frac{?}{18}$

25. Reduce $\frac{18}{24}$ to its lowest terms.

26. What is the lowest common denominator of $\frac{4}{9}$ and $\frac{5}{6}$?

27. Which is bigger: $\frac{3}{4}$ or $\frac{13}{16}$?

28. Change $3\frac{4}{5}$ to an improper fraction.

29. Change $\frac{23}{3}$ to a mixed number.

Skill Unit 7

30. $\frac{5}{11} + \frac{3}{11}$

31. $\frac{2}{9} + \frac{1}{3}$

32. $\frac{10}{13} - \frac{6}{13}$

33. $\frac{3}{4} - \frac{2}{5}$

34. $2\frac{1}{6} - \frac{5}{6}$

35. Henry is $6\frac{1}{4}$ feet tall. Suzanne is $5\frac{1}{2}$ feet tall. How much taller is Henry?

Skill Unit 8

36. $\frac{2}{3} \times \frac{4}{9} =$

37. $\frac{6}{11} \times 5$

38. $1\frac{1}{3} \times 3\frac{3}{4}$

39. $\frac{5}{6} \div \frac{1}{2}$

40. $\frac{3}{4} \div 2\frac{1}{9}$

41. A fence is made out of 12 boards, each measuring $3\frac{1}{4}$ inches. How long is the fence?

Skill Unit 9

42. Write twenty three thousandths in decimals.

43. Which is larger: 1.033 or 1.3?

44. Round off 2.496 to the nearest tenth.

45. 0.247 + 0.891 =

46. 2.913 − 1.672 =

47. Doug is riding in a 15-kilometer bicycle race. He has ridden 9.65 miles. How much farther does he have to ride?

Skill Unit 10

48. 34.72×1.33

49. $1.44 \div 1.2$

50. Robert has run 5.5 times around a track measuring .75 miles. How far has he run?

Skill Unit 11

51. A school has 300 students and 24 teachers. What is the ratio of students to teachers?

52. $\frac{20}{16} = \frac{?}{12}$

53. 2 ounces of gold costs $672. How much does 5 ounces cost?

Skill Unit 12

54. $\frac{93}{100} = \_\_\_\%$

55. Write 67% as a decimal.

56. Write 2.31 as a percent.

57. Write 75% as a fraction.

58. $\frac{7}{16} = \_\_\_\%$

Skill Unit 13

59. ____ = 15% of 40

60. 12 = ____% of 60

61. 25 = 60% of ____

62. You have $900 in a bank account that pays 6.5% yearly simple interest. How much interest would you earn in one year?

Skills Correlation Chart for Pretest

After you check your answers, look at the following chart. Circle the numbers of any problems you missed. Then review the subskill in which the skills for the problem you missed are explained.

	QUESTION NO.	SUBSKILL NO.	SUBSKILL NAME	PAGE NUMBERS
Skill Unit One Reading and Writing Numbers	1	1A	Writing Whole Numbers	pages 1–11
	2	1A	Writing Whole Numbers	pages 1–11
	3	1B	Comparing Numbers	pages 11–15
	4	1C	Rounding Numbers Off	pages 15–19
Skill Unit Two Adding Whole Numbers	5	2A	Adding One-Digit Numbers	pages 21–24
	6	2B	Adding Two-Digit Numbers Without Carrying	pages 24–27
	7	2C	Adding Three or More Numbers	pages 27–29
	8	2D	Adding Numbers With Carrying	pages 30–33
	9	2E	Solving Word Problems	pages 33–36
Skill Unit Three Subtracting Whole Numbers	10	3A	Subtracting One- and Two-Digit Numbers	pages 37–44
	11	3B	Subtracting Without Borrowing	pages 42–44
	12	3C	Subtracting With Borrowing	pages 44–49
	13	3D	Solving Word Problems	pages 50–52
Skill Unit Four Multiplying Whole Numbers	14	4A	Using the Multiplication Table	pages 54–58
	15	4B	Multiplying by One-Digit Numbers	pages 58–62
	16	4C	Multiplying by a Two-Digit Number	pages 62–66
	17	4D	Multiplying by Three Digit Numbers	pages 66–71
	18	4E	Solving Word Problems	pages 71–73
Skill Unit Five Dividing Whole Numbers	19	5A	Understanding Division	pages 75–80
	20	5B	Dividing by One-Digit Numbers	pages 80–89
	21	5C	Dividing by Two-Digit Numbers	pages 89–93
	22	5D	Dividing Larger Numbers	pages 94–97
	23	5E	Solving Word Problems	pages 97–101
Skill Unit Six Fractions	24	6B	Equivalent Fractions	pages 107–111
	25	6C	Reducing a Fraction to Its Lowest Terms	pages 111–114
	26	6D	Finding the Least Common Denominator	pages 114–123
	27	6E	Telling Larger Fractions From Smaller Ones	pages 123–127
	28	6F	Changing Improper Fractions to Mixed Numbers	pages 128–133
	29	6F	Changing Improper Fractions to Mixed Numbers	pages 128–133
Skill Unit Seven Adding and Subtracting Fractions	30	7A	Adding Like Fractions	pages 135–140
	31	7B	Adding Unlike Fractions	pages 140–145
	32	7C	Subtracting Like Fractions	pages 145–148
	33	7D	Subtracting Unlike Fractions	pages 148–158
	34	7E	Borrowing	pages 151–158
	35	7F	Solving Word Problems	pages 158–162
Skill Unit Eight Multiplying and Dividing Fractions	36	8A	Multiplying a Fraction by a Fraction	pages 164–171
	37	8B	Multiplying a Fraction by a Whole Number	pages 171–175
	38	8C	Multiplying Mixed Numbers	pages 175–179
	39	8D	Dividing Fractions	pages 179–182
	40	8E	Dividing Fractions, Whole Numbers and Mixed Numbers	pages 182–186
	41	8F	Solving Word Problems	pages 186–189

	QUESTION NO.	SUBSKILL NO.	SUBSKILL NAME	PAGE NUMBERS
Skill Unit Nine — Adding and Subtracting Decimals	42	9A	Reading and Writing Decimals	pages 191–199
	43	9B	Telling Higher Decimals from Lower Ones	pages 199–203
	44	9C	Rounding Off Decimals	pages 203–206
	45	9D	Adding Decimals	pages 206–209
	46	9E	Subtracting Decimals	pages 209–211
	47	9F	Solving Word Problems	pages 211–214
Skill Unit Ten — Multiplying and Dividing Decimals	48	10A	Multiplying Decimals	pages 216–219
	49	10B	Dividing Decimals	pages 219–225
	50	10C	Solving Word Problems	pages 225–228
Skill Unit Eleven — Ratio & and Proportion	51	11A	Reading Ratios	pages 229–233
	52	11B	Solving Proportions	pages 233–238
	53	11C	Solving Word Problems	pages 238–242
Skill Unit Twelve — Percents	54	12A	Reading and Writing Percents	pages 243–247
	55	12B	Changing Percents to Decimals	pages 247–249
	56	12C	Changing Decimals to Percents	pages 249–252
	57	12D	Changing Percents to Fractions	pages 252–256
	58	12E	Changing Fractions to Percents	pages 256–259
Skill Unit Thirteen — Solving Percent Problems	59	13A	Finding What Number Is a Certain Percent of Another Number	pages 261–265
	60	13B	Finding What Percent One Number Is of Another	pages 266–269
	61	13C	Finding an Unknown Number When Another Number Is a Certain Percent of It	pages 269–272
	62	13D	Figuring Interest	pages 272–275

Skill Unit 1
READING AND WRITING NUMBERS

What Skills You Need to Begin: None.

What Skills You Will Learn: After studying this skill unit, you will be able to read and write numbers and identify place values. You will be able to compare numbers and put them in order, and you will be able to round numbers.

Why You Need These Skills: This book will help you improve your skills in working with numbers. You will learn how to add, subtract, multiply, and divide whole numbers and decimals. To perform these skills, however, you must be able to read and write numbers.

How You Will Show What You Have Learned: At the end of this skill unit is a Self-Check consisting of ten problems in reading, writing, comparing, and rounding numbers. You should allow yourself thirty minutes to complete the Self-Check. To prove that you have mastered these skills, you must correctly answer eight of the ten problems.

If you feel that you have already mastered reading and writing numbers, complete the Self-Check on pages 19 and 20.

Subskill 1A: Writing Whole Numbers

Studying this subskill will enable you to read and write whole numbers.

We have ten numerals for writing numbers. They are 0, 1, 2, 3, 4, 5, 6, 7, 8, and 9. Another way of writing numbers is to spell them out. That is, we can write the number in words instead of numerals—"zero" instead of 0, "one" instead of 1, "two" instead of 2, and so on. If we want to, we can also represent a number by drawing a picture of it.

Numerals	Words	Dots
0	zero	
1	one	·
2	two	· ·
3	three	· · ·
4	four	· · · ·
5	five	· · · · ·
6	six	· · · · · ·
7	seven	· · · · · · ·
8	eight	· · · · · · · ·
9	nine	· · · · · · · · ·

Now we have used up all our numerals, and we have only counted up to nine. How can we write higher numbers in numerals? By combining the numerals according to a regular system.

10 ten (· · · · · · · · · ·)

Perhaps because we have ten fingers on both hands, our number system is based on groups of ten. It is called the **decimal system.**

We need two numerals, 1 and 0, to write 10. These two numerals take up two places, a place for the 1 and a place for the 0. The place occupied by a numeral is very important. Different places have different values. The place on the right is the "ones" place. The place just to the left of it is the "tens" place.

When we write 10, we put the 1 in the tens place to show that there is one group of ten. And we put the 0 in the ones place to show that there are no ones in this number.

1	0
tens	ones

To get the next higher number, add one dot to the group of ten.

11 eleven (· · · · · · · · · ·)
·

Two dots added to a group of ten will mean a group of ten plus two ones.

12 twelve (· · · · · · · · · ·)
· ·

Written in numerals, 12 has a 1 in the tens place to show that there is one group of ten and a 2 in the ones place to show that there are two ones in this number.

Here is how we write the next numbers that have a 1 in the tens place. You can see why these numbers are called the "teens."

13 thirteen (· · · · · · · · · ·)
· · ·

14 fourteen (· · · · · · · · · ·)
· · · ·

15 fifteen (· · · · · · · · · ·)
· · · · ·

16 sixteen (· · · · · · · · · ·)
· · · · · ·

17 seventeen (· · · · · · · · · ·)
· · · · · · ·

18 eighteen (· · · · · · · · · ·)
· · · · · · · ·

19 nineteen (· · · · · · · · · ·)
· · · · · · · · ·

Make sure you can spell these words correctly.

When we reach 19, we have once again used up all our numerals in the ones places. How can we write the number that comes next? By putting a 2 in the tens place to show that we now have two groups of ten.

20	twenty	(· · · · · · · · · ·) (· · · · · · · · · ·)

Like 10, the number 20 has a 0 in the ones place to show that there are no ones in it.

The next number is

21	twenty-one

Then come

22	twenty-two
23	twenty-three
24	twenty-four
25	twenty-five
26	twenty-six
27	twenty-seven
28	twenty-eight
29	twenty-nine

How can we write the number that comes next? By putting a 3 in the tens place and starting over with a 0 in the ones place.

30	thirty

We use the same system to write numbers up to 99.

		40	forty
31	thirty-one	41	forty-one
32	thirty-two	42	forty-two
33	thirty-three	43	forty-three
34	thirty-four	44	forty-four
35	thirty-five	45	forty-five
36	thirty-six	46	forty-six
37	thirty-seven	47	forty-seven
38	thirty-eight	48	forty-eight
39	thirty-nine	49	forty-nine

50	fifty	75	seventy-five
51	fifty-one	76	seventy-six
52	fifty-two	77	seventy-seven
53	fifty-three	78	seventy-eight
54	fifty-four	79	seventy-nine
55	fifty-five	80	eighty
56	fifty-six	81	eighty-one
57	fifty-seven	82	eighty-two
58	fifty-eight	83	eighty-three
59	fifty-nine	84	eighty-four
60	sixty	85	eighty-five
61	sixty-one	86	eighty-six
62	sixty-two	87	eighty-seven
63	sixty-three	88	eighty-eight
64	sixty-four	89	eighty-nine
65	sixty-five	90	ninety
66	sixty-six	91	ninety-one
67	sixty-seven	92	ninety-two
68	sixty-eight	93	ninety-three
69	sixty-nine	94	ninety-four
70	seventy	95	ninety-five
71	seventy-one	96	ninety-six
72	seventy-two	97	ninety-seven
73	seventy-three	98	ninety-eight
74	seventy-four	99	ninety-nine

In spelling these words, note that most of them from twenty-one to ninety-nine have a hyphen.

Reading and Writing Larger Numbers

What number comes after ninety-nine? One hundred. How can we write one hundred in numerals? When we reached 99, we used up all our numerals in the ones place *and* in the tens place. To write numbers above 99, we need another place. This place is called the "hundreds" place.

100 one hundred

The number 100 has a 1 in the hundreds place to show that there is one group of hundreds, a 0 in the tens place to show that there are no tens, and a 0 in the ones place to show that there are no ones in this number.

The numbers that follow 100 are

101	one hundred one
102	one hundred two
103	one hundred three
104	one hundred four
105	one hundred five
106	one hundred six
107	one hundred seven
108	one hundred eight
109	one hundred nine

The 0 in the middle is a place holder to show that there are no tens. For example, 101 means one hundred, no tens, and one one. The number 11 is different. It only has two places, a tens place and a ones place. It means that there is one group of tens plus one one.

The next number is

110 one hundred ten

Note the 1 in the middle. It means that this number has one group of tens.

Can you write all the numbers from 110 to 199 in numerals and words? Here is a sample to help you with the spelling.

137 one hundred thirty-seven

↑ ↑ ↑

no hyphens hyphen

What number comes after 199? The answer is 200. We put a 2 in the hundreds place to show that this number has two groups of hundreds.

200 two hundred

Place Values

To write the number that comes after 999, we need another place.

1,000 one thousand

Now we have four places: the "thousands" place, the hundreds place, the tens place, and the ones place. Look at some of the other numbers that have four places.

1,001	one thousand one
1,010	one thousand ten
1,011	one thousand eleven
1,100	one thousand one hundred
1,110	one thousand one hundred ten
1,111	one thousand one hundred eleven
9,999	nine thousand nine hundred ninety-nine

As we write larger and larger numbers, we need more and more places.

After 9,999 comes 10,000 (ten thousand).

After 99,999 comes 100,000 (one hundred thousand).

After 999,999 comes 1,000,000 (one million).

After 9,999,999 comes 10,000,000 (ten million).

After 99,999,999 comes 100,000,000 (one hundred million).

After 999,999,999 comes 1,000,000,000 (one billion).

Here are the values of all the places in 1,000,000,000.

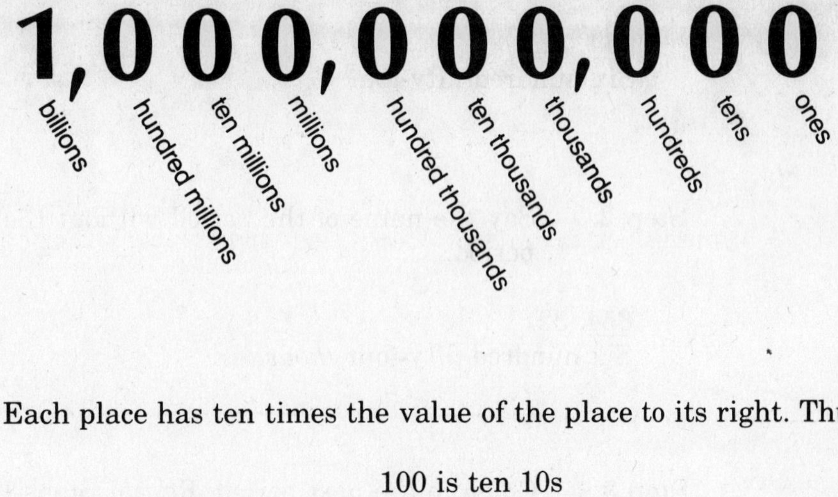

Each place has ten times the value of the place to its right. Thus,

100 is ten 10s

1,000 is ten 100s

10,000 is ten 1,000s

100,000 is ten 10,000s

Commas in Large Numbers

The commas in a large number make it easier to read. They divide the numerals into groups of three. Each group is called a **period.**

places	*hundred* billions	*ten* billions	billions	*hundred* millions	*ten* millions	millions	*hundred* thousands	*ten* thousands	thousands	*hundreds*	*tens*	ones (units)
	1	0	0,	0	0	0,	0	0	0,	0	0	0
periods	billions			millions			thousands			ones		

Reading Large Numbers

Practice reading large numbers by using the chart above and by following the steps below.

EXAMPLE: Read 654, 321 in words.

Step 1: Start at the left and read the numbers to the first comma.

<u>**654**</u>, 321
Six hundred fifty-four

Step 2: Say the name of the period without the s, except the *ones* period.

<u>**654**</u>, 321
Six hundred fifty-four *thousand*

Step 3: Go on to the next period. Repeat Steps 1 and 2.

654, <u>**321**</u>
three hundred twenty-one
NOTE: Do not say the name of the *ones* (units) period.

EXAMPLE: Read 53,497,655 in words.

53,497,655
Fifty-three million

53,**497**,655
four hundred ninety-seven thousand

53,497,**655**
six hundred fifty-five

EXAMPLE: Read 987,654,321 in words

987,654,321
Nine hundred eighty-seven million

987,**654**,321
six hundred fifty-four thousand

987,564,**321**
three hundred twenty-one

Can you read and write numbers of all sizes now? Check your skill by doing this exercise.

Exercise for Subskill 1A

What number follows each of these? Write your answers both in numerals and in words.

1. 31
2. 40
3. 69
4. 299
5. 500

In 5,870,439, what number is in the

6. hundreds place?
7. ten thousands place?
8. thousands place?
9. tens place?
10. millions place?

Write these numbers in numerals.

11. Ten thousand four
12. Fifteen thousand three hundred fifty-five
13. One hundred thousand two hundred three

14. Three hundred seventy-nine thousand
15. Four million eight hundred ninety-nine thousand six hundred twenty-eight

Write these numbers in words.

16. 1,020
17. 29,348
18. 301,103
19. 79,453,000
20. 99,009,009

Check your answers on page 1 in the Answer Key for Book One. If you correctly answered sixteen of twenty items, go to the next subskill. If not, complete the following Supplemental Exercise.

Supplemental Exercise for Subskill 1A

What number follows each of these? Write your answers both in numerals and in words.

1. 65
2. 70
3. 89
4. 599
5. 900

In 27,908,613, what number is in the

6. tens place?
7. thousands place?
8. ten thousands place?
9. hundreds place?
10. ten millions place?

Write these numbers in numerals.

11. Twelve thousand ten
12. Ninety-nine thousand eight hundred seventy-six
13. Five hundred one thousand eight hundred
14. Eight hundred thirty-two thousand
15. Nine million ten thousand fifty-five

Write these numbers in words.

16. 20,007
17. 55,555
18. 909,090

19. 4,012,568
20. 14,483,764

Check your answers on page 1 in the Answer Key for Book One. If you correctly answered sixteen of twenty items, go to the next subskill. If not, ask your instructor for help.

Subskill 1B: Comparing Numbers

Studying this subskill will enable you to tell larger numbers from smaller ones.

You are looking at two used cars. One has 31,729 miles on the odometer, and the other has 38,115. Which car has more miles on it?

To tell which of any two numbers is larger, first count the places in each number. If one number has more places than the other, it is larger.

EXAMPLE: Which is larger, 19,000,000 or 19?
Answer: 19,000,000 is larger, because it has eight places while 19 only has two.

EXAMPLE: Which is larger, 31 or 301?
Answer: 301 is larger, because it has three places while 31 only has two.

EXAMPLE: Which is smaller, 10,212 or 9,899?
Answer: 9,899 is smaller, because it only has four places while 10,212 has five.

If you find that both numbers have the same number of places, look at the first number on the left of each. If one has a larger first number than the other, it is larger.

EXAMPLE: Which is larger 204,053 or 197,968?
Answer: 201,023 is larger, because 2 is larger than 1.

EXAMPLE: Which is smaller, 87 or 90?
Answer: 87 is smaller, because 8 is smaller than 9.

If you find that both numbers have the same number of places and the first number on the left of each is the same, find the next number to the left that is larger. The one that has a larger second number than the other is larger.

EXAMPLE: Which is larger, 5,611,833 or 5,711,833?
Answer: 5,711,833 is larger, because 7 is larger than 6.

EXAMPLE: Which is smaller, 192 or 102?
Answer: 102 is smaller, because 0 is smaller than 9.

Now you can answer the question about the two used cars. The car with 38,115 miles has more miles on it, because the 8 in 38,115 is larger than the 1 in 31,729.

What if you find that both numbers have the same number of places and the first two numbers on the left of each are the same? Look at the third number from the left. If this is also the same, go on to the fourth, and so on, place by place, until you find a place where the two numbers are different.

EXAMPLE: Which is larger, 999,000,001 or 999,000,000?

Answer: 999,000,001 is larger, because the 1 in the last place is larger than 0.

EXAMPLE: Which is larger, 798,615,958 or 798,625,958?
Answer: 798,625,958 is larger, because the 2 in the ten thousands place is larger than 1.

EXAMPLE: Which is smaller, 213,741 or 213,841?

Answer: 213,741 is smaller, because the 7 in the hundreds place is smaller than 8.

EXAMPLE: Which is larger, 571,619 or five hundred seventy-one thousand six hundred nineteen?

Answer: Neither. This is the same number written in two ways, in numerals and in words.

Putting Several Numbers in Order From Largest to Smallest

Here are several numbers:

86 1,550 707 91 899 2,302 708 290

How can you put them in order from largest to smallest?

First count the places in each number. Group the numbers with the same number of places together. Put the group with the most places first, then the group with the next most places, and so on.

1,550 2,302	707 899 708 290	86 91
four places	three places	two places

Take the group with the most places.

1,550 2,302

Look at the first number on the left of each number in this group. If either one has a higher first number than the other, it is larger. Put it first.

2,302 1,550 ___

Now take the group with the next most places.

707 899 708 290

Look at the first number on the left of each number in this group. If any has a higher first number than the others, it is larger. Put it before the others.

899 707 ___ 708 290

This group has one number with an 8 on the left, two numbers with a 7 on the left, and one number with a 2 on the left. As far as the place on the left is concerned, these numbers are now arranged in order from largest to smallest. But are the two numbers that both start with a 7 in the correct order?

707 708

No. These two numbers are the same in the first two places, but different in the last place. Since we are putting them in order from largest to smallest, we must put the larger one before the other.

708 707 ___

Now this group is correctly arranged.

899 708 707 290

We have one more group to look at, the group with the least places.

86 91

Are these two numbers already in correct order? No. Looking at the first number on the left, we see that the 9 in this place is larger than the 8. We must put 91 before 86.

91 86 ___

Finally we have put all the numbers in order from largest to smallest.

2,302 1,550 899 708 707 290 91 86

Check your skill at telling larger numbers from smaller ones by doing this exercise.

Exercise for Subskill 1B

Which number is smaller?

1. 34 or 39
2. 463 or 513
3. 104 or 98
4. 5,450 or 5,451
5. 348 or 319

Which number is larger?

6. 75 or 80
7. 103 or 130
8. 666 or 665
9. 804 or 725
10. 1,987 or 999

Write these numbers from smallest to largest.

11. 12 10 11
12. 101 98 111
13. 456 453 455
14. 997 991 983 989
15. 1,053 984 1,101 768

Write these numbers from largest to smallest.

16. 20 19 29
17. 88 99 77
18. 1,111 111 11
19. 1,003 1,009 1,010 1,013
20. 980 989 1,053 1,051

Check your answers on page 1 in the Answer Key for Book One. If you correctly answered sixteen of twenty items, go on to the next subskill. If not, complete the following Supplemental Exercise.

Supplemental Exercise for Subskill 1B

Reread Subskill 1B, working through the examples. Then try this exercise.

Which number is smaller?

1. 9 or 18
2. 74 or 70
3. 69 or 96
4. 1,098 or 999
5. 483 or 4,803

Which number is larger?

6. 103 or 130
7. 999 or 9,990
8. 777 or 778
9. 513 or 514
10. 2,011 or 983

Write these numbers from smallest to largest.

11. 9 11 10
12. 1,001 998 1,010
13. 701 703 702
14. 363 366 374 375
15. 2,220 222 2,020 2,022

Write these numbers from largest to smallest.

16. 89 91 90
17. 68 86 66
18. 97 908 980
19. 9,001 9,010 9,011 9,100
20. 561 1,472 2,472 733

Check your answers on page 1 in the Answer Key for Book One. If you correctly answered sixteen of twenty items, go to the next subskill. If not, ask your instructor for help.

Subskill 1C: Rounding Numbers Off

When you read about the federal budget in the newspaper, you seldom find the figure given in full, exact numbers. You do not see, for example, that the President submitted a budget of $936,044,257,801. Instead, you see that the President submitted a budget of $936 billion.

Where does this figure $936 billion come from? It comes from **rounding off** the full number $936,044,257,801.

Being able to round numbers off is a useful skill to have not only if you work for the government but also in estimating costs and quantities of all kinds.

Numbers are always rounded to a certain place. The federal budget figure above, for example, is rounded to the nearest billion. Let's see how you can round a number off to the nearest thousand.

EXAMPLE: Round 38,297 to the nearest thousand.

To do this, first underline the number in the place you are rounding to.

3<u>8</u>,297 — 8 is in the thousands place.

Then look at the number in the next place to the right. Is it 5 or more? If not, leave the underlined number as it is.

3<u>8</u>,↓297 — 2 is less than 5. Leave the underlined number as it is.

Finally, change all the numbers to the right of the underlined number to 0.

3<u>8</u>,297 (with 0 0 0 written over 297)

Answer: 38,000

If you want to, you can round the same number to a different place.

EXAMPLE: Round 38,297 to the nearest hundred.

First, underline the number in the place you are rounding to.

38,<u>2</u>97 — 2 is in the hundreds place.

Then look at the number in the next place to the right. Is it 5 or more? If so, change the underlined number. Increase it by 1.

38,<u>2</u>↓97 — 9 is more than 5.

38,<u>2</u>97 (with 3 written over 2) — Change the underlined number. Increase it by 1.

Finally, change all the numbers to the right of the underlined number to 0.

  300
38,297

Answer: 38,297 rounded to the nearest hundred is 38,300.

EXAMPLE: Round 61,584,723 to the nearest million.

61,584,723 — 1 is in the millions place.

Look at the number in the next place to the right. Is it 5 or more?

 ↓
61,584,723

It is exactly 5. Here again you must change the underlined number, increasing it by 1.

 2
61,584,723

Finally, change all the numbers to the right of the underlined number to 0.

 2,000,000
61,584,723

Answer: 61,584,723 rounded to the nearest million is 62,000,000.

Let's summarize these steps. To round a number, first underline the number in the place you are rounding to. Then look at the number in the next place to the right. Is it 5 or more? If not, leave the underlined number as it is. If so, change the underlined number, increasing it by 1. Finally, change all the numbers to the right of the underlined number to 0.

Here's one more example. It's interesting because it's tricky.

EXAMPLE: Round 89,541 to the nearest thousand.

89,541 — 9 is in the thousands place.

 ↓
89,541 — The number in the next place to the right is 5, so you must change the underlined number, increasing it by 1.

 0
89,541 — But when you change the 9 to 10, you can only put the 0 in the thousands place. What should you do with the 1?

90 89,541	Add it to the 8 in the ten thousands place.
90,000 89,541	Now you can change all the numbers to the right to 0.

Answer: 89,541 rounded to the nearest thousand is 90,000.

Now try rounding these numbers.

Exercise for Subskill 1C

Round to the nearest ten.

1. 24
2. 19
3. 38
4. 108
5. 5,453

Round to the nearest hundred.

6. 216
7. 562
8. 984
9. 3,214
10. 15,499

Round to the nearest thousand.

11. 20,109
12. 54,830
13. 89,541
14. 206,983
15. 5,477,162

Round each number to the place that is underlined.

16. 5$\underline{0}$8
17. 1,$\underline{4}$92
18. $\underline{2}$,853
19. 74,$\underline{9}$46
20. 1,208,9$\underline{9}$9

Check your answers on page 2 in the Answer Key for Book One. If you correctly answered sixteen of twenty items, go on to the Self-Check. If not, complete the following Supplemental Exercise.

Supplemental Exercise for Subskill 1C

Round to the nearest ten.

1. 25
2. 598
3. 91
4. 1,450
5. 9,687

Round to the nearest hundred.

6. 605
7. 980
8. 1,246
9. 1,947
10. 6,997

Round to the nearest thousand.

11. 5,403
12. 9,099
13. 78,286
14. 598,598
15. 4,444

Round each number to the place that is underlined.

16. $\underline{9}83$
17. $2{,}\underline{4}87$
18. $\underline{3}5{,}008$
19. $4\underline{0}8{,}197$
20. $2{,}95\underline{1}{,}000$

Check your answers on page 2 in the Answer Key for Book One. If you correctly answered sixteen of twenty items, go on to the Self-Check. If not, ask your instructor for help.

SELF-CHECK FOR SKILL UNIT 1

Write these numbers in numerals.

1. One hundred forty thousand ninety-three
2. Three hundred thousand two hundred four

Write these numbers in words.

3. 92,468
4. 4,208,050
5. Which number is smaller, 548 or 584?
6. Which number is larger, 490 or 4,090?
7. Write these numbers from smallest to largest:
   103 97 99 113
8. Write these numbers from largest to smallest:
   998 1,018 989 999 1,110
9. Round 9,999 to the nearest hundreds.
10. Round 154,875 to the nearest ten thousands.

Check your answers on page 2 in the Answer Key for Book One. If you correctly answered eight of ten items, go on to Skill Unit 2. If not, ask your instructor for help.

Skill Unit 2
ADDING WHOLE NUMBERS

What Skills You Need to Begin: Ability to read and write numbers and identify place values (Skill Unit 1).

What Skills You Will Learn: After studying this skill unit, you will be able to add whole numbers of all sizes. You will also be able to solve word problems involving addition of whole numbers.

Why You Need These Skills: In order to earn money or to spend it wisely, you should be able to add. Your job may require only a little arithmetic, but you do use it—often without thinking about what you are doing. For example, you worked four hours before lunch and five hours after lunch. How many hours did you work today? Or, you have deposited $135 into a bank account containing $1560. How much money do you now have in the account?

You also use arithmetic when you play games. If you bowl or play tennis, baseball, football, basketball, or just about any sport, you must be able to keep score. Addition is the procedure that you use to solve these and many other problems from day to day.

How You Will Show What You Have Learned: At the end of this skill unit is a Self-Check consisting of ten problems in adding whole numbers. You should allow yourself one hour to complete the Self-Check. To prove that you have mastered these skills, you must correctly answer eight of the ten problems.

If you feel that you have already mastered adding whole numbers, complete the Self-Check on page 36.

Subskill 2A: Adding One-Digit Numbers

After studying this subskill, you will be able to add one-digit numbers.

Addition means to combine or put together. A plus sign (+) is used to show that two or more numbers are to be added together.

Using an Addition Table

You can use the following addition table to find the sum (the result of adding two or more numbers) of any two one-digit numbers.

+	0	1	2	3	4	5	6	7	8	9
0	0	1	2	3	4	5	6	7	8	9
1	1	2	3	4	5	6	7	8	9	10
2	2	3	4	5	6	7	8	9	10	11
3	3	4	5	6	7	8	9	10	11	12
4	4	5	6	7	8	9	10	11	12	13
5	5	6	7	8	9	10	11	12	13	14
6	6	7	8	9	10	11	12	13	14	15
7	7	8	9	10	11	12	13	14	15	16
8	8	9	10	11	12	13	14	15	16	17
9	9	10	11	12	13	14	15	→ 16	17	18

EXAMPLE: Find 7 + 9.

To find the sum of 7 + 9, find 7 in the row of numbers across the top of the table. Move your finger straight down from the 7 until you find the row that starts with 9. You can see that the sum of 7 and 9 is 16, or 7 + 9 = 16. This is read "seven plus nine equals 16."

EXAMPLE: Find 9 + 7.

Find 9 in the row of numbers across the top of the table. Move down until you find the row that starts with 7. Do you see that the sum of 9 and 7 is 16, or 9 + 7 = 16?

We have found that 7 + 9 = 16 and 9 + 7 = 16. Since the sums are equal, 7 + 9 = 9 + 7. You will find that two numbers can be added in any order. The sum will always be the same.

Adding Two One-Digit Numbers Without the Table

You won't always have an addition table available. Even if you did, it takes time to use the table to find the sum of two one-digit numbers. For these reasons, it is very important that you memorize the addition facts from the table and practice using them to increase your speed. Because addition of numbers can be done in any order, if you know that 4 + 6 = 10, you also know that 6 + 4 = 10.

Now that you know the addition facts, let's practice for speed and accuracy. But first, note that addition problems may be written left to right (horizontally) or up and down (vertically). Here is an example of both ways of writing a problem.

$$\begin{array}{r} 7 \\ +9 \\ \hline 16 \end{array}\updownarrow \qquad \text{or} \qquad \overleftrightarrow{7 + 9} = 16$$

Exercise for Subskill 2A

Write the sum for each problem below. *Do not use the addition table.*

1.	2	4	6	3	1	2	0	6
	+3	+1	+2	+4	+0	+5	+8	+3
2.	7	4	5	2	8	7	3	5
	+2	+3	+6	+9	+4	+6	+7	+8
3.	9	7	4	9	8	9	4	5
	+0	+7	+9	+7	+8	+3	+8	+7
4.	3	5	2	4	6	9	8	3
	+1	+5	+8	+7	+6	+6	+9	+9
5.	9	5	6	3	9	6	8	3
	+9	+4	+9	+5	+8	+7	+7	+6
6.	4	9	6	8	3	7	6	8
	+4	+5	+3	+6	+8	+9	+4	+7

Check your answers on page 2 in the Answer Key for Book One. If you correctly answered forty of the forty-eight items, go to the next subskill. If not, complete the following Supplemental Exercise.

Supplemental Exercise for Subskill 2A

Study the addition table until you have memorized all of the facts. If you are having difficulty, flash cards may help. These can be purchased in a store or you can make them. See your instructor if you need flash cards.

Now do this exercise.

1.	3 +6	8 +0	5 +2	0 +1	4 +4	5 +9	2 +3	6 +8
2.	4 +3	2 +6	1 +4	3 +2	8 +3	9 +7	4 +6	7 +8
3.	8 +5	7 +3	6 +7	4 +8	9 +2	6 +5	3 +4	2 +7
4.	7 +5	8 +4	3 +9	8 +8	7 +9	9 +4	7 +7	0 +9
5.	9 +3	9 +8	6 +9	6 +6	7 +4	8 +2	5 +5	1 +3
6.	6 +3	7 +8	7 +6	8 +9	5 +3	9 +6	4 +5	9 +9

Check your answers on page 2 in the Answer Key for Book One. If you correctly answered forty of the forty-eight items go to the next subskill. If not ask your instructor for help.

Subskill 2B: Adding Two Numbers Without Carrying

After studying this subskill, you will be able to add two numbers when carrying is not required.

Adding Without Carrying

Now we are going to practice adding numbers that have more than one digit. It is important to remember that place values must be lined up. For example, 32 + 145 would be written as follows:

hundreds tens ones

$$\begin{array}{r} 32 \\ +145 \\ \hline \end{array}$$

Put the numerals in the ones place (2 and 5) in the same column. Put the numerals in the tens place (3 and 4) in the same column. Put the numeral in the hundreds place (1) in the hundreds column.

$$\begin{array}{r} 32 \\ +145 \\ \hline 7 \end{array}$$

Add each column. Start with the ones column.

$$\begin{array}{r} 32 \\ +145 \\ \hline 77 \end{array}$$

Next add the tens column.

$$\begin{array}{r} 32 \\ +145 \\ \hline 177 \end{array}$$

Finally, add the hundreds column. Since there is nothing to add to the 1 in the hundreds column, just bring it down as part of the sum.

Continue adding columns until you have found the sum of the last column on the left. Remember to start at the right and move toward the left.

$$\begin{array}{r} 351 \\ +213 \\ \hline \leftarrow \end{array} \qquad \begin{array}{r} 351 \\ +213 \\ \hline 4 \end{array} \qquad \begin{array}{r} 351 \\ +213 \\ \hline 64 \end{array} \qquad \begin{array}{r} 351 \\ +213 \\ \hline 564 \end{array}$$

Here is an example of the trouble that happens if place values are not lined up:

$$\begin{array}{l} 16 \\ +\ 23 \\ \hline 183 \end{array} \text{ WRONG!} \qquad \begin{array}{r} 16 \\ +\ 23 \\ \hline 39 \end{array} \text{ RIGHT}$$

Checking Your Answer

You can often avoid mistakes if you check your answer. Check an addition problem by adding again or adding in the opposite direction. In other words, if you first added from top to bottom, check by adding from bottom to top.

$$\begin{array}{r} 17 \\ +481 \\ \hline 498 \end{array}\downarrow \qquad \text{Check: } \begin{array}{r} 17 \\ +481 \\ \hline 498 \end{array}\uparrow$$

Exercise for Subskill 2B

Find the sum of each of the problems below. Check your answers.

1. $\begin{array}{r} 33 \\ +45 \\ \hline \end{array}$

2. $\begin{array}{r} 6 \\ +52 \\ \hline \end{array}$

3. $\begin{array}{r} 81 \\ +\ 4 \\ \hline \end{array}$

4. $\begin{array}{r} 73 \\ +21 \\ \hline \end{array}$

5. $\begin{array}{r} 103 \\ +220 \\ \hline \end{array}$

6. $\begin{array}{r} 863 \\ +111 \\ \hline \end{array}$

7. $\begin{array}{r} 1{,}354 \\ +\ \ 214 \\ \hline \end{array}$

8. $\begin{array}{r} 8{,}006 \\ +11{,}983 \\ \hline \end{array}$

Rewrite these problems vertically (up and down). Then find the sums.

9. 204 + 553 =

10. 82 + 1,214 =

Check your answers on page 2 in the Answer Key for Book One. If you correctly answered eight of the ten items, go on to the next subskill. If not, complete the following Supplemental Exercise.

Supplemental Exercise for Subskill 2B

Read Subskill 2B again. Work through the examples as you read.

Remember to start at the right and add each column of numbers. Check your answers by adding again or by adding in the opposite direction.

If you are still having problems with your addition facts, review them before going on.

Now that you know your addition facts, practice them by finding the sums for these problems. Check your answers.

1. $\begin{array}{r} 30 \\ +25 \\ \hline \end{array}$

2. $\begin{array}{r} 7 \\ +41 \\ \hline \end{array}$

3. $\begin{array}{r} 62 \\ +\ 6 \\ \hline \end{array}$

4. $\begin{array}{r} 88 \\ +11 \\ \hline \end{array}$

5. $\begin{array}{r} 552 \\ +124 \\ \hline \end{array}$

6. $\begin{array}{r} 653 \\ +200 \\ \hline \end{array}$

7. $\begin{array}{r} 3{,}051 \\ +\ \ 418 \\ \hline \end{array}$

8. $\begin{array}{r} 7{,}213 \\ +31{,}786 \\ \hline \end{array}$

Rewrite these problems vertically (up and down). Then find the sums.

9. 457 + 321 =

10. 302 + 9,590 =

Check your answers on page 2 in the Answer Key for Book One. If you correctly answered eight of the ten items, go on to the next subskill. If not, ask your instructor for help.

Subskill 2C: Adding Three or More Numbers

After studying this subskill, you will be able to add three or more numbers when carrying is not required.

Adding Three or More One-Digit Numbers

Groups of more than two numbers can be added in any order: the first and second can be added, and their sum can be added to the third; or, the first and third numbers can be added, and their sum added to the second number. The sum will be the same.

EXAMPLE: Find the sum of 1 + 2 + 5.

$\underbrace{1 + 2} + 5 =$ First, find the sum of 1 and 2.

$3 \quad + 5 = 8$ Then, add 5.

Answer: 8

Let's look at the example again. This time try a different order.

EXAMPLE: $1 + \underbrace{2 + 5} =$ First, find the sum of 2 and 5.

$1 + \quad 7 \quad = 8$ Then, add 1.

Answer: 8

The answer is the same. Remember, you can add numbers in any order.

Adding Three or More Numbers with More than One Digit

To add three or more numbers, first find the sum of the ones column. Then find the sum of the tens column, then the hundreds column, and so on.

EXAMPLE: Add 23, 40, and 16.

Line up the place values. Then add each column, starting at the right.

```
23      23 }
40      40 }  3
16      16
         9
```

Add the ones column. First add the 3 and the 0. The sum is 3. Then add this sum to 6. The total for the ones column is 9.

```
6  { 23
   { 40
     16
     79
```

Add the tens column. First add the 2 and the 4. The sum is 6. Then add this sum to 1. The total for the ones column is 7. Your answer is 79.

Answer: 79

Here is another example. (Note that the plus sign may or may not be written.)

EXAMPLE: Find the sum of 503, 65, and 411.

```
5 0 3 }        3 + 5 = 8
  6 5 }  8
4 1 1          8 + 1 = 9
    9
```

```
5 0 }      3     0 + 6 = 6
  6 }  6   5
4 1        1     6 + 1 = 7
  7        9
```

```
5 0 3            5 + 4 = 9
  6 5
4 1 1
9 7 9
```

Answer: 979

You can check your answers by adding in the opposite direction:

```
5 0 3            5 + 1 = 6
  6 5 }          3 + 6 = 9
4 1 1 }  6
    9
```

```
5 0        3     6 + 1 = 7
  6 }      5     7 + 0 = 7
4 1 }  7   1
  7        9
```

```
5 0 3            5 + 4 = 9
  6 5
4 1 1
9 7 9
```

Answer: 979

Check your understanding of adding three or more numbers by completing this exercise.

Exercise for Subskill 2C

Find the sums and check your answers.

1.	2.	3.	4.	5.
3	5	3	2	1
4	2	3	3	2
1	1	3	4	3
				3

6.	7.	8.	9.	10.
21	53	42	4	13
30	5	102	71	23
18	1	53	111	140
				812

Check your answers on page 3 in the Answer Key for Book One. If you correctly answered eight of the ten items, go on to the next subskill. If not, complete the following Supplemental Exercise.

Supplemental Exercise for Subskill 2C

Read Subskill 2C again. Work through the examples as you read.

Now do this exercise. Find the sums and check your answers.

1.	2.	3.	4.	5.
1	4	1	2	5
2	3	1	2	1
3	2	5	4	2
				1

6.	7.	8.	9.	10.
43	66	50	44	231
13	21	804	621	114
22	11	145	133	322
				211

Check your answers on page 3 in the Answer Key for Book One. If you correctly answered eight of the ten items, go on to the next subskill. If not, ask your instructor for help.

Subskill 2D: Adding Numbers With Carrying

After studying this subskill, you will be able to add numbers when carrying is required.

If the sum of a column is more than 9, you will need to **carry.** A single column cannot hold more than one digit, so you will need to move to first digit of the sum into the next column.

EXAMPLE: Add 24 and 68.

$$\begin{array}{r} {}^{1} \\ 24 \\ +68 \\ \hline 2 \end{array}$$

$4 + 8 = 12$
Write the 2 in the ones column. Because the numeral 1 in 12 means one ten, add the 1 to the other numerals in the tens column. Write the 1 over the tens column.

$$\begin{array}{r} {}^{1} \\ 24 \\ +68 \\ \hline 92 \end{array}$$

Add the tens column. Remember to include the 1 you carried from the ones column.
$1 + 2 + 6 = 9$

Answer: 92

EXAMPLE: Add 27, 116, and 542.

$$\begin{array}{r} {}^{1} \\ 27 \\ 116 \\ 542 \\ \hline 5 \end{array}$$

$7 + 6 + 2 = 15$
Write the 5 in the ones column. Carry the 1.

$$\begin{array}{r} {}^{1} \\ 27 \\ 116 \\ 542 \\ \hline 85 \end{array}$$

Add the tens column.
$1 + 2 + 1 + 4 = 8$

$$\begin{array}{r} 27 \\ 116 \\ 542 \\ \hline 685 \end{array}$$

Add the hundreds column.

Answer: 685

You may have to carry more than once.

EXAMPLE: Add 482, 687, and 296.

```
  1
482     2 + 8 + 6 = 16
678     Carry the 1 over into the tens place.
296
----
  6
```

```
 21
482     1 + 8 + 7 + 9 = 25
678     The 2 in 25 means two hundreds. Carry the 2 over
296     into the hundreds place.
----
 56
```

```
  2
  482   2 + 4 + 6 + 2 = 14
  678   The 1 in 14 is carried to the thousands column and
  296   brought down.
-----
1,456
```

Answer: 1,456

EXAMPLE: Add 547 and 536.

```
   1
  547   7 + 6 = 13
 +536   Carry the 1 over into the tens place.
-----
    3
```

```
  1
  547   1 + 4 + 3 = 8
 +536
-----
   83
```

```
  1
  547   5 + 5 = 10
 +536   Write the 1 in the thousands place and the 0 in the
-----
1,083   hundreds place.
```

Answer: 1,083

Check your understanding of carrying by doing this exercise.

Exercise for Subskill 2D

Find the sum to each problem and check your work.

1.	2.	3.	4.
6	5	1	34
7	8	9	+18
3	4	5	

5. 77 +23	**6.** 81 +19	**7.** 65 +89	**8.** 106 + 98
9. 526 +635	**10.** 154 +937	**11.** 788 +225	**12.** 384 +789
13. 1,254 +6,957	**14.** 15,265 + 7,954	**15.** 376 498 +254	

16. 14,379 + 4,674 =

17. 1,562 + 435 + 2,016 =

18. 162,574 + 59,076 + 1,386 =

Check your answers on page 3 in the Answer Key for Book One. If you correctly answered fourteen of the eighteen items, go to the next subskill. If not, complete the following Supplemental Exercise.

Supplemental Exercise for Subskill 2D

Read Subskill 2D again. Work through the examples as you study them.

Now try this exercise. Find the sums and check your answers.

1. 2 4 6	**2.** 7 4 7	**3.** 5 6 8	**4.** 48 +60
5. 63 +76	**6.** 35 +35	**7.** 19 +41	**8.** 68 +35
9. 379 +662	**10.** 408 +293	**11.** 924 + 67	**12.** 2,346 + 899

13. $\begin{array}{r} 3{,}058 \\ +4{,}967 \\ \hline \end{array}$ **14.** $\begin{array}{r} 27{,}989 \\ +\ 9{,}164 \\ \hline \end{array}$ **15.** $\begin{array}{r} 554 \\ 163 \\ 789 \\ \hline \end{array}$

16. 28,520 + 9,491 =

17. 2,562 + 765 + 418 =

18. 76,504 + 198 + 270 =

Check your answers on page 3 in the Answer Key for Book One. If you correctly answered fourteen of the eighteen items, go to the next subskill. If not, ask your instructor for help.

Subskill 2E: Solving Word Problems

After studying this subskill, you will be able to solve word problems involving addition.

Many of the problems you must solve are in the form of word problems. These are the steps you should follow in solving word problems.

Read and Reread the Problem

Read the entire problem carefully. Read the problem again to make sure you understand what you are being asked to do.

EXAMPLE: Joyce Johnson had $258 in her checking account. She deposited her paycheck into her account, increasing the amount in her account by $435. What was the new balance in Ms. Johnson's account? (In a bank account, the balance is the amount of money in the account.)

Now that you have read the problem, go to the next step.

Determine What You Are to Find

What does the problem ask you to do? In other words, what will you have to do to get the answer?

In the example above, you are asked to find the new balance.

Determine What You Are Given

What facts do you know? Also, what facts are not needed to solve the problem?

In the example above, you know the beginning balance and the amount of the deposit.

Decide What Operation(s) to Use

Addition problems may ask for a **total** or a **sum.** Sometimes the following words can be used as clues that you will need to add:

Total	In all	Both
Sum	Increase	Raise
	Together	

In the above example, the beginning balance is increased by the amount of the deposit. Therefore, you must add the deposit to the original balance to find the new balance.

Solve the Problem

$$\begin{array}{r} \$258 \\ 435 \\ \hline \end{array} \quad \begin{array}{l} \text{Original balance} \\ + \qquad \text{Deposit} \\ \hline \end{array}$$

$$\begin{array}{r} \$258 \\ 435 \\ \hline 3 \end{array} \quad \begin{array}{l} 8 + 5 = 13 \\ \text{Carry the 1 into the tens column.} \end{array}$$

$$\begin{array}{r} \$258 \\ 435 \\ \hline 93 \end{array} \quad 1 + 5 + 3 = 9$$

$$\begin{array}{r} \$258 \\ 435 \\ \hline \$693 \end{array} \quad \begin{array}{l} 2 + 4 = 6 \\ \text{The new balance equals \$693.} \end{array}$$

Check Your Answer

Check your solution by adding again.

Now check your understanding of solving addition word problems by doing this exercise.

Exercise for Subskill 2E

1. Find the sum of five hundred eighty-eight thousand and two hundred thousand eighty-four.

2. The rent on an apartment was $185. The landlord raised the rent $45. What is the rent now?

3. A stereo system cost $1,069 last year. This year the price was increased by $155. How much does the stereo cost now?

4. The base price of a car is $6,098. The following accessories are available:

AM Radio	$168
Air Conditioning	507
Power Steering	165
Power Brakes	245

What is the total price of the car with all accessories?

5. Marlene worked eight hours on Monday, seven hours on Tuesday, nine hours on Wednesday, six hours on Thursday, and eight hours on Friday. How many hours did she work this week?

Check your answers on page 3 in the Answer Key for Book One. If you correctly answered four of the five items, go on to the Self-Check. If not, complete the following Supplemental Exercise.

Supplemental Exercise for Subskill 2E

Review the steps for solving word problems. Work through the examples as you read them. Now do this exercise.

1. Find the sum of one hundred fourteen thousand six hundred forty-eight and thirty-three thousand seventy-five.

2. While on vacation, a family drove 320 miles one day and 288 miles the next day. How many miles did they drive in the two days?

3. The price of a daily newspaper currently is 30 cents. Soon it will be increased by 5 cents. What will the new price be?

4. You pay $210 a month for rent. This month you had the following bills:

Electricity	$48
Gas	23
Water	19
Telephone	37
Cable TV	12

What is the total cost for the month for rent and utilities?

5. A telephone with a dial (rotary phone) costs $23 to buy. A telephone with push buttons (touch-tone phone) costs $15 more. What is the price of a push button phone?

Check your answers on page 3 in the Answer Key for Book One. If you correctly answered four of the five items, go on to the Self-Check. If not, ask your instructor for help.

SELF-CHECK FOR SKILL UNIT 2

Solve each problem. Check your answers.

1. $\begin{array}{r} 21 \\ +68 \\ \hline \end{array}$ **2.** $\begin{array}{r} 99 \\ +88 \\ \hline \end{array}$ **3.** $\begin{array}{r} 26 \\ 3 \\ 5 \\ 8 \\ \hline \end{array}$ **4.** $\begin{array}{r} 2{,}507 \\ +1{,}530 \\ \hline \end{array}$

5. $\begin{array}{r} 58 \\ 12 \\ 21 \\ 15 \\ \hline \end{array}$ **6.** $\begin{array}{r} 4{,}369 \\ 204 \\ 16{,}998 \\ 1{,}316 \\ \hline \end{array}$ **7.** $105 + 7 + 20 =$

8. Find the sum of two hundred sixteen thousand three hundred fifty-three and seventy-four thousand six hundred eighty-nine.

9. Mike Hanley wants to fence in his backyard. The four sides measure 111 feet, 216 feet, 127 feet, and 175 feet. What is the total amount of fencing that Mike must buy?

10. Estelle borrowed $900. Interest on this loan is $108. How much will Estelle have to repay?

Check your answers on page 3 in the Answer Key for Book One. If you correctly answered eight of the ten items, go on to Skill Unit 3. If not, ask your instructor for help.

Skill Unit 3
SUBTRACTING WHOLE NUMBERS

What Skills You Need to Begin: Ability to read and write numbers and identify place values (Skill Unit 1). Ability to add whole numbers (Skill Unit 2).

What Skills You Will Learn: After studying this skill unit, you will be able to subtract whole numbers of all sizes. You will also be able to solve word problems involving subtraction of whole numbers.

Why You Need These Skills: When you buy an item that is on sale, the amount you save is figured by subtracting the sale price from the original price. If you want to determine your take-home pay, you must subtract the deductions (withholding tax, health insurance, etc.) from your gross (total) wages. When you purchase something, you must subtract the price of the item from the amount of money you gave the cashier in order to determine whether you received the correct change. These are only a few examples of the uses of subtraction.

How You Will Show What You Have Learned: At the end of this skill unit is a Self-Check consisting of fifteen problems in subtracting whole numbers. You should allow yourself one hour to complete the Self-Check. To prove that you have mastered these skills, you must correctly answer twelve of the fifteen problems.

If you feel that you have already mastered subtracting whole numbers, complete the Self-Check on pages 52 and 53.

Subskill 3A: Subtracting One- and Two-Digit Numbers

After studying this subskill, you will be able to subtract one- and two-digit numbers.

Addition is the combination of two or more items. Subtraction is the opposite of addition. To **subtract** means to take things away. A minus sign (−) is used to show that one number is to be taken away, or subtracted, from another.

Using an Addition Table for Subtraction

Because subtraction is the opposite of addition, the addition table below can be used to find the answer, or the **difference,** to a subtraction problem.

–	0	1	2	3	4	5	6	7	8	9
0	0	1	2	3	4	5	6	7	8	9
1	1	2	3	4	5	6	7	8	9	10
2	2	3	4	5	6	7	8	9	10	11
3	3	4	5	6	7	8	9	10	11	12
4	4	5	6	7	8	9	10	11	12	13
5	5	6	7	8	9	10	11	12	13	14
6	6	7	8	9	10	11	12	13	14	15
7	7	8	9	10	11	12	13	14	15	16
8	8	9	10	11	12	13	14	15	16	17
9	9	10	11	12	13	14	15	16	17	18

EXAMPLE: Find 6 − 2.

To find the answer to 6 − 2, find 2 in the top row. Move straight down to the 6 in the column under the 2. Then follow the arrow from the 6 all the way to the left side of the table. Do you see that 6 − 2 = 4? This is read "six minus two equals four." Check your answer by adding the number that you subtracted to your answer. Does 2 + 4 = 6? Yes. Your answer is correct.

Use the table to find the answer to 11 − 4. Was your answer 7? Check this answer by adding. Does 7 + 4 = 11? Yes.

Memorizing the Subtraction Facts

As with addition facts, you must memorize certain subtraction facts. If you know your addition facts, you can easily learn the subtraction facts. For example, to find the answer to

$$8 - 3 = ?$$

ask yourself what number must be added to 3 to make 8. In other words, change

$$8 - 3 = ? \quad \text{to} \quad 3 + ? = 8$$

Do you recall that $3 + 5 = 8$? Therefore, $8 - 3 = 5$.

What is the answer to $9 - 5$? What must be added to 5 to make 9? If you said four, you're right. Therefore, $9 - 5 = 4$.

Check your understanding of subtraction of one- and two-digit numbers by completing the following exercise.

Exercise for Subskill 3A

Write the difference for each subtraction problem below. *Do not use the addition table.* Check your answers by adding.

1.	9 −7	6 −3	4 −1	8 −8	7 −2	5 −5	3 −0	9 −1
2.	0 −0	6 −5	8 −7	4 −2	5 −3	7 −6	9 −3	3 −2
3.	7 −5	8 −3	6 −0	4 −3	9 −2	8 −4	5 −2	8 −0
4.	8 −6	3 −3	5 −4	7 −2	2 −0	4 −4	6 −2	7 −4
5.	1 −1	6 −4	9 −5	3 −1	5 −0	8 −5	7 −7	9 −8

6.	9	4	8	7	9	5	6	8
	−4	−0	−4	−1	−6	−1	−6	−2
7.	14	11	12	10	12	7	10	9
	− 6	− 7	− 7	− 4	− 5	−5	− 2	−3
8.	12	10	17	13	11	16	8	15
	− 4	− 6	− 9	− 4	− 8	− 9	−8	− 7
9.	14	16	11	12	17	13	10	13
	− 7	− 8	− 6	− 9	− 8	− 6	− 7	− 8
10.	11	10	13	16	15	12	10	14
	− 9	− 9	− 9	− 7	− 8	− 3	− 3	− 5
11.	15	12	11	10	14	13	15	11
	− 6	− 8	− 7	− 8	− 9	− 7	− 7	− 2
12.	11	15	12	18	10	14	11	13
	− 5	− 9	− 6	− 9	− 5	− 8	− 3	− 5

Check your answers on page 3 in the Answer Key for Book One. If you correctly answered eighty-four of the ninety-six items, go to the next subskill. If not, complete the following Supplemental Exercise.

Supplemental Exercise for Subskill 3A

The best way to memorize something is to practice. Here is another exercise to try.

1.	2	9	7	3	9	8	6	5
	−0	−8	−4	−2	−1	−0	−6	−1
2.	7	6	9	3	7	8	5	4
	−7	−2	−3	−0	−6	−4	−2	−4

3.	6 −5	4 −1	9 −6	5 −5	8 −4	6 −0	4 −3	7 −1
4.	8 −8	5 −3	4 −2	3 −1	9 −5	8 −7	5 −0	6 −3
5.	0 −0	9 −7	8 −6	6 −0	5 −4	7 −5	8 −3	1 −1
6.	9 −4	3 −3	7 −2	6 −4	8 −2	4 −0	9 −2	6 −3
7.	13 − 5	11 − 2	14 − 5	13 − 8	15 − 7	9 −3	10 − 2	11 − 4
8.	10 − 7	11 − 3	15 − 7	8 −8	14 − 8	13 − 7	12 − 3	11 − 9
9.	16 − 9	7 −5	12 − 5	11 − 8	17 − 8	15 − 8	14 − 9	10 − 5
10.	18 − 9	10 − 8	16 − 7	12 − 9	13 − 4	11 − 6	12 − 7	17 − 9
11.	10 − 4	13 − 9	11 − 7	12 − 6	15 − 9	12 − 8	10 − 9	16 − 8
12.	10 − 6	13 − 6	14 − 6	12 − 4	14 − 7	10 − 3	15 − 6	11 − 5

Check your answers on page 4 in the Answer Key for Book One. If you correctly answered eighty-four of the ninety-six items, go to the next subskill. If not, ask your instructor for help.

Subskill 3B: Subtracting Without Borrowing

Studying this subskill will enable you to subtract numbers when borrowing is not required.

Numbers are easier to subtract if you write the smaller number *under* the larger number. Place values must be lined up. For example, 183 − 71 would be written as follows.

EXAMPLE:

$$\begin{array}{r} 183 \\ -\ \ 71 \\ \hline \end{array}$$

Notice that place values are lined up.

$$\begin{array}{r} 183 \\ -\ \ 71 \\ \hline 2 \end{array}$$

Subtract each column. Start with the ones column. $3 - 1 = 2$

$$\begin{array}{r} 183 \\ -\ \ 71 \\ \hline 12 \end{array}$$

Next subtract the tens column. $8 - 7 = 1$

$$\begin{array}{r} 183 \\ -\ \ 71 \\ \hline 112 \end{array}$$

Finally, subtract the hundreds column. Since there is nothing to subtract from the 1 in the hundreds column, just bring it down as part of the difference.

Answer: 112

Continue subtracting columns until you have found the difference of the last column on the left. Remember to start at the right and move toward the left.

$$\begin{array}{r} 869 \\ -243 \\ \hline \end{array} \qquad \begin{array}{r} 869 \\ -243 \\ \hline 6 \end{array} \qquad \begin{array}{r} 869 \\ -243 \\ \hline 26 \end{array} \qquad \begin{array}{r} 869 \\ -243 \\ \hline 626 \end{array}$$

Sometimes the difference will contain zeros. If the zeros are at the left end of the number, they should be dropped.

$$\begin{array}{r} 348 \\ -321 \\ \hline \mathbf{0}27 \end{array}$$ is written 27.

$$\begin{array}{r} 982 \\ -981 \\ \hline \mathbf{00}1 \end{array}$$ is written 1.

If a zero appears in the difference but has other digits to its left, it cannot be removed. The zero is needed as a placeholder.

$$\begin{array}{r} 493 \\ -\ 391 \\ \hline 102 \end{array} \qquad \begin{array}{r} 1,764 \\ -\ 644 \\ \hline 1,120 \end{array} \qquad \begin{array}{r} 988 \\ -\ 488 \\ \hline 500 \end{array}$$

Checking Your Answer

You can often avoid getting the wrong answer to a problem if you check your answer. Check a subtraction problem by adding the difference and the smaller of the two numbers in the problem. The sum should be the larger number.

$$\begin{array}{r} 869 \\ -\ 243 \\ \hline 626 \end{array} \qquad \text{Check:} \qquad \begin{array}{r} 626 \\ +\ 243 \\ \hline 869 \end{array}$$

Check your understanding of subtraction without borrowing by completing this exercise.

Exercise for Subskill 3B

Solve the following subtraction problems. Use addition to check your answers.

1. $\begin{array}{r} 48 \\ -33 \\ \hline \end{array}$ **2.** $\begin{array}{r} 59 \\ -\ 7 \\ \hline \end{array}$ **3.** $\begin{array}{r} 222 \\ -\ 12 \\ \hline \end{array}$ **4.** $\begin{array}{r} 527 \\ -425 \\ \hline \end{array}$

5. $\begin{array}{r} 986 \\ -941 \\ \hline \end{array}$ **6.** $\begin{array}{r} 666 \\ -665 \\ \hline \end{array}$ **7.** $\begin{array}{r} 747 \\ -426 \\ \hline \end{array}$ **8.** $\begin{array}{r} 3,986 \\ -1,024 \\ \hline \end{array}$

Rewrite these problems vertically (up and down). Then find the differences.

9. 16,249 − 4,125 =

10. 9,064 − 21 =

Check your answers on page 4 in the Answer Key for Book One. If you correctly answered eight of the ten problems, go to the next subskill. If not, complete the following Supplemental Exercise.

Supplemental Exercise for Subskill 3B

Remember to start at the right and subtract each column of numbers. Check your answers by adding.

If you are still having problems with your subtraction facts, review them before going on.

Now that you know your subtraction facts, practice them by finding the difference for these problems. Check your answers.

1. 78 − 44	**2.** 62 − 2	**3.** 495 − 83	**4.** 668 − 561
5. 843 − 822	**6.** 977 − 970	**7.** 734 − 223	**8.** 4,679 − 1,508

Rewrite these problems vertically (up and down). Then find the differences.

9. 26,925 − 6,603 =

10. 108,504 − 8,301 =

Check your answers on page 4 in the Answer Key for Book One. If you correctly answered eight of the ten problems, go to the next subskill. If not, ask your instructor for help.

Subskill 3C: Subtracting With Borrowing

After studying this subskill, you will be able to subtract numbers when borrowing is required.

Subtracting When Borrowing Is Required in One Column

Often one or more digits in the number you are subtracting will be larger than the digits in the number they are being subtracted from. To find the difference, you must **borrow**.

Look at the following example. You cannot subtract 8 from 3. You must borrow, as shown on page 45.

EXAMPLE:

$$\begin{array}{r} 6\ 3 \\ -\quad 8 \\ \hline \end{array}$$

Borrow 1 from the 6 in the tens column. You have borrowed 1 ten or 10. Add this to the 3 in the ones column (10 + 3 = 13).

$$\begin{array}{r} {\scriptstyle 5\ 13} \\ \not{6}\ \not{3} \\ -\quad 8 \\ \hline \end{array}$$

Subtract the 1 you borrowed from the 6 to make it a 5.

$$\begin{array}{r} {\scriptstyle 5\ 13} \\ \not{6}\ \not{3} \\ -\quad 8 \\ \hline 5 \end{array}$$

Now subtract 8 from 13.

$$\begin{array}{r} {\scriptstyle 5\ 13} \\ \not{6}\ \not{3} \\ -\quad 8 \\ \hline 5\ 5 \end{array}$$

Finally, subtract the tens column.
5 − 0 = 5.

Don't forget to check your answer.

$$\begin{array}{r} {\scriptstyle 1\quad} \\ 5\ 5 \\ +\quad 8 \\ \hline 3 \end{array} \qquad \begin{array}{r} {\scriptstyle 1\quad} \\ 5\ 5 \\ +\quad 8 \\ \hline 6\ 3 \end{array}$$

Answer: 55

Let's try another problem:

EXAMPLE:

$$\begin{array}{r} 5\ 2\ 7 \\ -\ 1\ 8\ 4 \\ \hline 3 \end{array}$$

Subtract the digits in the ones column.
7 − 4 = 3

$$\begin{array}{r} {\scriptstyle 4\ 12\quad} \\ \not{5}\ 2\ 7 \\ -\ 1\ 8\ 4 \\ \hline 3 \end{array}$$

You cannot subtract 8 from 2. Borrow 1 from the next column, changing the 5 to a 4. Since this is the hundreds column, you have really borrowed 10 tens. Add this to the 2 already in the tens column. Now you can subtract.
12 − 8 = 4

$$\begin{array}{r} {\scriptstyle 4\ 12\quad} \\ \not{5}\ 2\ 7 \\ -\ 1\ 8\ 4 \\ \hline 4\ 3 \end{array}$$

$$\begin{array}{r} {\scriptstyle 4\ 12\quad} \\ \not{5}\ 2\ 7 \\ -\ 1\ 8\ 4 \\ \hline 3\ 4\ 3 \end{array}$$

Finally, subtract the hundreds column.
4 − 1 = 3
The difference is 343.

Check:
$$\begin{array}{r} 343 \\ +\,184 \\ \hline 527 \end{array}$$

Answer: 343

Subtracting When Borrowing is Required in More Than One Column

Sometimes you must borrow more than once, as shown in the following example:

EXAMPLE: Subtract 389 from 584.

$$\begin{array}{r} {\scriptstyle 7\;14} \\ 5\,\not{8}\,\not{4} \\ -\,3\,8\,9 \\ \hline 5 \end{array}$$

You cannot subtract 9 from 4. Borrow 1 from the 8 in the tens column. You have really borrowed 10. Add this 10 to the 4 in the ones column. Now subtract the ones column.
14 − 9 = 5

$$\begin{array}{r} {\scriptstyle 4\;17\;14} \\ \not{5}\,\not{8}\,\not{4} \\ -\,3\,8\,9 \\ \hline 9\,5 \end{array}$$

You cannot subtract 8 from 7. Borrow 1 from the 5 in the hundreds column. You have really borrowed 10 tens. Add this 10 to the 7 in the tens column. Subtract.
17 − 8 = 9

$$\begin{array}{r} {\scriptstyle 4\;17\;14} \\ \not{5}\,\not{8}\,\not{4} \\ -\,3\,8\,9 \\ \hline 1\,9\,5 \end{array}$$

Finally, subtract the hundreds column.
4 − 3 = 1

Check:
$$\begin{array}{r} 195 \\ +\,389 \\ \hline 584 \end{array}$$

Answer: 195

When the number that you are subtracting from has a zero in it, borrowing can be tricky.

EXAMPLE: Subtract 399 from 807.

$$\begin{array}{r} 8\,0\,7 \\ -\,3\,9\,9 \\ \hline \end{array}$$

You cannot subtract 9 from 7. However, you cannot borrow from the tens column because you cannot subtract anything from 0. You must go to the hundreds column to borrow.

```
  7 10
  8 0 7
- 3 9 9
```

Borrow 1 from the 8 in the hundreds column. Add 10 to the 0 in the tens column.

```
    9
  7 10 17
  8 0 7
- 3 9 9
      8
```

Now you can borrow 1 from the 10 in the tens column. Add 10 to the 7 in the ones column. Now you can subtract.
17 − 9 = 8

```
    9
  7 10 17
  8 0 7
- 3 9 9
    0 8
```

Subtract the tens column.
9 − 9 = 0

```
    9
  7 10 17
  8 0 7
- 3 9 9
  4 0 8
```

Subtract the hundreds column.
7 − 3 = 4
The difference is 408.

```
Check:     4 0 8
         + 3 9 9
           8 0 7
```

Answer: 408

Here is another problem in which you must borrow from 0.

EXAMPLE: Subtract 387 from 3,000.

```
  3 0 0 0
-   3 8 7
```

You cannot subtract 7 from 0. However, you cannot borrow from either the tens or the hundreds column. You must go to the thousands column to borrow.

```
  2 10
  3 0 0 0
-   3 8 7
```

Borrow 1 from the 3 in the thousands column. Add 10 to the 0 in the hundreds column.

```
     9
  2 10 10
  3 0 0 0
-   3 8 7
```

Borrow 1 from the 10 in the hundreds column. Add 10 to the 0 in the tens column.

```
     9  9
  2 10 10 10
  3 0 0 0
-   3 8 7
        3
```

Borrow 1 from the 10 in the tens column. Add 10 to the 0 in the ones column. Now you can subtract.
10 − 7 = 3

9 9 2 ~~10~~~~10~~10 ~~3~~ ~~0~~ ~~0~~ ~~0~~ − 3 8 7 1 3	Subtract the tens column. 9 − 8 = 1
9 9 2 ~~10~~~~10~~10 ~~3~~ ~~0~~ ~~0~~ ~~0~~ − 3 8 7 6 1 3	Subtract the hundreds column. 9 − 3 = 6
9 9 2 ~~10~~~~10~~10 ~~3~~ ~~0~~ ~~0~~ ~~0~~ − 3 9 7 2 6 1 3	Finally, subtract the thousands column. 2 − 0 = 2 The difference is 2,613.

Check: 2 6 1 3
+ 3 8 7
3 0 0 0

Answer: 2,613

Check your skill at subtracting when borrowing is required by completing this exercise.

Exercise for Subskill 3C

Find the difference for each problem. Check your answers.

1. 29 − 6

2. 87 − 15

3. 37 − 24

4. 62 − 8

5. 70 − 3

6. 139 − 57 =

7. 472 − 57

8. 902 − 71

9. 611 − 40

10. 600 − 85

11. 300 − 147

12. 1,280 − 93

13. 2,864 − 159

14. 562 − 173 =

15. 6,773 − 824

16. 3,200 − 495

17. 14,629 − 2,537

18. 16,000 − 9,738

19. 207,401 − 19,512

20. 650,000 − 43,168 =

Check your answers on page 4 in the Answer Key for Book One. If you correctly answered sixteen of the twenty items, go to the next Subskill. If not, complete the following Supplemental Exercise.

Supplemental Exercise for Subskill 3C

Find the difference for each problem below. Check your answers.

1. 56 − 3

2. 79 − 53

3. 68 − 24

4. 34 − 6

5. 51 − 9

6. 703 − 40 =

7. 561 − 28

8. 703 − 81

9. 566 − 70

10. 860 − 70

11. 1,257 − 389

12. 2,340 − 62

13. 1,953 − 227

14. 635 − 248 =

15. 7,336 − 419

16. 6,300 − 596

17. 12,814 − 1,763

18. 13,000 − 8,937

19. 506,307 − 27,418

20. 720,005 − 52,317 =

Check your answers on page 4 in the Answer Key for Book One. If you correctly answered sixteen of the twenty items, go to the next subskill. If not, ask your instructor for help.

Subskill 3D: Solving Word Problems

After studying this subskill, you will be able to solve word problems involving subtraction.

Many of the problems you must solve are in the form of word problems. These are the steps you should follow in solving word problems that require subtraction.

Read and Reread the Problem

Read the *entire* problem carefully. Read the problem again to make sure you understand what you are being asked to do.

EXAMPLE: Joyce Johnson had $693 in her checking account. She wrote a check for $285 for rent. What was the new balance remaining in Ms. Johnson's account?

Now that you have read the problem, go to the next step.

Determine What You Are to Find

What does the problem ask you to do? In other words, what will you have to do to find the answer?

In the example above, you are asked to find the new balance in Ms. Johnson's account.

Determine What You Are Given

What facts do you know? Also, what facts are not needed to solve the problem?

In the example above, you know the beginning balance and the amount of the check.

Decide What Operation(s) to Use

Subtraction problems ask for *what is left* after something is *taken away*. They also may ask for how much greater one number is than another. Sometimes these key words or phrases may be used:

Difference	How much less
Remainder	Decreased by
How much more	Reduced by
How many are left	Discount

In the example above, the beginning balance is decreased by the amount of the check. By subtracting $285 from $693, you can find the balance *remaining* in Joyce Johnson's account.

Solve the Problem

$$\begin{array}{r} \$693 \\ -\ 285 \\ \hline \$408 \end{array}$$

Check Your Answer

$$\begin{array}{r} \$408 \\ +\ 285 \\ \hline \$693 \end{array}$$

Here's another example.

EXAMPLE: The heating-oil tank in Tom's house holds 175 gallons when it is full. The gauge says the tank now holds 37 gallons. How many gallons are needed to fill up the tank?

$$\begin{array}{r} 175 \\ -\ 37 \\ \hline 138 \end{array}$$

To find the space remaining in the tank, subtract what is still in the tank from the full amount it will hold.

Check:

$$\begin{array}{r} 138 \\ +\ 37 \\ \hline 175 \end{array}$$

Answer: 138 gallons

Now check your skill at solving word problems by doing this exercise.

Exercise for Subskill 3D

1. What is the difference between seventy-five thousand and nine thousand four hundred eighty-three?

2. Before a trip, the odometer (mileage counter) on your car read 57,938 miles. After the trip, the odometer read 60,023. How far did you travel on your trip?

3. Amanda's total monthly car expenses are $243. She pays an average of $55 a month for gas, oil, and repairs. What are Amanda's remaining car expenses each month?

4. Ryan owes $2,374 in income taxes for the year. He has already paid $2,538 that has been withheld from his wages by his employer. How much of a refund should he receive?

5. Tom's salary is now $495. That includes a raise of $21. What was his old salary before the raise?

Check your answers on page 4 in the Answer Key for Book One. If you correctly answered four of the five items, go to the Self-Check. If not, complete the Supplemental Exercise for Subskill 3D.

Supplemental Exercise for Subskill 3D

Reread the explanation of solving subtraction word problems. Work through the examples, then try this exercise.

1. Find the difference between twelve thousand and ten thousand two hundred nine.

2. Donald Jones's weekly gross income (before deductions) is $788. His deductions total $119. What is Mr. Jones's net income (take-home pay)?

3. A factory employs 902 people. On Monday 47 employees were absent. How many employees were at work on Monday?

4. Mr. Simpson's hospital bill was $610. Mr. Simpson's insurance company paid $440 of this bill. How much did Mr. Simpson have to pay?

5. A bookcase requires 35 board feet of lumber to build. You have 25 board feet of lumber. How much more lumber is needed to build the bookcase?

Check your answers on page 4 in the Answer Key for Book One. If you correctly answered four of the five problems, go on to the Self-Check. If not, ask your instructor for help.

SELF-CHECK FOR SKILL UNIT 3

Solve each problem. Check your answer.

1. $\begin{array}{r} 4,236 \\ -2,548 \\ \hline \end{array}$ **2.** $\begin{array}{r} 14,379 \\ -\ 4,674 \\ \hline \end{array}$ **3.** $\begin{array}{r} 10,004 \\ -\ 9,248 \\ \hline \end{array}$

4. 3,641 − 208

5. 8,484 − 6,537

6. 505 − 502

7. 17,998 − 9,320

8. 688 − 472

9. 5,183 − 4,495

10. 126 − 87

11. 345 − 234

12. A bakery had 205 loaves of bread at 9:00 a.m. By 5:00 p.m. 19 loaves were left. How many loaves of bread were sold that day?

13. Oscar ran seven miles on Saturday and three miles on Sunday. How many more miles did he run on Saturday than he did on Sunday?

14. A camera and lens together cost $238. The lens costs $92. What is the cost of the camera alone?

15. Mrs. Franklin put a coat costing $89 on layaway. She paid $9 down. How much remains to be paid on the coat?

Check your answers on page 4 in the Answer Key for Book One. If you correctly answered eight of the ten items, go on to Skill Unit 4. If not, ask your instructor for help.

Skill Unit 4
MULTIPLYING WHOLE NUMBERS

What Skills You Need to Begin: Ability to read and write numbers and identify place values; ability to add and subtract whole numbers (Skill Units 1 through 3).

What Skills You Will Learn: After studying this skill unit, you will be able to multiply by one-digit, two-digit, and three-digit numbers and to solve word problems involving multiplication.

Why You Need These Skills: You work eight hours a day four days a week. How many hours do you work each week?

Your rent is $220 a month. How much do you pay for rent each year?

You want to count the number of chairs in a room. There are eight rows. Each row contains twelve chairs.

The answer to each of these problems can be found by multiplication.

How You Will Show What You Have Learned: At the end of this skill unit is a Self-Check consisting of fifteen problems in multiplying whole numbers. You should allow yourself one hour to complete the Self-Check. To prove that you have mastered these skills, you must correctly answer twelve of the fifteen problems.

If you feel that you have already mastered multiplying whole numbers, complete the Self-Check on page 74.

Subskill 4A: Using the Multiplication Table

Studying this subskill will enable you to use the multiplication table and memorize basic multiplication facts.

Multiplication is a fast way to add a number to itself. A times sign (×) shows multiplication. For example, instead of adding 2 together five times, you can multiply 5 times 2 to obtain the answer quickly.

Adding:

$$\begin{array}{r} 2 \\ 2 \\ 2 \\ 2 \\ +\ 2 \\ \hline 10 \end{array}$$

Multiplying:

$$5 \times 2 = 10 \quad \text{or} \quad \begin{array}{r} 2 \\ \times\ 5 \\ \hline 10 \end{array}$$

The numbers that are multiplied together are called **factors.** The answer is called the **product.** In the problem $5 \times 2 = 10$, 5 and 2 are the factors and 10 is the product.

$$\begin{array}{rl} 2 & \text{factor} \\ \times\ 5 & \text{factor} \\ \hline 10 & \text{product} \end{array} \qquad \begin{array}{ccccc} 5 & \times & 2 & = & 10 \\ \text{factor} & & \text{factor} & & \text{product} \end{array}$$

This table shows the multiplication facts for all one-digit numbers.

×	0	1	2	3	4	5	6	7	8	9
0	0	0	0	0	0	0	0	0	0	0
1	0	1	2	3	4	5	6	7	8	9
2	0	2	4	6	8	10	12	14	16	18
3	0	3	6	9	12	15	18	21	24	27
4	0	4	8	12	16	20	24	28	32	36
5	0	5	10	15	20	25	30	35	40	45
6	0	6	12	18	24	30	36	42	48	54
7	0	7	14	21	28	35	42	49	56	63
8	0	8	16	24	32	40	48	56	64	72
9	0	9	18	27	36	45	54	63	72	81

EXAMPLE: Find 5×2.

To find the product of 5 × 2, locate 2 in the top row. Follow the arrow straight down to the row that starts with 5. Do you see that 5 × 2 = 10?

EXAMPLE: Now find 2 × 5.

Locate 5 in the top row. Move straight down to the row that starts with 2. Do you see that 2 × 5 = 10?

Since 5 × 2 = 10 and 2 × 5 = 10, 5 × 2 = 2 × 5. You can multiply numbers in any order and still get the same product.

Here's another example. Can you use the table to find the product of 7 × 6? Did you get 42 as your answer? What is the product of 6 × 7? Right—it's also 42.

Notice from the table that if you multiply any number by 1, the product is always the same as the original number. If you multiply any number by 0, the answer is always 0.

Memorizing the Multiplication Facts

As with addition facts, you must memorize certain multiplication facts. Study the multiplication table and memorize all the numbers. Check your understanding of these facts by completing the following exercise.

Exercise for Subskill 4A

Find the product for each multiplication problem below

1.	2 ×3	4 ×5	1 ×0	7 ×6	3 ×0	5 ×2	9 ×7	6 ×1	0 ×9	8 ×8
2.	5 ×3	1 ×8	7 ×0	4 ×2	0 ×6	6 ×5	9 ×4	3 ×7	8 ×1	2 ×9
3.	3 ×3	7 ×1	0 ×8	2 ×7	6 ×2	9 ×0	4 ×6	8 ×9	5 ×4	1 ×5
4.	6 ×0	8 ×2	7 ×3	5 ×5	0 ×7	3 ×8	9 ×9	1 ×7	4 ×1	2 ×4
5.	4 ×0	6 ×3	2 ×8	8 ×0	3 ×1	5 ×8	1 ×9	0 ×5	9 ×6	7 ×8

6.	1	3	5	7	9	0	8	6	4	2
	×3	×9	×0	×4	×2	×4	×3	×9	×4	×1
7.	7	1	5	9	3	6	2	0	8	4
	×2	×1	×1	×5	×4	×7	×0	×3	×5	×3
8.	6	9	0	7	1	4	5	3	8	2
	×8	×1	×2	×5	×6	×7	×9	×6	×7	×5
9.	7	2	4	8	0	3	6	1	9	5
	×9	×2	×9	×4	×0	×5	×4	×2	×3	×6
10.	5	8	1	9	7	2	4	3	6	0
	×7	×6	×4	×8	×7	×6	×8	×2	×6	1

Check your answers on pages 4 and 5 in the Answer Key for Book One. If you correctly answered eighty of the one hundred problems, go to the next subskill. If not, complete the following Supplemental Exercise.

Supplemental Exercise for Subskill 4A

Study the multiplication table until you have learned all of the facts. If you are having difficulty, flash cards may help. These can be purchased in a store or you can make them. See your instructor if you need flash cards.

Now do this exercise.

1.	2 × 9 =	8 × 8 =	1 × 5 =	2 × 4 =
2.	7 × 8 =	2 × 1 =	4 × 3 =	2 × 5 =
3.	0 × 9 =	8 × 1 =	5 × 4 =	4 × 1 =
4.	9 × 6 =	4 × 4 =	8 × 5 =	8 × 7 =
5.	9 × 3 =	6 × 6 =	6 × 1 =	3 × 7 =
6.	8 × 9 =	1 × 7 =	0 × 5 =	6 × 9 =
7.	0 × 3 =	3 × 6 =	1 × 2 =	3 × 2 =

8.	$9 \times 7 =$	$4 \times 6 =$	$8 \times 3 =$	$9 \times 4 =$
9.	$9 \times 9 =$	$2 \times 0 =$	$1 \times 9 =$	$5 \times 1 =$
10.	$6 \times 4 =$	$4 \times 8 =$	$5 \times 2 =$	$6 \times 5 =$
11.	$9 \times 0 =$	$3 \times 8 =$	$5 \times 8 =$	$0 \times 4 =$
12.	$6 \times 7 =$	$4 \times 7 =$	$3 \times 5 =$	$2 \times 6 =$
13.	$3 \times 0 =$	$6 \times 2 =$	$0 \times 7 =$	$3 \times 1 =$
14.	$9 \times 2 =$	$3 \times 4 =$	$0 \times 6 =$	$0 \times 0 =$
15.	$7 \times 7 =$	$1 \times 6 =$	$4 \times 2 =$	$7 \times 6 =$
16.	$2 \times 7 =$	$5 \times 5 =$	$8 \times 0 =$	$7 \times 4 =$
17.	$9 \times 5 =$	$8 \times 4 =$	$1 \times 0 =$	$7 \times 5 =$
18.	$7 \times 0 =$	$2 \times 8 =$	$9 \times 8 =$	$7 \times 3 =$
19.	$5 \times 9 =$	$0 \times 8 =$	$1 \times 4 =$	$4 \times 5 =$
20.	$5 \times 0 =$	$7 \times 1 =$	$4 \times 9 =$	$1 \times 8 =$
21.	$8 \times 2 =$	$6 \times 3 =$	$0 \times 2 =$	$3 \times 9 =$
22.	$1 \times 1 =$	$9 \times 1 =$	$2 \times 2 =$	$8 \times 6 =$
23.	$2 \times 3 =$	$5 \times 3 =$	$3 \times 3 =$	$6 \times 0 =$
24.	$4 \times 0 =$	$1 \times 3 =$	$7 \times 2 =$	$6 \times 8 =$
25.	$7 \times 9 =$	$5 \times 7 =$	$0 \times 1 =$	$5 \times 6 =$

Check your answers on page 5 in the Answer Key for Book One. If you correctly answered eighty of the one hundred items, go to the next subskill. If not, ask your instructor for help.

Subskill 4B: Multiplying by One-Digit Numbers

After studying this subskill, you will be able to multiply by one-digit numbers.

Line Up the Place Values

Before multiplying two factors, first write one below the other. It is usually easier to work the problem if you write the factor containing the most digits on top. For example, change

$2 \times 32 =$ $\quad\quad$ $3 \times 28 =$

to

$$\begin{array}{r} 32 \\ \times\ \ 2 \\ \hline \end{array} \qquad \begin{array}{r} 28 \\ \times\ \ 3 \\ \hline \end{array}$$

Multiply the Ones Digit

Multiply the digit in the ones position of the top number by the number on the bottom, which is called the **multiplier.** Write the product of these two digits in the ones place of the answer. If the product is greater than nine, write the ones digit and carry the tens digit.

$$\begin{array}{r} 32 \\ \times\ \ 2 \\ \hline 4 \end{array} \qquad 2 \times 2 = 4$$

$$\begin{array}{r} {\scriptstyle 2}\ \ \\ 28 \\ \times\ \ 3 \\ \hline 4 \end{array}$$

$3 \times 8 = 24$
Write 4 in the ones place of the answer. Carry the 2.

Multiply the Tens Digit

Next, multiply the number on the bottom by the tens digit in the top number. Add any number that you carried to this product and write this result in the tens place of the answer.

$$\begin{array}{r} 32 \\ \times\ \ 2 \\ \hline 64 \end{array} \qquad 2 \times 3 = 6$$

$$\begin{array}{r} {\scriptstyle 2}\ \ \\ 28 \\ \times\ \ 3 \\ \hline 84 \end{array}$$

$3 \times 2 = 6$
Add the 2 you carried and write 8 in the answer.

Continue Until You Have Multiplied All Digits

Turn to page 60 for an example that contains more digits.

EXAMPLE:

$$\begin{array}{r} {}^{2} \\ 1{,}045 \\ \times\quad 4 \\ \hline 0 \end{array}$$

$5 \times 4 = 20$

Multiply the ones digit (5) by the multiplier (4). Write the 0 of the product in the ones place. Carry the 2.

$$\begin{array}{r} {}^{1\,2} \\ 1{,}045 \\ \times\quad 4 \\ \hline 80 \end{array}$$

$4 \times 4 = 16$
$16 + 2 = 18$

Multiply the tens digit (4) by the multiplier (4). Add the 2 you carried to the 6 of the product. Write the 8 in the tens place. Carry the 1.

$$\begin{array}{r} {}^{1\,2} \\ 1{,}045 \\ \times\quad 4 \\ \hline 480 \end{array}$$

$4 \times 0 = 0$
$0 + 1 = 1$

Multiply the hundreds digit (0) by the multiplier (4). Add the 1 you carried to the product. Write the 1 in the hundreds place.

$$\begin{array}{r} {}^{1\,2} \\ 1{,}045 \\ \times\quad 4 \\ \hline 4{,}180 \end{array}$$

$4 \times 1 = 4$

Multiply the thousands digit (1) by the multiplier (4). Write the product in the thousands place.

Answer: 4,180

Be very careful when one of the factors contains a zero. Remember, zero times any number equals zero.

$$\begin{array}{r} 200 \\ \times\quad 5 \\ \hline 0 \end{array}$$

$5 \times 0 = 0$

$$\begin{array}{r} 200 \\ \times\quad 5 \\ \hline 00 \end{array}$$

$5 \times 0 = 0$

$$\begin{array}{r} 200 \\ \times\quad 5 \\ \hline 1{,}000 \end{array}$$

$5 \times 2 = 10$

Now work through this example step-by-step.

EXAMPLE:

$$\begin{array}{r} {}^{8} \\ 5{,}309 \\ \times\quad 9 \\ \hline 1 \end{array}$$

$9 \times 9 = 81$

$$\begin{array}{r} {}^{8} \\ 5,309 \\ \times \quad 9 \\ \hline 81 \end{array} \qquad \begin{array}{l} 0 \times 9 = 0 \\ 0 + 8 = 8 \end{array}$$

$$\begin{array}{r} {}^{2\ \ 8} \\ 5,309 \\ \times \quad 9 \\ \hline 781 \end{array} \qquad 3 \times 9 = 27$$

$$\begin{array}{r} {}^{2\ \ 8} \\ 5,309 \\ \times \quad 9 \\ \hline 47,781 \end{array} \qquad \begin{array}{l} 5 \times 9 = 45 \\ 45 + 2 = 47 \end{array}$$

Answer: 47,781

Check your skill at multiplying by one-digit numbers by doing this exercise.

Exercise for Subskill 4B

1. $\begin{array}{r} 32 \\ \times\ 4 \\ \hline \end{array}$ **2.** $\begin{array}{r} 51 \\ \times\ 2 \\ \hline \end{array}$ **3.** $73 \times 3 =$

4. $\begin{array}{r} 64 \\ \times\ 2 \\ \hline \end{array}$ **5.** $\begin{array}{r} 14 \\ \times\ 4 \\ \hline \end{array}$ **6.** $53 \times 5 =$

7. $\begin{array}{r} 321 \\ \times\ \ 4 \\ \hline \end{array}$ **8.** $\begin{array}{r} 612 \\ \times\ \ 3 \\ \hline \end{array}$ **9.** $714 \times 5 =$

10. $\begin{array}{r} 516 \\ \times\ \ 6 \\ \hline \end{array}$ **11.** $\begin{array}{r} 925 \\ \times\ \ 4 \\ \hline \end{array}$ **12.** $452 \times 8 =$

13. $\begin{array}{r} 508 \\ \times\ \ 5 \\ \hline \end{array}$ **14.** $\begin{array}{r} 2,863 \\ \times\ \ \ 7 \\ \hline \end{array}$ **15.** $\begin{array}{r} 4,060 \\ \times\ \ \ 3 \\ \hline \end{array}$

Check your answers on page 5 in the Answer Key for Book One. If you correctly answered twelve of the fifteen problems, go to the next subskill. If not, complete the following Supplemental Exercise.

Supplemental Exercise for Subskill 4B

Review the explanation of how to multiply by one-digit numbers. Work through the examples. Then solve these multiplication problems.

1. $\begin{array}{r} 24 \\ \times\ 2 \\ \hline \end{array}$ 2. $\begin{array}{r} 41 \\ \times\ 4 \\ \hline \end{array}$ 3. $62 \times 3 =$

4. $\begin{array}{r} 72 \\ \times\ 4 \\ \hline \end{array}$ 5. $\begin{array}{r} 25 \\ \times\ 3 \\ \hline \end{array}$ 6. $49 \times 2 =$

7. $\begin{array}{r} 813 \\ \times\ 3 \\ \hline \end{array}$ 8. $\begin{array}{r} 911 \\ \times\ 4 \\ \hline \end{array}$ 9. $524 \times 3 =$

10. $\begin{array}{r} 715 \\ \times\ 6 \\ \hline \end{array}$ 11. $\begin{array}{r} 654 \\ \times\ 9 \\ \hline \end{array}$ 12. $396 \times 8 =$

13. $\begin{array}{r} 480 \\ \times\ 5 \\ \hline \end{array}$ 14. $\begin{array}{r} 909 \\ \times\ 8 \\ \hline \end{array}$ 15. $\begin{array}{r} 2{,}476 \\ \times\ 6 \\ \hline \end{array}$

Check your answers on page 5 in the Answer Key for Book One. If you correctly answered twelve of the fifteen problems, go on to the next subskill. If not, ask your instructor for help.

Subskill 4C: Multiplying by Two-Digit Numbers

After studying this subskill, you will be able to multiply by two-digit numbers.

Line Up Place Values

Before multiplying two factors, first write one below the other, with the larger one on top. For example, change

$24 \times 31 =$ $45 \times 163 =$

to

$\begin{array}{r} 31 \\ \times\ 24 \\ \hline \end{array}$ $\begin{array}{r} 163 \\ \times\ 45 \\ \hline \end{array}$

Multiply the Top Factor by the Ones Digit of the Bottom Factor

Starting at the right, multiply each digit of the top factor by the ones digit of the bottom factor. When the multiplier has more than one digit, the result of multiplying each digit is called a partial product.

EXAMPLE:

```
                1
   31         163     5 × 3 = 15
×  24      ×   45     Write 5 in the ones place of the
    4           5     answer. Carry the 1.

               3 1
   31         163     5 × 6 = 30
×  24      ×   45     Add the 1 you carried.
  124          15     30 + 1 = 31
                      Write 1 in the tens place of the
                      answer. Carry the 3.

               3 1
   31         163     5 × 1 = 5
×  24      ×   45     Add the 3 you carried.
  124 partial 815     5 + 3 = 8
      product         Write 8 in the hundreds place.
```

Multiply the Top Factor by the Tens Digit of the Bottom Factor

Again starting at the right, multiply each digit of the top factor by the tens digit of the bottom factor. Since you are multiplying by the tens digit, the first digit of the product is written in the tens place.

```
                1
   31         163     4 × 3 = 12
×  24      ×   45     Write 2 in the tens place of the
  124         815     answer because the multiplier (4)
   2           2      is in the tens place. Carry the 1.

               2 1
   31         163     4 × 6 = 24
×  24      ×   45     Add the 1 you carried.
  124         815     24 + 1 = 25
  62          52      Write 5 in the hundreds place of
                      the answer. Carry the 2.
```

$$\begin{array}{r} 31 \\ \times\ 24 \\ \hline 124 \\ 62\ \ \\ \hline \end{array} \quad \text{partial product} \qquad \begin{array}{r} {}^{2\,1}\ \ \ \\ 163 \\ \times\ \ 45 \\ \hline 815 \\ 652\ \ \end{array}$$

4 × 1 = 4
Add the 2 you carried.
4 + 2 = 6
Write 6 in the thousands place.

Add the Partial Products

The last step is to add the partial products to find the answer (product) to the multiplication problem.

$$\begin{array}{r} 31 \\ \times\ 24 \\ \hline 124 \\ 62\ \ \\ \hline 744 \end{array} \qquad \begin{array}{r} 163 \\ \times\ \ \ 45 \\ \hline 815 \\ 652\ \ \\ \hline 7,335 \end{array}$$

Answer: 744 and 7,335

Let's try another example.

EXAMPLE:

$$\begin{array}{r} 346 \\ \times\ \ 54 \\ \hline \end{array}$$

Line up the place values.

$$\begin{array}{r} {}^{2}\ \ \ \\ 346 \\ \times\ \ 54 \\ \hline 4 \end{array}$$

Multiply by the ones digit of the multiplier.
4 × 6 = 24
Write 4 in the ones place of the answer. Carry the 2.

$$\begin{array}{r} {}^{1\,2}\ \ \ \\ 346 \\ \times\ \ 54 \\ \hline 84 \end{array}$$

4 × 4 = 16
Add the 2 you carried.
16 + 2 = 18
Write 8 in the tens column of the answer. Carry the 1.

$$\begin{array}{r} {}^{1\,2}\ \ \ \\ 346 \\ \times\ \ 54 \\ \hline 1384 \end{array} \quad \text{1st partial product}$$

4 × 3 = 12
Add the 1 you carried.
12 + 1 = 13
Since the 3 is the last digit to be multiplied, it is not necessary to carry the 1, because there is nothing to add it to. Simply write 13 in the hundreds and thousands place of the answer.

```
    3
  346
×  54
 1384
   0
```

Multiply by the tens digit of the multiplier.
$5 \times 6 = 30$
Write 0 in the tens place of the answer. Carry the 3.

```
   2 3
  346
×  54
 1384
  30
```

$5 \times 4 = 20$
Add the 3 you carried.
$20 + 3 = 23$
Write 3 in the hundreds place of the answer. Carry the 2.

```
   2 3
   346
×   54
  1384
 1730     2nd partial product
```

$5 \times 3 = 15$
Add the 2 you carried.
$15 + 2 = 17$
Write 17 in the thousands and ten thousands place of the answer.

```
     346
×     54
   1 384
  17 30
  18,684
```

Add the partial products.
Now add the two partial products to arrive at the final answer.

Answer: 18,684

Check your skill at multiplying by a two-digit number by doing this exercise.

Exercise for Subskill 4C

1. $\begin{array}{r} 13 \\ \times 32 \\ \hline \end{array}$ **2.** $\begin{array}{r} 41 \\ \times 26 \\ \hline \end{array}$ **3.** $74 \times 43 =$

4. $\begin{array}{r} 68 \\ \times 76 \\ \hline \end{array}$ **5.** $\begin{array}{r} 55 \\ \times 97 \\ \hline \end{array}$ **6.** $86 \times 39 =$

7. $\begin{array}{r} 62 \\ \times 93 \\ \hline \end{array}$ **8.** $\begin{array}{r} 98 \\ \times 95 \\ \hline \end{array}$ **9.** $\begin{array}{r} 554 \\ \times\ 16 \\ \hline \end{array}$

10. $\begin{array}{r} 4{,}188 \\ \times\ \ 97 \\ \hline \end{array}$

Check your answers on page 5 in the Answer Key for Book One. If you correctly answered eight of the ten problems, go on to the next subskill. If not, complete the following Supplemental Exercise.

Supplemental Exercise for Subskill 4C

Reread the instructions for multiplying by two-digit numbers, working through the examples. Then try these multiplication problems.

1. $\begin{array}{r} 32 \\ \times 31 \\ \hline \end{array}$ **2.** $\begin{array}{r} 52 \\ \times 44 \\ \hline \end{array}$ **3.** $67 \times 42 =$

4. $\begin{array}{r} 74 \\ \times 57 \\ \hline \end{array}$ **5.** $\begin{array}{r} 48 \\ \times 18 \\ \hline \end{array}$ **6.** $93 \times 37 =$

7. $\begin{array}{r} 86 \\ \times 36 \\ \hline \end{array}$ **8.** $\begin{array}{r} 57 \\ \times 86 \\ \hline \end{array}$ **9.** $939 \times 64 =$

10. $2{,}476 \times 67 =$

Check your answers on page 5 in the Answer Key for Book One. If you correctly answered eight of the ten problems, go on to the next subskill. If not, ask your instructor for help.

Subskill 4D: Multiplying by Three-Digit Numbers

Studying this subskill will enable you to multiply by three-digit numbers.

Line Up Place Values

Before multiplying two factors, first write one below the other. It is usually easier to work the problem if you write the larger factor on top.

EXAMPLE:

$$\begin{array}{r} 5\,2\,6 \\ \times\ 3\,7\,1 \\ \hline \end{array}$$

Multiply the Ones Digit

Multiply the ones digit of the bottom factor by each digit of the top factor. Be sure to start at the right and go to the left.

```
  526     1 × 6 = 6
× 371     1 × 2 = 2
  526     1 × 5 = 5
```

There is no carrying involved in this part of the problem.

Multiply the Tens Digit

Remember to start writing this partial product in the tens place.

```
      14
     526
×    371
     526
   3682
```

7 × 6 = 42
Write the 2 in the tens place and carry the 4.
7 × 2 = 14
Add 4 to 14 to get 18. Write the 8 in the hundreds place and carry the 1.
7 × 5 = 35
Add 1 to 35 to get 36. Write the 6 in the thousands place and write the 3 in the ten thousands place.

Multiply the Hundreds Digit

```
       1
     526
×    371
     526
   3682
  1578
```

3 × 6 = 18
Write the 8 in the hundreds place and carry the 1.
3 × 2 = 6
Add 1 to 6 to get 7. Write 7 in the thousands place.
3 × 5 = 15
Write the 5 in the ten thousands place and write the 1 in the hundred thousands place.

Complete the Problem

Continue multiplying until you have multiplied the top factor by every digit of the bottom factor. Then add the partial products.

```
       526
×      371
       526
     3682
    1578
   195,146
```

Answer: 195,146

Here's another example to work through.

EXAMPLE:

4, 0 4 8 × 1 7 0 ———	Line up the place values.
4, 0 4 8 × 1 7 0 ——— 0 0 0 0	Multiply the ones digits. Any number multiplied by zero equals zero.
5 4, 0 4 8 × 1 7 0 ——— 0 0 0 0 6	Multiply the tens digit. 7 × 8 = 56 Write 6 in the tens place of the answer. Carry the 5.
5 4, 0 4 8 × 1 7 0 ——— 0 0 0 0 3 3 6	7 × 4 = 28 Add the 5 you carried. 28 + 5 = 33 Write 33 in the hundred and thousand places of the answer. This is possible because the next multiplication, 7 × 0, equals 0, so it does not affect the preceding number.
5 4, 0 4 8 × 1 7 0 ——— 0 0 0 0 2 8 3 3 6	7 × 4 = 28 Since this is the last digit, write 28 in the ten thousand and hundred thousand places in the answer.
4, 0 4 8 × 1 7 0 ——— 0 0 0 0 2 8 3 3 6 4 0 4 8	Multiply the hundreds digit. Any number times 1 equals the original number. Just bring down the 4,048, making sure the place values are correctly lined up.
4, 0 4 8 × 1 7 0 ——— 0 0 0 0 2 8 3 3 6 4 0 4 8 ——— 6 8 8, 1 6 0	Complete the problem. Now add the partial products and arrive at the final solution.

Answer: 688,160

Problems involving multiplication by numbers containing zeros can be simplified. Let's look at 4,048 × 170 again.

4,048 × 170 0 000	When you multiplied by zero, you obtained a partial product containing only zeros.
4,048 × 170 0 000 283 36	Next you multiplied by 7 and wrote this partial product.

These two steps can be combined as follows.

4,048 × 170 0	When you multiply by zero, write only one zero as the partial product.
4,048 × 170 283 360	Write the next partial product on the same line. Since you are multiplying by the tens digit, the partial product starts in the tens place.
4,048 × 170 283 360 404 8 688,160	Finish by multiplying by the hundreds digit. Be sure to start the partial product in the hundreds place. Then add the partial products.

Here are more examples:

EXAMPLE:

643 × 400 0	Multiply by the ones digit. Write only one zero in the ones place.
643 × 400 00	Multiply by the tens digit. Write only one zero in the tens place.
643 × 400 267,200	Multiply by the hundreds digit.

Answer: 267,200

EXAMPLE:

```
   40
 × 90
 ----
    0
```

Multiply by the ones digit. Write one zero in the ones place.

```
    40
 ×  90
 -----
 3,600
```

Multiply by the tens digit. Write one zero in the tens place.

Answer: 3,600

EXAMPLE:

```
   156
 × 307
 -----
  1092
```

Multiply by the ones digit.

```
   156
 × 307
 -----
  1092
     0
```

Multiply by the tens digit. Write one zero in the tens place.

```
      156
 ×    307
 --------
     1092
    4680
 --------
   47,892
```

Multiply by the hundreds digit.

Answer: 47,892

Check your skill at multiplying whole numbers by doing this exercise.

Exercise for Subskill 4D

1. 49 × 23

2. 376 × 79

3. 981 × 357

4. 806 × 206

5. 321 × 413

6. 542 × 631

7. 756 × 381

8. 3,968 × 793

9. 698 × 320 =

10. 7,801 × 500 =

Check your answers on page 5 in the Answer Key for Book One. If you correctly answered eight of the ten problems, go on to the next subskill. If not, complete the following Supplemental Exercise.

Supplemental Exercise for Subskill 4D

Reread the explanation for multiplying by three-digit numbers. Work through the examples as you read.

Now try these problems.

1. $\begin{array}{r} 412 \\ \times\ 32 \\ \hline \end{array}$	**2.** $\begin{array}{r} 68 \\ \times 99 \\ \hline \end{array}$	**3.** $\begin{array}{r} 543 \\ \times 643 \\ \hline \end{array}$	**4.** $\begin{array}{r} 509 \\ \times 902 \\ \hline \end{array}$
5. $\begin{array}{r} 183 \\ \times 657 \\ \hline \end{array}$	**6.** $\begin{array}{r} 937 \\ \times 487 \\ \hline \end{array}$	**7.** $\begin{array}{r} 786 \\ \times 659 \\ \hline \end{array}$	**8.** $\begin{array}{r} 9{,}684 \\ \times\ 863 \\ \hline \end{array}$

9. $939 \times 740 =$ **10.** $507 \times 200 =$

Check your answers on page 5 in the Answer Key for Book One. If you correctly answered eight of the ten problems, go on to the next subskill. If not, ask your instructor for help

Subskill 4E: Solving Word Problems

After studying this subskill, you will be able to solve word problems involving multiplication.

You have already had practice solving word problems using addition and subtraction. Multiplication word problems require the same procedure in finding their solutions.

Read and Reread the Problem

Read the entire problem carefully. Read the problem again to make sure you understand what you are being asked to do.

EXAMPLE:

Joyce Johnson earns $1,400 each month. How much does she earn in a year?

Now that you have read the problem, go to the next step.

Determine What You Are to Find

What does the problem ask you to do? In other words, what will you need to do to find the answer?

In the example on page 71, you are asked to find Ms. Johnson's annual salary.

Determine What You Are Given

What facts do you know? Also, what facts are not needed to solve the problem?

In the example on page 71, you know Ms. Johnson's monthly salary. In order to work the problem, you must also know that there are twelve months in a year.

Decide What Operation(s) to Use

"Multi" means many. Multiplication problems ask for a *combination of items*. "Product" and "times" are common key words in multiplication problems. Look also for any problem that gives you a number for one item, and asks you to find that number for several such items.

In the example on page 71, you are given the salary for one-twelfth of the year. You must multiply by 12 to obtain the annual salary.

Solve the Problem

$$\begin{array}{r} \$1,400 \\ \times \quad 12 \\ \hline 2\,800 \\ 14\,00 \\ \hline \$16,800 \end{array}$$

Joyce earns $16,800 in a year.

Check Your Answer

Check your multiplication by multiplying again.

Now check your skill at solving word problems by doing this exercise.

Exercise for Subskill 4E

1. Find the product of four thousand nine hundred eight and seven hundred thirty.

2. A used car can be purchased by making 24 payments of $145 each. How much does the car cost?

3. John's fixed salary each week is $195. How much did John earn in a whole year (52 weeks)?

4. A stadium contains 150 rows of seats. There are 110 seats in each row. How many people can be seated in the stadium?

5. A room contains 39 square yards of floor space. If carpeting costs $14 a square yard, including padding and installation, what is the cost of carpeting the room?

Check your answers on page 6 in the Answer Key for Book One. If you correctly answered four of the five problems, go on to the Self-Check. If not, complete the following Supplemental Exercise.

Supplemental Exercise for Subskill 4E

Review the steps in solving word problems. Work through the example problem and study the word problems in previous chapters. Then try these problems.

1. Find the product of one thousand ninety-three and two hundred twenty.

2. An orchard contains 125 rows of trees. Each row consists of 105 trees. How many trees are in the orchard?

3. A stadium holds 43,127 people. One Saturday afternoon the stadium was full. Each person had paid $5.00 to get in. Find the total price paid for tickets at the stadium on that day.

4. Liza was throwing a party. She ordered four cases of cola, three cases of ginger ale, and four cases of fruit punch. Each case contained twenty-four cans. How many cans did she order?

5. Michelle earns $205 a week. How much does she earn in a year (52 weeks)?

Check your answers on page 6 in the Answer Key for Book One. If you correctly answered four of the five problems, go to the Self-Check. If not, ask your instructor for help.

SELF-CHECK FOR SKILL UNIT 4

Solve each problem in the exercise below. You must show your work.

1. 937×487 **2.** 967×36 **3.** 803×904

4. $358 \times 1{,}986 =$ **5.** $182 \times 5{,}099 =$

6. $213 \times 32{,}014 =$ **7.** $29 \times 784 =$

8. 438×500 **9.** 690×321 **10.** 641×399

11. Mr. Jackson has 76 cows. He gets about 6 gallons of milk every day from each cow. How much milk should he get in one day?

12. It costs $23 a day, without mileage, to rent a car. How much does it cost, without mileage charges, to rent a car for a month that has 31 days?

13. It costs $1,850 a year to educate one student at Lincoln School. There are 230 students in the school. What is the total cost for educating all the students at Lincoln School for one year?

14. The Warren County stadium can hold 52,532 people. One Saturday afternoon, the stadium was full. Each ticket cost $6. What was the total amount of money paid for tickets at the stadium that day?

15. Mr. Seltzer ordered seven cases of tomato soup, nine cases of chicken soup, and three cases of bean soup for his store. Each case contained twelve cans of soup. How many cans of soup did he order altogether?

Check your answer on page 6 in the Answer Key for Book One. If you correctly answered twelve of fifteen items, go on to Skill Unit 5. If not, ask your instructor for help.

Skill Unit 5
DIVIDING WHOLE NUMBERS

What Skills You Need to Begin: Ability to read and write numbers and identify place values; ability to add, subtract, and multiply whole numbers (Skill Units 1 through 4).

What Skills You Will Learn: After studying this skill unit, you will be able to divide whole numbers. You will also be able to solve word problems involving division.

Why You Need These Skills: You have $15 to spend each week for lunch at work. You work five days each week. How much can you spend each day?

A portable television set costs $399. You can pay for it in three equal payments. What is the amount of each payment?

You drove 440 miles on a tank of gasoline. The tank holds 20 gallons of gasoline. How many mpg (miles per gallon) did your car average?

All of these problems can be solved by division.

How You Will Show What You Have Learned: At the end of this skill unit is a Self-Check consisting of fifteen problems in dividing whole numbers. You should allow yourself one hour to complete the Self-Check. To prove that you have mastered these skills, you must correctly answer twelve of the fifteen problems.

If you feel that you have already mastered dividing whole numbers, complete the Self-Check on pages 101 and 102.

Subskill 5A: Understanding Division

This subskill will give you different ways to look at what happens to a number when it is **divided.** This subskill will also help you to memorize basic division facts.

Division is a way to subtract a number several times. For example, take the number 12 and keep subtracting 3 until zero is left.

$$\begin{array}{r} 12 \\ -\ 3 \\ \hline 9 \end{array} \qquad \begin{array}{r} 9 \\ -\ 3 \\ \hline 6 \end{array} \qquad \begin{array}{r} 6 \\ -\ 3 \\ \hline 3 \end{array} \qquad \begin{array}{r} 3 \\ -\ 3 \\ \hline 0 \end{array}$$

You can see that four 3's were taken away.

In division, you would say: How many 3's are in 12? You would show it in this form: $3\overline{)12}$

There are four 3's in 12: $\begin{array}{r} 4 \\ 3\overline{)12} \end{array}$

Other ways of writing this division example are:

$$12 \div 3 \qquad \frac{12}{3} \qquad 12/3$$

These forms could be expressed as "12 divided by 3."

The number that is being divided is the **dividend.** The number you are dividing by is the **divisor.** The answer is the **quotient.**

$$\begin{array}{rrl} & 4 & \text{quotient} \\ \text{divisor} & 3\overline{)12} & \text{dividend} \end{array}$$

$$\begin{array}{ccccc} 12 & \div & 3 & = & 4 \\ \text{dividend} & & \text{divisor} & & \text{quotient} \end{array}$$

Division and Multiplication

Division and multiplication are related. As you can see in the following two examples, they use the same numbers as facts.

$$4 \times 3 = 12$$

$$12 \div 3 = 4$$

As with multiplication facts, you must memorize certain basic division facts. If you know your multiplication facts, you can easily learn the division facts. For example, to find the answer to

$$12 \div 3 = ?$$

ask yourself: What number must be multiplied by 3 to make 12? In other words, change

$$12 \div 3 = ? \quad \text{to} \quad 3 \times ? = 12$$

Because $3 \times \underline{4} = 12$

Then $12 \div 3 = \underline{4}$

EXAMPLE: Find the quotient of $36 \div 4$.

To find the quotient of $36 \div 4$, think to yourself: What must be multiplied by 4 to make 36? If you said 9, you're right.

Answer: 9

NOTE: If you need to review multiplication facts, study the multiplication table on page 55.

You can check a division problem by multiplying. The product of the quotient and the divisor should be the dividend. Does $4 \times 9 = 36$? Yes.

Division and Zero

ZERO DIVIDED BY A NUMBER. What is the quotient of $0 \div 8$? $0 \div 8 = 0$ because $8 \times 0 = 0$. In fact, 0 divided by any number is 0 because 0 multiplied by any number is 0.

$0 \div 1 = 0$	$0 \div 6 = 0$
$0 \div 2 = 0$	$0 \div 7 = 0$
$0 \div 3 = 0$	$0 \div 8 = 0$
$0 \div 4 = 0$	$0 \div 9 = 0$
$0 \div 5 = 0$	

YOU CANNOT DIVIDE BY ZERO. For example, if $5 \div 0 =$ a number, then the number multiplied by 0 must equal 5. However, any number multiplied by 0 equals 0. Therefore, no number can be divided by 0.

Check your understanding of division facts by completing the exercise on page 78.

Exercise for Subskill 5A

Find the quotient for each division problem below.

1.	$0 \div 0 =$	$4 \div 0 =$	$7 \div 0 =$	$3 \div 0 =$	$5 \div 0 =$
2.	$35 \div 5 =$	$16 \div 8 =$	$27 \div 9 =$	$28 \div 7 =$	$9 \div 3 =$
3.	$6 \div 3 =$	$5 \div 1 =$	$2 \div 2 =$	$3 \div 1 =$	$4 \div 2 =$
4.	$9 \div 1 =$	$7 \div 1 =$	$5 \div 1 =$	$8 \div 1 =$	$6 \div 1 =$
5.	$8 \div 2 =$	$4 \div 2 =$	$0 \div 2 =$	$6 \div 2 =$	$2 \div 2 =$
6.	$48 \div 6 =$	$72 \div 8 =$	$28 \div 7 =$	$9 \div 9 =$	$27 \div 3 =$
7.	$30 \div 5 =$	$0 \div 4 =$	$12 \div 3 =$	$15 \div 3 =$	$8 \div 4 =$
8.	$7 \div 7 =$	$48 \div 8 =$	$0 \div 5 =$	$24 \div 4 =$	$40 \div 5 =$
9.	$63 \div 7 =$	$45 \div 9 =$	$12 \div 2 =$	$32 \div 8 =$	$24 \div 3 =$
10.	$81 \div 9 =$	$54 \div 9 =$	$63 \div 9 =$	$36 \div 6 =$	$20 \div 4 =$
11.	$18 \div 2 =$	$72 \div 9 =$	$21 \div 7 =$	$0 \div 7 =$	$4 \div 4 =$
12.	$28 \div 4 =$	$5 \div 5 =$	$45 \div 5 =$	$18 \div 3 =$	$16 \div 8 =$
13.	$0 \div 8 =$	$10 \div 5 =$	$49 \div 7 =$	$20 \div 5 =$	$40 \div 8 =$
14.	$14 \div 7 =$	$0 \div 9 =$	$0 \div 6 =$	$12 \div 4 =$	$36 \div 4 =$
15.	$6 \div 6 =$	$18 \div 9 =$	$30 \div 6 =$	$42 \div 7 =$	$16 \div 2 =$
16.	$14 \div 2 =$	$12 \div 6 =$	$21 \div 3 =$	$27 \div 9 =$	$36 \div 9 =$
17.	$35 \div 7 =$	$8 \div 8 =$	$64 \div 8 =$	$54 \div 6 =$	$3 \div 3 =$

18. $56 \div 7 =$ $56 \div 8 =$ $25 \div 5 =$ $18 \div 6 =$ $24 \div 8 =$

19. $24 \div 6 =$ $10 \div 2 =$ $16 \div 4 =$ $35 \div 5 =$ $0 \div 3 =$

20. $32 \div 4 =$ $15 \div 5 =$ $9 \div 3 =$ $6 \div 3 =$ $42 \div 6 =$

Check your answers on page 6 in the Answer Key for Book One. If you correctly answered eighty of the one hundred problems, go to the next subskill. If not, complete the following Supplemental Exercise.

Supplemental Exercise for Subskill 5A

Study the division facts until you have memorized all of them. If you are having difficulty, flash cards may help. These can be purchased in a store, or you can make your own. See your instructor if you think you might need flash cards.

Find the quotient for each division problem below.

1. $3\overline{)6}$ $5\overline{)20}$ $0\overline{)0}$ $6\overline{)42}$ $0\overline{)3}$

2. $2\overline{)10}$ $7\overline{)63}$ $1\overline{)6}$ $9\overline{)0}$ $8\overline{)64}$

3. $3\overline{)15}$ $8\overline{)8}$ $0\overline{)7}$ $2\overline{)8}$ $5\overline{)30}$

4. $0\overline{)6}$ $4\overline{)36}$ $7\overline{)21}$ $1\overline{)8}$ $9\overline{)18}$

5. $3\overline{)9}$ $1\overline{)7}$ $8\overline{)0}$ $7\overline{)14}$ $2\overline{)12}$

6. $0\overline{)9}$ $6\overline{)24}$ $9\overline{)72}$ $4\overline{)20}$ $5\overline{)5}$

7. $0\overline{)6}$ $2\overline{)16}$ $3\overline{)21}$ $5\overline{)25}$ $7\overline{)0}$

8. $8\overline{)24}$ $9\overline{)81}$ $7\overline{)7}$ $1\overline{)4}$ $4\overline{)8}$

9. $0\overline{)4}$ $3\overline{)18}$ $8\overline{)16}$ $0\overline{)8}$ $1\overline{)3}$

10. $8\overline{)40}$ $9\overline{)9}$ $5\overline{)0}$ $6\overline{)54}$ $8\overline{)56}$

11. $3\overline{)3}$ $9\overline{)27}$ $0\overline{)5}$ $4\overline{)28}$ $2\overline{)18}$

12.	$4\overline{)0}$	$3\overline{)24}$	$9\overline{)54}$	$4\overline{)16}$	$1\overline{)2}$
13.	$2\overline{)14}$	$1\overline{)1}$	$1\overline{)5}$	$5\overline{)45}$	$4\overline{)12}$
14.	$7\overline{)42}$	$0\overline{)2}$	$3\overline{)0}$	$5\overline{)40}$	$3\overline{)12}$
15.	$8\overline{)48}$	$1\overline{)9}$	$2\overline{)0}$	$5\overline{)35}$	$6\overline{)6}$
16.	$7\overline{)28}$	$9\overline{)45}$	$6\overline{)18}$	$7\overline{)56}$	$5\overline{)10}$
17.	$9\overline{)63}$	$2\overline{)4}$	$9\overline{)36}$	$4\overline{)32}$	$0\overline{)1}$
18.	$5\overline{)15}$	$4\overline{)24}$	$2\overline{)2}$	$3\overline{)27}$	$6\overline{)30}$
19.	$7\overline{)35}$	$6\overline{)48}$	$4\overline{)4}$	$8\overline{)72}$	$7\overline{)49}$
20	$6\overline{)12}$	$8\overline{)32}$	$2\overline{)6}$	$6\overline{)36}$	$1\overline{)0}$

Check your answers on page 6 in the Answer Key for Book One. If you correctly answered eighty of the one hundred problems, go to the next subskill. If not, ask your instructor for help.

Subskill 5B: Dividing by One-Digit Numbers

After studying this subskill, you will be able to divide by one-digit numbers.

There are four steps that must be followed in solving any division problem. They are:

Divide
Multiply
Subtract
Bring Down

These are repeated as often as needed. Repeat these four steps to yourself until you have memorized them.

EXAMPLE: Divide 624 by 4.

First, write 624 under the division sign and 4 outside the division sign.

$$4\overline{)6\,2\,4}$$

Divide

$$\begin{array}{r} 1 \\ 4\overline{)6\,2\,4} \end{array}$$

Divide the divisor into the first digit of the dividend. Can you divide 6 by 4? Yes, it goes 1 time. Write 1 in the quotient over the 6.

Multiply

$$\begin{array}{r} 1 \\ 4\overline{)6\,2\,4} \\ \underline{4} \end{array}$$

Multiply the 1 in the quotient times the divisor. Write the product, 4, under the 6.

Subtract

$$\begin{array}{r} 1 \\ 4\overline{)6\,2\,4} \\ -\underline{4} \\ 2 \end{array}$$

Subtract 4 from 6. Write the difference, 2, under the 4.

Bring Down

$$\begin{array}{r} 1 \\ 4\overline{)6\,2\,4} \\ -\underline{4} \\ 2\,2 \end{array}$$

Bring down the next digit, 2, from the dividend. Write it next to the 2.

Repeat the four steps.

$$\begin{array}{r} 1\,5 \\ 4\overline{)6\,2\,4} \\ -\underline{4} \\ 2\,2 \end{array}$$

Divide 22 by 4. It goes 5 times. Write 5 in the quotient above the 2.

$$\begin{array}{r} 1\,5 \\ 4\overline{)6\,2\,4} \\ -\underline{4} \\ 2\,2 \\ \underline{2\,0} \end{array}$$

Multiply 5 × 4. Write the product, 20, under the 22.

$$
\begin{array}{r}
15\\
4\overline{)624}\\
-4\\
\hline
22\\
-20\\
\hline
2
\end{array}
$$

Subtract 20 from 22. Write the difference, 2, under the 20.

$$
\begin{array}{r}
15\\
4\overline{)624}\\
-4\\
\hline
22\\
-20\\
\hline
24
\end{array}
$$

Bring down the next digit, 4, from the dividend.

Repeat

$$
\begin{array}{r}
156\\
4\overline{)624}\\
-4\\
\hline
22\\
-20\\
\hline
24
\end{array}
$$

Divide 24 by 4. It goes 6 times. Write 6 in the quotient above the 4.

$$
\begin{array}{r}
156\\
4\overline{)624}\\
-4\\
\hline
22\\
-20\\
\hline
24\\
24\\
\hline
\end{array}
$$

Multiply 6 × 4. Write the product, 24, under the 24.

$$
\begin{array}{r}
156\\
4\overline{)624}\\
-4\\
\hline
22\\
-20\\
\hline
24\\
-\quad 24\\
\hline
0
\end{array}
$$

Subtract 24 from 24. Write the difference, 0, under 24.

There are no more digits in the dividend to bring down, so the division is finished. The result of dividing 624 by 4 is 156. There is no remainder.

Check your answer. Multiply the quotient by the divisor.

$$\begin{array}{r} 156 \\ \times \quad 4 \\ \hline 624 \end{array} \qquad \begin{array}{r} \text{quotient} \\ \times \quad \text{divisor} \\ \hline \text{dividend} \end{array}$$

Answer: 156

Here is another example. Don't just read the example—work it through.

EXAMPLE: Divide 2,136 by 8.

Write the problem.

$$8\overline{)2,136}$$

Divide

$$8\overline{)2,136}$$

Can 2 be divided by 8? No. You must use the first 2 digits in this problem.

$$\begin{array}{r} 2 \\ 8\overline{)2,136} \end{array}$$

Can 21 be divided by 8? Yes. It goes 2 times. Write 2 in the quotient over the 1.

Multiply

$$\begin{array}{r} 2 \\ 8\overline{)2,136} \\ \underline{16} \end{array}$$

Multiply 2 × 8. Write the product, 16, under the 21.

Subtract

$$\begin{array}{r} 2 \\ 8\overline{)2,136} \\ -\underline{16} \\ 5 \end{array}$$

Subtract 16 from 21. Write the difference, 5, under the 16.

Bring Down

$$\begin{array}{r} 2 \\ 8\overline{)2,136} \\ -\underline{16} \\ 53 \end{array}$$

Bring down the next digit, 3, from the dividend. Write it next to the 5.

Repeat the four steps.

$$\begin{array}{r} 26 \\ 8\overline{)2,136} \\ -\underline{16} \\ 53 \end{array}$$

Divide 53 by 8. It goes 6 times. Write 6 in the quotient over the 3.

```
     2 6
 8)2,1 3 6
 - 1 6
     5 3
     4 8
```

Multiply 6 × 8. Write the product, 48, under the 53.

```
     2 6
 8)2,1 3 6
 - 1 6
     5 3
   - 4 8
       5
```

Subtract 48 from 53. Write the difference, 5, under the 48.

```
     2 6
 8)2,1 3 6
 - 1 6
     5 3
   - 4 8
       5 6
```

Bring down the next digit, 6, from the dividend. Write it next to the 5.

Repeat

```
     2 6 7
 8)2,1 3 6
 - 1 6
     5 3
   - 4 8
       5 6
```

Divide 56 by 8. It goes 7 times. Write 7 in the quotient over the 6.

```
     2 6 7
 8)2,1 3 6
 - 1 6
     5 3
   - 4 8
       5 6
     - 5 6
```

Multiply 7 × 8. Write the product, 56, under the 56.

```
     2 6 7
 8)2,1 3 6
 - 1 6
     5 3
   - 4 8
       5 6
     - 5 6
         0
```

Subtract 56 from 56. Write the difference, 0, under 56.

There are no more digits in the dividend to bring down, so the division is finished. The result of dividing 2,136 by 8 is 267.

Check

$$\begin{array}{r} 267 \\ \times \quad 8 \\ \hline 2,136 \end{array} \qquad \begin{array}{r} \text{quotient} \\ \times \ \text{divisor} \\ \hline \text{dividend} \end{array}$$

Answer: 267

If the number you get when you subtract (the difference) is equal to or bigger than the divisor, the divisor will go into the dividend more times. Here is an example:

EXAMPLE: Divide 396 by 4.

Divide

$$\begin{array}{r} 8 \\ 4\overline{)396} \end{array} \qquad 39 \div 4 = 8$$

Multiply

$$\begin{array}{r} 8 \\ 4\overline{)396} \\ \underline{32} \end{array} \qquad 8 \times 4 = 32$$

Subtract

$$\begin{array}{r} 8 \\ 4\overline{)396} \\ -\underline{32} \\ 7 \end{array} \qquad 39 - 32 = 7$$

The difference of 7 is greater than the 4 of the divisor.

Increase the 8 in the quotient by 1 to make it 9, and try again.

Divide

$$\begin{array}{r} 9 \\ 4\overline{)396} \end{array} \qquad 39 \div 4 = 9$$

Multiply

$$\begin{array}{r} 9 \\ 4\overline{)396} \\ 36 \end{array} \qquad 9 \times 4 = 36$$

Subtract

```
    9
4)3 9 6
 -3 6
    3
```

39 − 36 = 3
The difference of 3 is less than the 4 of the divisor.

Bring Down

```
    9
4)3 9 6
 -3 6
    3 6
```

Bring down the 6 from the dividend.

Repeat

```
    9 9
4)3 9 6
 -3 6
    3 6
    3 6
      0
```

36 ÷ 4 = 9
9 × 4 = 36
36 − 36 = 0

Check

```
   9 9
×    4
 3 9 6
```

Answer: 99

Sometimes the remainder is not zero. The following example shows you how to write the remainder and check the problem. Work the problem through.

EXAMPLE: Divide 387 by 4.

Divide

```
    9
4)3 8 7
```

38 ÷ 4 = 9

Multiply

```
    9
4)3 8 7
  3 6
```

9 × 4 = 36

Subtract

$$\begin{array}{r} 9 \\ 4\overline{)387} \\ -36 \\ \hline 2 \end{array}$$

$38 - 36 = 2$

Bring Down

$$\begin{array}{r} 9 \\ 4\overline{)387} \\ -36 \\ \hline 27 \end{array}$$

Bring down the 7 from the dividend.

Repeat

$$\begin{array}{r} 96 \\ 4\overline{)387} \\ -36 \\ \hline 27 \end{array}$$

$27 \div 4 = 6$

$$\begin{array}{r} 96 \\ 4\overline{)387} \\ -36 \\ \hline 27 \\ -24 \\ \hline \end{array}$$

$6 \times 4 = 24$

$$\begin{array}{r} 96 \text{ R}3 \\ 4\overline{)387}\phantom{\text{ R}3} \\ -36\phantom{\text{ R}3} \\ \hline 27\phantom{\text{ R}3} \\ -24\phantom{\text{ R}3} \\ \hline 3\phantom{\text{ R}3} \end{array}$$

$27 - 24 = 3$

The remainder is 3. Write R3 (R = remainder) after the quotient.

Check

$$\begin{array}{rl} 96 & \text{quotient} \\ \times \quad 4 & \text{divisor} \\ \hline 384 & \\ + \quad 3 & \text{remainder} \\ \hline 387 & \text{dividend} \end{array}$$

In checking the answer, you must consider the remainder. Add it to the amount obtained by multiplying the quotient by the divisor.

Answer: 96 R3

Finally, the most common error in division is the omission of zeros in the quotient. These problems show the correct placement of zeros.

EXAMPLE:

$$\begin{array}{r} 2 \\ 5\overline{)1,025} \\ -\underline{10} \\ 2 \end{array} \qquad \begin{array}{r} 20 \\ 5\overline{)1,025} \\ -\underline{10} \\ 2 \end{array} \qquad \begin{array}{r} 205 \\ 5\overline{)1,025} \\ -\underline{10} \\ 25 \\ \underline{25} \end{array}$$

EXAMPLE:

$$\begin{array}{r} 2, \\ 5\overline{)10,000} \\ -\underline{10} \end{array} \qquad \begin{array}{r} 2,000 \\ 5\overline{)10,000} \\ -\underline{10} \end{array}$$

Remember, every time you bring down a digit, you must place a digit above it in the quotient.

You must add a zero in the quotient above each zero in the dividend that was not used.

Check your skill at dividing by one-digit numbers by completing this exercise.

Exercise for Subskill 5B

Find the quotients. Show your work and check your answers by multiplication.

1. $6\overline{)288}$ **2.** $3\overline{)282}$ **3.** $5\overline{)425}$

4. $7\overline{)1,778}$ **5.** $4\overline{)2,544}$ **6.** $8\overline{)1,632}$

7. $2\overline{)1,596}$ **8.** $9\overline{)5,589}$ **9.** $6\overline{)3,432}$

10. $5\overline{)3,295}$ **11.** $7\overline{)5,475}$ **12.** $3\overline{)2,898}$

13. $5\overline{)1,025}$ **14.** $7\overline{)42,577}$ **15.** $5\overline{)10,000}$

Check your answers on page 6 in the Answer Key for Book One. If you correctly answered twelve of fifteen items, go to the next subskill. If not, complete the following Supplemental Exercise.

Supplemental Exercise for Subskill 5B

Read Subskill 5B again. Work through the examples as you read. Then find the following quotients. Show your work and check your answers.

1. $5\overline{)175}$ **2.** $7\overline{)448}$ **3.** $3\overline{)285}$

4. $2\overline{)1{,}588}$ **5.** $4\overline{)1{,}872}$ **6.** $9\overline{)1{,}377}$

7. $6\overline{)2{,}244}$ **8.** $8\overline{)2{,}848}$ **9.** $4\overline{)3{,}420}$

10. $5\overline{)4{,}935}$ **11.** $7\overline{)2{,}912}$ **12.** $8\overline{)6{,}160}$

13. $5\overline{)2{,}005}$ **14.** $7\overline{)2{,}860}$ **15.** $3\overline{)18{,}300}$

Check your answers on pages 6 and 7 in the Answer Key for Book One. If you correctly answered twelve of the fifteen items, go to the next subskill. If not, ask your instructor for help.

Subskill 5C: Dividing by Two-Digit Numbers

After studying this subskill, you will be able to divide by two-digit numbers.

Division by a two-digit number is done the same way as division by a one-digit number. The only difference is that you will be working with larger numbers.

EXAMPLE: Divide 6,164 by 46.

$46\overline{)6{,}164}$ First, write 6,164 under the division sign and 46 outside the division sign.

Divide

$$\begin{array}{r} 1 \\ 46\overline{)6{,}164} \end{array}$$

Divide the divisor into the first two digits of the dividend. 46 goes into 61 one time. Write the 1 in the quotient over the 1 in 6,164.

Multiply

```
      1
46)6,164
   46
```

Multiply the 1 in the quotient times the divisor. Write the product, 46, under the 61.

Subtract

```
      1
46)6,164
  -46
   15
```

Subtract 46 from 61. Write the difference, 15, under the 46.

Bring Down

```
      1
46)6,164
  -46
   156
```

Bring down the 6 in the dividend.

Repeat the last four steps.

```
      13
46)6,164
  -46
   156
```

Divide 156 by 46. It goes 3 times. Write 3 in the quotient.

```
      13
46)6,164
  -46
   156
  -138
```

Multiply 3 × 46. Write the product, 138, under the 156.

```
      13
46)6,164
  -46
   156
  -138
    18
```

Subtract 138 from 156. Write the difference, 18, under the 138.

```
      13
46)6,164
  -46
   156
  -138
    184
```

Bring down the next digit.

```
      134
46)6,164
  - 46
    156
  - 138
     184
```

Divide 184 by 46. It goes 4 times. Write 4 in the quotient.

```
      134
46)6,164
  - 46
    156
  - 138
     184
     184
```

Multiply 4 × 46. Write the product, 184, under the 184.

```
      134
46)6,164
  - 46
    156
  - 138
     184
   - 184
       0
```

Subtract 184 from 184. Write the difference, 0, under the 184.

The result of dividing 6,164 by 46 is 134. There is no remainder.

Check

```
     134
×     46
     804
    536
   6,164
```

Answer: 134

Here is another example for you to study.

EXAMPLE:

```
         6
68)41,140
```

Can you divide 41 by 68? No. Can you divide 411 by 68? Yes. It goes 6 times.

```
         6
68)41,140
   408
```

Multiply 6 × 68. Write the product, 408, under the 411.

$$\begin{array}{r} 6 \\ 68\overline{)41,140} \\ -\underline{408} \\ 3 \end{array}$$

Subtract 408 from 411. Write the difference, 3, under 408.

$$\begin{array}{r} 6 \\ 68\overline{)41,140} \\ -\underline{408} \\ 34 \end{array}$$

Bring down the next digit.

$$\begin{array}{r} 60 \\ 68\overline{)41,140} \\ -\underline{408} \\ 34 \end{array}$$

Does 68 go into 34? No. Put a 0 in the quotient as a place holder.

$$\begin{array}{r} 60 \\ 68\overline{)41,140} \\ -\underline{408} \\ 340 \end{array}$$

Bring down the next digit.

$$\begin{array}{r} 605 \\ 68\overline{)41,140} \\ \underline{408} \\ 340 \end{array}$$

Can you divide 340 by 68? Yes. It goes 5 times. Write 5 in the quotient.

$$\begin{array}{r} 605 \\ 68\overline{)41,140} \\ -\underline{408} \\ 340 \\ \underline{340} \end{array}$$

Multiply the divisor by 5. Place the product under the 340.

$$\begin{array}{r} 605 \\ 68\overline{)41,140} \\ -\underline{408} \\ 340 \\ -\underline{340} \\ 0 \end{array}$$

Subtract 340 from 340. The difference is zero. There is no remainder.

Check

$$\begin{array}{r} 605 \\ \times\ \ 68 \\ \hline 4\,840 \\ 36\,30 \\ \hline 41,140 \end{array}$$

Answer: 605

Check your skill in dividing by two-digit numbers by completing the following exercise.

Exercise for Subskill 5C

Do these problems. Show your work and check your answers by multiplication.

1. 21)756	**2.** 14)1,218	**3.** 36)1,656
4. 73)2,482	**5.** 17)986	**6.** 57)13,395
7. 61)6,893	**8.** 89)41,118	**9.** 75)63,525
10. 45)41,625	**11.** 26)14,664	**12.** 68)43,384
13. 35)17,525	**14.** 29)30,752	**15.** 40)2,400

Check your answers on page 7 in the Answer Key for Book One. If you correctly answered twelve of the fifteen items, go to the next subskill. If not, complete the following Supplemental Exercise.

Supplemental Exercise for Subskill 5C

Read Subskill 5C again, working through the examples. Then try these problems. Show your work and check your answers by multiplication.

1. 34)782	**2.** 54)648	**3.** 48)912
4. 65)8,775	**5.** 13)9,399	**6.** 27)22,329
7. 91)31,486	**8.** 76)47,728	**9.** 32)4,384
10. 29)15,863	**11.** 84)34,776	**12.** 25)15,825
13. 12)4,800	**14.** 15)60,135	**15.** 61)12,625

Check your answers on page 7 in the Answer Key for Book One. If you correctly answered twelve of the fifteen items, go to the next subskill. If not, ask your instructor for help.

Subskill 5D: Dividing Larger Numbers

After studying this subskill, you will be able to divide larger numbers.

You can use the process described in this Skill Unit to divide any whole number into another whole number. With divisors of three or more digits, it is helpful to find trial quotients and compare numbers before going through all the calculations. Let's review the steps again.

EXAMPLE: Divide 93,187 by 357.

First, write down the problem.

```
357)9 3, 1 8 7
```

Divide

```
        2
357)9 3, 1 8 7
```

357 will not go into 9 or 93. To find a trial quotient for 931 divided by 357, compare (trial divide) the first digit of each number: $9 \div 3 = 3$. Then trial multiply: $357 \times 3 = 1{,}071$. Since 1,071 is larger than 931, try 2.

Multiply

```
        2
357)9 3, 1 8 7
  - 7 1 4
```

$2 \times 357 = 714$

Subtract

```
        2
357)9 3, 1 8 7
  - 7 1 4
    2 1 7
```

$931 - 714 = 217$

Bring Down

```
        2
357)9 3, 1 8 7
  - 7 1 4
    2 1 7 8
```

Bring down the next digit.

Divide

```
        2 6
357)9 3, 1 8 7
  - 7 1 4
    2 1 7 8
```

To divide 2,178 by 357, compare (trial divide) the first digits: you cannot divide 2 by 3, but 21 ÷ 3 = 7. Then trial multiply. Since 357 × 7 = 2,499, which is larger than 2,178, try 6.

Multiply

```
        2 6
357)9 3, 1 8 7
  - 7 1 4
    2 1 7 8
    2 1 4 2
```

6 × 357 = 2142

Subtract

```
        2 6
357)9 3, 1 8 7
  - 7 1 4
    2 1 7 8
  - 2 1 4 2
        3 6
```

2178 − 2142 = 36

Bring Down

```
        2 6
357)9 3, 1 8 7
  - 7 1 4
    2 1 7 8
  - 2 1 4 2
        3 6 7
```

Bring down the next digit.

Divide

```
        2 6 1
357)9 3, 1 8 7
  - 7 1 4
    2 1 7 8
  - 2 1 4 2
        3 6 7
```

This time, no trial is really needed, because it is easy to see that 357 will go into 367 with a little left over, so put 1 in the quotient.

Multiply

```
      261
357)93,187
   -714
    2178
   -2142
      367
      357
```

$1 \times 357 = 357$

Subtract

```
      261 R10
357)93.187
   -714
    2178
   -2142
      367
     -357
       10
```

$367 - 357 = 10$
The remainder is 10. Write "R" in the quotient. Then write 10.

Check

```
     261   quotient
×    357   divisor
    1827
   1305
   783
   93177
+     10   remainder
   93,187  dividend
```

Multiply the quotient by the divisor. Then add the remainder to get the original dividend.

Answer: 261 R10

Exercise for Subskill 5D

Do these problems. Show your work and check your answers by multiplication.

1. 6)9,630 **2.** 16)128,112 **3.** 532)1,523,648

4. 9)67 **5.** 37)2,318 **6.** 98)3,491

7. 35)17,525 **8.** 125)6,663 **9.** 567)277,564

10. $12\overline{)53}$ **11.** $42\overline{)4,327}$ **12.** $63\overline{)2,986}$

13. $546\overline{)163,917}$ **14.** $29\overline{)30,768}$ **15.** $872\overline{)210,155}$

Check your answers on page 7 in the Answer Key for Book One. If you correctly answered twelve of the fifteen problems, go to the next subskill. If not, complete the following Supplemental Exercise.

Supplemental Exercise for Subskill 5D

Go back to the example at the beginning of this subskill. Work through it step by step. Then do this exercise. Show your work and check your answers by multiplication.

1. $8\overline{)5,600}$ **2.** $5\overline{)6,005}$ **3.** $41\overline{)123,082}$

4. $8\overline{)79}$ **5.** $55\overline{)1,885}$ **6.** $78\overline{)4,821}$

7. $48\overline{)43,237}$ **8.** $623\overline{)29,572}$ **9.** $318\overline{)229,983}$

10. $17\overline{)107}$ **11.** $63\overline{)31,989}$ **12.** $31\overline{)1,711}$

13. $429\overline{)257,513}$ **14.** $87\overline{)262,765}$ **15.** $119\overline{)98,989}$

Check your answers on page 7 in the Answer Key for Book One. If you correctly answered twelve of the fifteen problems, go to the next subskill. If not, ask your instructor for help.

Subskill 5E: Solving Word Problems

After studying this subskill, you will be able to solve word problems involving division.

Many of the problems you must solve are in the form of word problems. These are the steps you should follow in solving word problems that require division.

Read and Reread the Problem

Read the entire problem carefully. Read the problem again to make sure you understand what you are being asked to do.

EXAMPLE: Joyce Johnson wants to buy a washer and dryer on the installment plan. The total cost of the washer and dryer is $720. Joyce can pay the $720 in 12 equal monthly payments. What is the amount of each payment?

Now that you have read the problem, go to the next step.

Determine What You Are to Find

What does the problem ask you to do? In other words, what do you need to do to find the answer?

In the example above, you are asked to find the amount of the monthly payment Ms. Johnson must make on her washer and dryer.

Determine What You Are Given

What facts do you know? Also, what facts are not needed to solve the problem?

In the example above, you know that there will be 12 payments, and the total cost is $720.

Decide What Operation(s) to Use

Division problems ask for **part of something.** These key words and phrases might be used in a division word problem:

Shared equally	Split
Divided into	Average
How many times	Equal parts

In the example above, you are given the total of 12 payments. You must divide the total by 12 to find the amount of one payment.

Solve the Problem

$12\overline{)720}$ Write the problem.

$$\begin{array}{r} 6 \\ 12\overline{)720} \end{array}$$

Divide the divisor into the first two digits of the dividend. A trial quotient digit shows that 12 goes into 72 six times.

```
     6
12)7 2 0
   7 2
```

Multiply the divisor by 6.
6 × 12 = 72

```
     6
12)7 2 0
 - 7 2
     0
```

Subtract 72 from 72. The difference is zero.

```
   $ 6 0
12)7 2 0
 - 7 2
     0 0
```

Bring down the zero from the dividend. At the same time, put a 0 in the quotient.

Check Your Answer

```
   $ 6 0
 ×   1 2
   1 2 0
   6 0
 $ 7 2 0
```

Multiply the amount of one payment by the number of payments. The product is the total that Joyce needs to pay.

Answer: $60

Some problems require more than one operation. For example, to find an average, you must first add and then divide.

EXAMPLE: Ron bowled three games. His scores were 185, 170, and 177. What is his average for the three games?

To find the average of a group of figures, first add them together. Then divide this total by the number of figures.

Add the scores.

```
1 8 5
1 7 0
1 7 7
5 3 2
```

Divide by the number of games.

```
  1 7 7  R 1
3)5 3 2
- 3
  2 3
  2 1
    2 2
    2 1
      1
```

Ron's average can be rounded off to 177.

Answer: 177

Check your skill at solving division word problems by completing this exercise.

Exercise for Subskill 5E

1. Find the quotient of five thousand ninety-two divided by six.

2. Two thousand four hundred sixty-four chairs are placed in rows for school graduation. There are to be twenty-two chairs in each row. How many rows will be made?

3. A car used 21 gallons of gasoline to go 378 miles. What is the mpg (miles per gallon) for the car?

4. Mr. Dumas wants to buy a car that costs $8,995. He can pay $1,800 down (when he gets the car). Mr. Dumas must pay the remainder in 48 equal monthly installments. How much will each installment payment be? Round your answer to the nearest dollar.

5. Mr. and Mrs. Thompson recorded their food expenses for six months. Their monthly bills are shown below:

December	$425
January	$350
February	$295
March	$282
April	$278
May	$306

What is the average food expense for each month? Round your answer to the nearest dollar.

Check your answers on page 7 in the Answer Key for Book One. If you correctly answered four of the five problems, go to the Self-Check. If not, complete the following Supplemental Exercise for Subskill 5E.

Supplemental Exercise for Subskill 5E

Although you can add, subtract, multiply, and divide, you may be having difficulty deciding which operation or operations to use in a word problem. Here is another exercise to practice on.

1. Find the quotient of nine thousand four hundred three divided by nine.

2. A family traveled 984 miles in 3 days. What was the average number of miles traveled each day?

3. Mr. and Mrs. Quinn bought a house for $58,000. They financed the purchase price for 20 years. Finance charges (interest) for the term of the loan total $72,000.
   (a) What is the total cost of the house?
   (b) What is the amount of each monthly payment (240 payments)?

4. A bingo prize of $5,000 must be divided equally among four winners. How much money will each winner receive?

5. The Kiwanis Club sold tickets to the circus. Ticket sales totaled $10,500. Each ticket cost $4. How many tickets were sold?

Check your answers on page 7 in the Answer Key for Book One. If you correctly answered four of the five problems, go to the Self-Check. If not, ask your instructor for help.

SELF-CHECK FOR SKILL UNIT 5

Solve each problem in the exercise below. You must show your work.

1. $12\overline{)912}$ **2.** $67\overline{)6{,}569}$ **3.** $123\overline{)37{,}392}$

4. $85{,}600 \div 107 =$ **5.** $276{,}547 \div 307 =$

6. $179{,}814 \div 293 =$ **7.** $999\overline{)963{,}706}$

8. $512\overline{)3{,}518{,}694}$ **9.** $326\overline{)21{,}842}$

10. $91{,}376 \div 28 =$ **11.** $37{,}418 \div 706 =$

12. Find the quotient of forty thousand ninety-five divided by five.

13. Jan's annual salary is $17,450. How much does Jan earn each month?

14. Jennifer paid a babysitter $2080 in a year, and used her for the same time every week. How much did she pay the babysitter each week?

15. At the beginning of a trip, the odometer (mileage counter) on Paul's car showed 17,486 miles. At the end of the trip, the odometer showed 20,025 miles. During the trip, Paul used 88 gallons of gasoline. How many mpg (miles per gallon) did Paul's car average on the trip?

Check your answers on page 7 in the Answer Key for Book One. If you correctly answered twelve of the fifteen problems, go on to Skill Unit 6. If not, ask your instructor for help.

Skill Unit 6
FRACTIONS

What Skills You Need to Begin: Basic skills with whole numbers (Skill Units 1 through 5).

What Skills You Will Learn: After studying this skill unit, you will understand fractions and be able to change a fraction to its equivalent, reduce a fraction to its lowest terms, find the least common denominator, tell larger fractions from smaller ones, and change improper fractions to mixed numbers and vice versa.

Why You Need This Skill: You use fractions almost every day, in measuring with a ruler, following a recipe, choosing tools and materials, and many other activities.

How You Will Show What You Have Learned: At the end of this skill unit is a Self-Check consisting of twenty problems involving fractions. You should allow yourself one hour to complete the Self-Check. To prove that you have mastered this skill, you must correctly answer sixteen of the twenty problems.

If you feel that you have already mastered fractions, complete the Self-Check on pages 133 and 134.

Subskill 6A: Understanding Fractions

After studying this subskill you will understand fractions.

What Is a Fraction?

A fraction is a part of a whole. For example, if you cut a whole pie into two parts, each part is one of two. In other words, each part is one half of the whole pie. "One half" means "one of two." In numerals, one half is written as the fraction:

$$\frac{1}{2}$$

Look at the pies in these pictures.

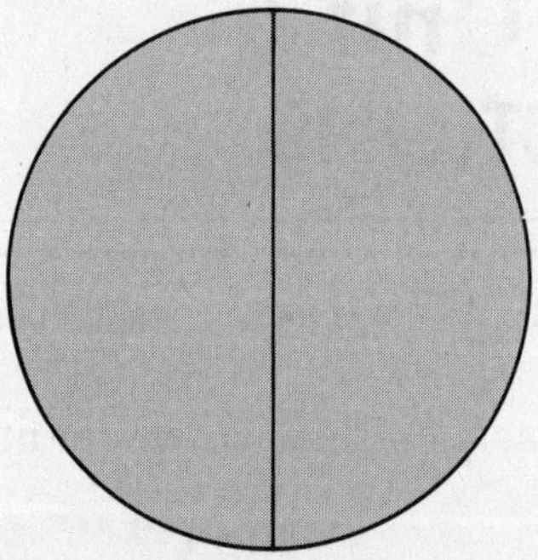

In this picture, both halves of the pie are shaded. Two halves is the fraction $\frac{2}{2}$. Two halves is the whole pie.

$$\frac{2}{2} = 1$$

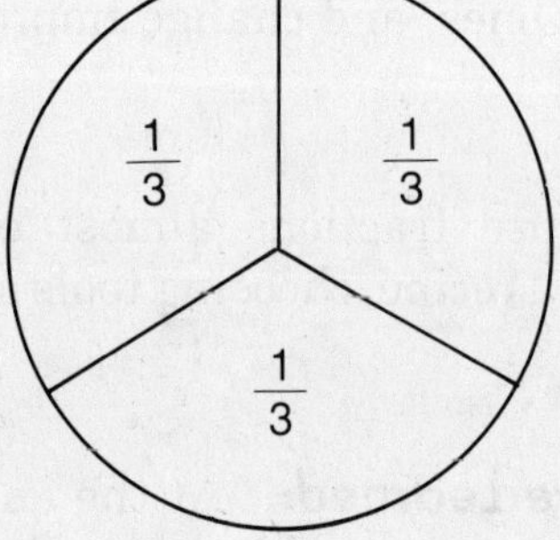

This pie is cut into three parts. Each part is one third of the whole pie. In numerals, one third is the fraction $\frac{1}{3}$.

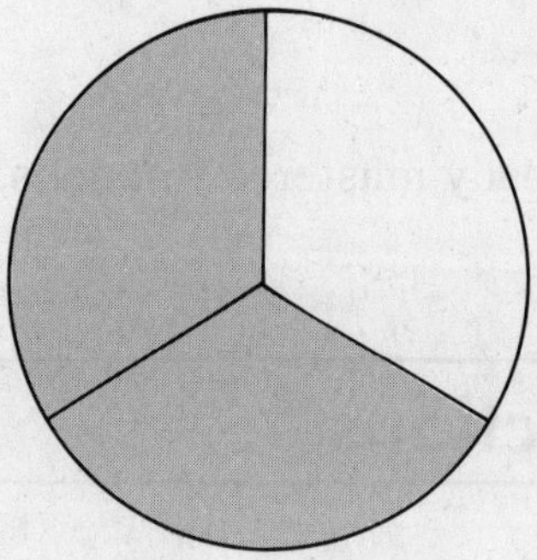

In this picture, two thirds of the pie are shaded. Two thirds is the fraction $\frac{2}{3}$.

Note: The bottom number of the fraction tells how many parts the pie has been divided into. The top number tells how many parts are shaded.

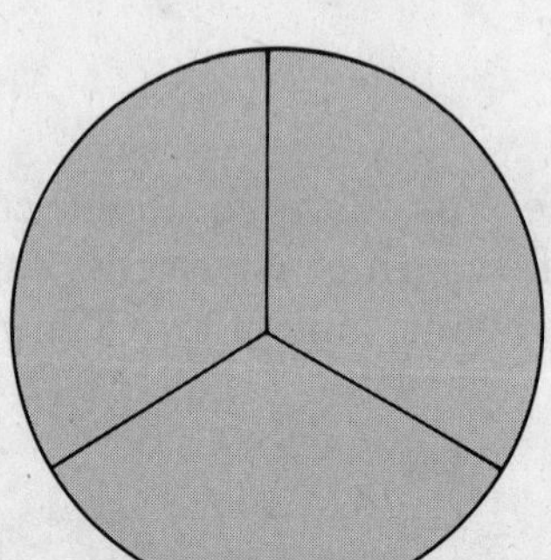

Now three thirds of the pie are shaded. Three thirds is the fraction $\frac{3}{3}$. Three thirds is the whole pie.

$$\frac{3}{3} = 1$$

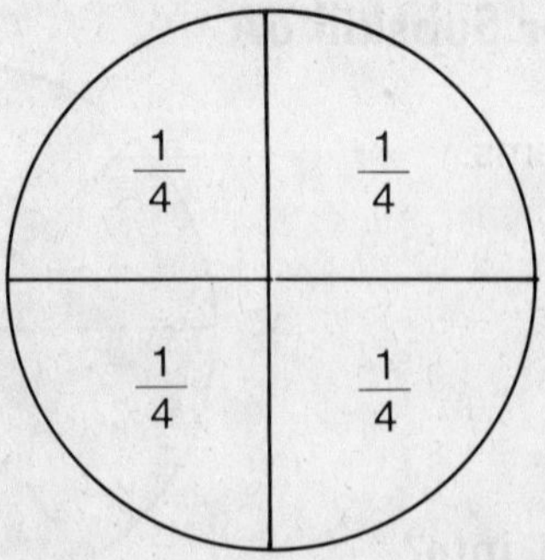

This pie is cut into four parts. Each part is one fourth of the whole pie. In numerals, one fourth is the fraction $\frac{1}{4}$.

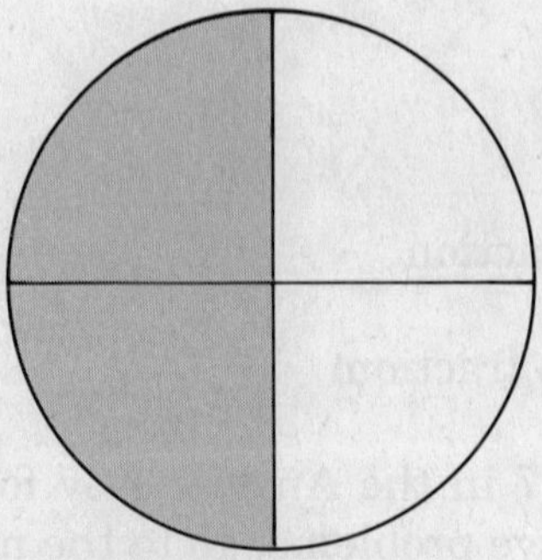

Two fourths of the pie are shaded here. Two fourths is the fraction $\frac{2}{4}$. Go back and look again at the first pie. Note that $\frac{2}{4}$ of a pie is the same as $\frac{1}{2}$ of a pie.

$$\frac{2}{4} = \frac{1}{2}$$

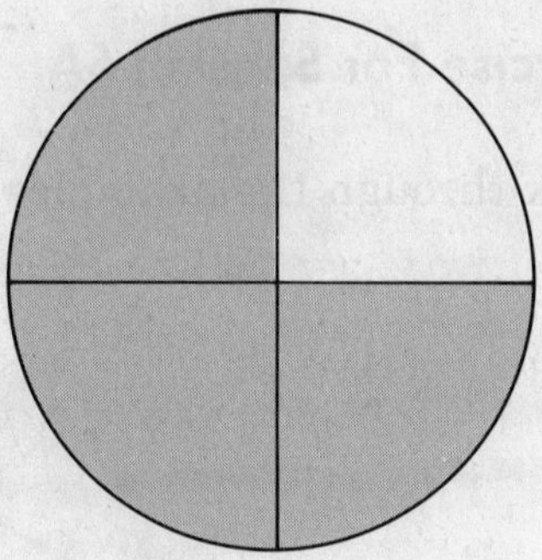

Three fourths of the pie are shaded. Three fourth is the fraction $\frac{3}{4}$. The unshaded part is $\frac{1}{4}$ of the pie.

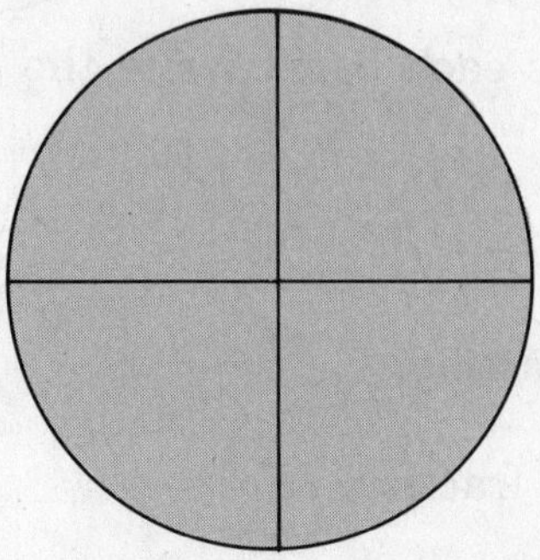

Now four fourths of the pie are shaded. Four fourths is the fraction $\frac{4}{4}$. Four fourths is the whole pie.

$$\frac{4}{4} = 1$$

Check your understanding of fractions by doing the exercise on page 106.

Exercise for Subskill 6A

Use this pie to solve the five problems.

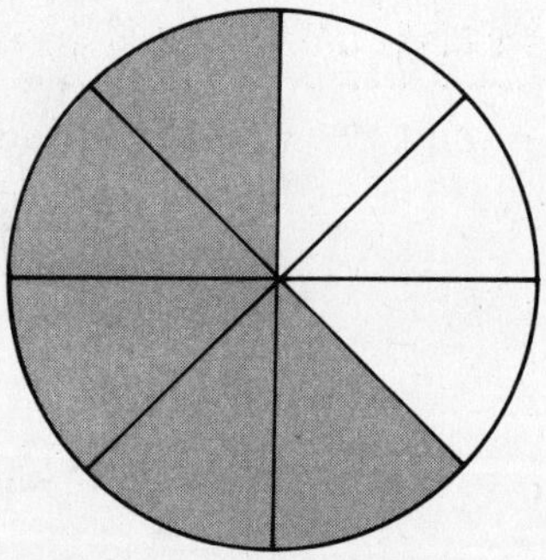

1. How many parts is the pie cut into?

2. How much of the whole pie is each part? Write the answer as a fraction.

3. How many parts are shaded?

4. Write the shaded parts as a fraction.

5. Write the unshaded parts as a fraction.

Check your answers on page 7 in the Answer Key for Book One. If you correctly answered four of five problems, go to the next subskill. If not, complete the following Supplemental Exercise.

Supplemental Exercise For Subskill 6A

Read Subskill 6A again. Work through the examples as you read them. Then do this exercise.

Use this pie to solve the five problems.

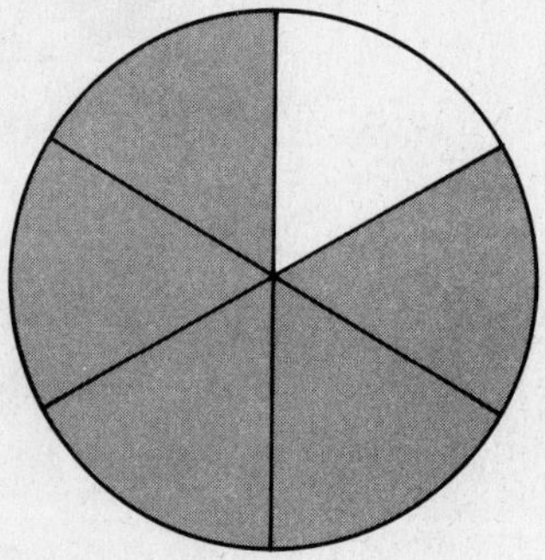

1. How many parts is the pie cut into?

2. How much of the whole pie is each part? Write the answer as a fraction.

3. How many parts are shaded?

4. Write the shaded parts as a fraction.

5. Write the unshaded parts as a fraction.

Check your answers on page 7 in the Answer Key for Book One. If you correctly answered four of the five problems, go to the next subskill. If not, ask your instructor for help.

Subskill 6B: Equivalent Fractions

After studying this subskill you will be able to change a fraction to its equivalent.

What Are Equivalent Fractions?

In the previous subskill you saw that $\frac{1}{2} = \frac{2}{4}$. Here are the pies again.

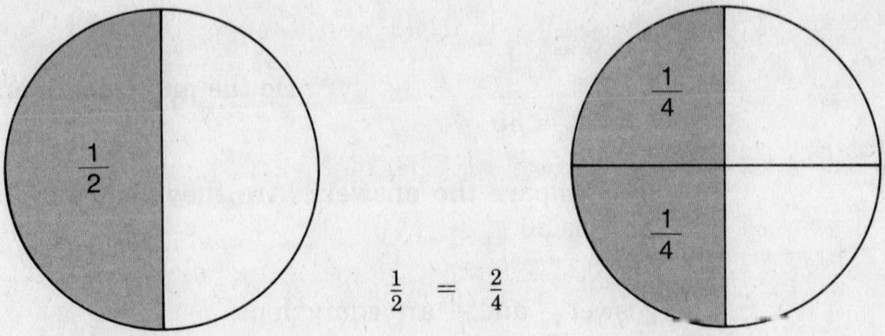

$\frac{1}{2} = \frac{2}{4}$

The fractions $\frac{1}{2}$ and $\frac{2}{4}$ are called **equivalent fractions.** Equivalent fractions are fractions that have the same value. Here are some more pies. All the fractions are equivalent to $\frac{1}{2}$.

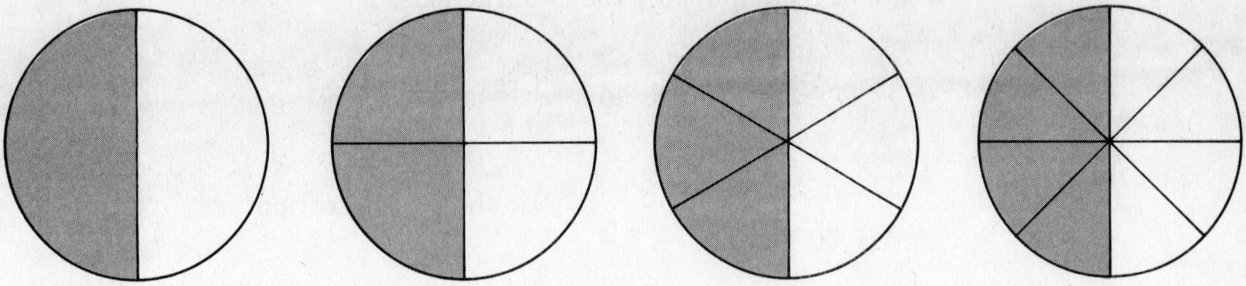

$\frac{1}{2} \quad = \quad \frac{2}{4} \quad = \quad \frac{3}{6} \quad = \quad \frac{4}{8}$

Fractions are equivalent if their cross products are equal.

$\frac{1}{2} = \frac{2}{4}$ since $1 \times 4 = 4$ and $2 \times 2 = 4$

$\frac{3}{6} = \frac{4}{8}$ since $3 \times 8 = 24$ and $6 \times 4 = 24$

How Can You Tell If Two Fractions Are Equivalent?

To tell if two fractions are equivalent, cross multiply them. If they *are* equivalent, the two answers will be the same.

EXAMPLE: Are $\frac{3}{4}$ and $\frac{9}{12}$ equivalent?

First, cross multiply the two fractions.

$\frac{3}{4} \times \frac{9}{12}$ $\quad$ 4×9, 3×12 $\quad$ Cross multiply.

$4 \times 9 = 36$

$3 \times 12 = 36$ $\quad$ Do the multiplication.

Compare the answers. Are they the same? Yes, 36 is the same as 36.

Answer: $\frac{3}{4}$ and $\frac{9}{12}$ are equivalent.

Here is another example.

EXAMPLE: Are $\frac{2}{3}$ and $\frac{8}{20}$ equivalent?

First, cross multiply the two fractions.

$\frac{2}{3} \times \frac{8}{20}$ $\quad$ 3×8, 2×20 $\quad$ Cross multiply.

$3 \times 8 = 24$

$2 \times 20 = 40$ $\quad$ Do the multiplication.

Compare the answers. Are they the same? No, 24 is not the same as 40.

Answer: $\frac{2}{3}$ and $\frac{8}{20}$ are *not* equivalent.

Changing a Fraction to its Equivalent

To change a fraction to its equivalent, multiply or divide both the top and the bottom by the same number.

For example, to change $\frac{1}{2}$ to an equivalent fraction, you can multiply both the top and the bottom by 2.

$$\frac{1}{2}\,\frac{\times 2}{\times 2} = \frac{2}{4} \qquad \frac{1}{2} = \frac{2}{4}$$

Or you can multiply by 3.

$$\frac{1}{2}\,\frac{\times 3}{\times 3} = \frac{3}{6} \qquad \frac{1}{2} = \frac{3}{6}$$

You can also multiply by 4.

$$\frac{1}{2}\,\frac{\times 4}{\times 4} = \frac{4}{8} \qquad \frac{1}{2} = \frac{4}{8}$$

Or by 5.

$$\frac{1}{2}\,\frac{\times 5}{\times 5} = \frac{5}{10} \qquad \frac{1}{2} = \frac{5}{10}$$

Here is another example. Change $\frac{75}{100}$ to an equivalent fraction.

You can divide by 5.

$$\frac{75}{100}\,\frac{\div 5}{\div 5} = \frac{15}{20} \qquad \frac{75}{100} = \frac{15}{20}$$

Or by 25.

$$\frac{75}{100}\,\frac{\div 25}{\div 25} = \frac{3}{4} \qquad \frac{75}{100} = \frac{3}{4}$$

Note: In using division to change a fraction to its equivalent, you must be able to divide both the top and the bottom *evenly*. No remainders allowed!

Check your skill at telling if two fractions are equivalent and changing a fraction to its equivalent by doing this exercise.

Exercise for Subskill 6B

Use cross multiplication to tell if the following pairs of fractions are equivalent. Write "yes" if the fractions are equivalent and "no" if they are not.

1. $\frac{1}{3}$ $\frac{3}{9}$ ______ **2.** $\frac{2}{3}$ $\frac{4}{5}$ ______

3. $\frac{3}{5}$ $\frac{6}{7}$ ______ **4.** $\frac{3}{4}$ $\frac{9}{12}$ ______

5. $\frac{3}{6}$ $\frac{4}{8}$ ______ **6.** $\frac{15}{18}$ $\frac{10}{12}$ ______

7. $\frac{16}{18}$ $\frac{8}{9}$ ______ **8.** $\frac{11}{12}$ $\frac{13}{14}$ ______

9. Change $\frac{5}{6}$ to an equivalent fraction.

10. Change $\frac{16}{20}$ to an equivalent fraction.

11. Change $\frac{3}{4}$ to an equivalent fraction.

12. Change $\frac{24}{36}$ to an equivalent fraction.

Check your answers on page 8 in the Answer Key for Book One. If you correctly answered ten of the twelve problems, go to the next subskill. If not, do the following Supplemental Exercise.

Supplemental Exercise for Subskill 6B

Read Subskill 6B again. Work through the examples as you read them. Then do this exercise.

Use cross multiplication to tell if the following pairs of fractions are equivalent. Write "yes" if the fractions are equivalent and "no" if they are not.

1. $\frac{1}{4}$ $\frac{8}{32}$ ______ **2.** $\frac{3}{8}$ $\frac{6}{11}$ ______

3. $\frac{6}{12}$ $\frac{1}{2}$ ______ **4.** $\frac{4}{5}$ $\frac{16}{25}$ ______

5. $\frac{25}{40}$ $\frac{5}{8}$ ______ **6.** $\frac{9}{10}$ $\frac{90}{100}$ ______

7. $\frac{7}{12}$ $\frac{15}{24}$ ______ **8.** $\frac{40}{50}$ $\frac{8}{10}$ ______

9. Change $\frac{40}{64}$ to an equivalent fraction.

10. Change $\frac{3}{5}$ to an equivalent fraction.

11. Change $\frac{32}{48}$ to an equivalent fraction.

12. Change $\frac{5}{6}$ to an equivalent fraction.

Check your answers on page 8 in the Answer Key for Book One. If you correctly answered ten of the twelve problems, go to the next subskill. If not, ask your instructor for help.

Subskill 6C: Reducing a Fraction to Its Lowest Terms

After studying this subskill you will be able to reduce a fraction to its lowest terms.

Look at these equivalent fractions:

$$\frac{16}{24} = \frac{2}{3}$$

Although the two fractions are equivalent, $\frac{2}{3}$ looks smaller because 2 and 3 are smaller than 16 and 24. In other words, $\frac{2}{3}$ has **lower terms.** Reducing a fraction to lower terms really means changing it to an equivalent fraction with lower terms.

To reduce a fraction to lower terms, divide both the top and the bottom by the same number. Remember, you must be able to divide them both *evenly*.

EXAMPLE: Reduce $\frac{12}{18}$ to lower terms.

What number will go into both 12 and 18 evenly? Try 2.

$$\frac{12 \div 2 = 6}{18 \div 2 = 9} \qquad \frac{12}{18} = \frac{6}{9}$$

Now, can you reduce $\frac{6}{9}$ to lower terms? Yes. Both 6 and 9 can be divided evenly by 3.

$$\frac{6 \div 3 = 2}{9 \div 3 = 3} \qquad \frac{6}{9} = \frac{2}{3}$$

Can you reduce $\frac{2}{3}$ to lower terms? No. There is no number except 1 that goes evenly into both 2 and 3.

Answer: $\frac{12}{18}$ reduced to its *lowest* terms is $\frac{2}{3}$.

To reduce a fraction to its *lowest* terms, keep dividing until there is no number except 1 that goes evenly into both the top and the bottom.

Note: Reducing $\frac{12}{18}$ to its lowest terms took two steps. First you divided by 2 and then you divided by 3. You could have reduced $\frac{12}{18}$ to its lowest terms in one step by dividing by 6:

$$\frac{12 \div 6 = 2}{18 \div 6 = 3} \qquad \frac{12}{18} = \frac{2}{3}$$

To save time in reducing a fraction to its lowest terms, try to think of the largest number that will go evenly into both the top and the bottom. Here are some hints for thinking of a number to divide by.

First, check to see if the top will go evenly into the bottom. If it will, divide by the top number.

EXAMPLE: Reduce $\frac{15}{90}$ to its lowest terms.

Does 15 go evenly into 90? Yes. Therefore divide both the top and the bottom by 15.

$$\frac{15 \div 15 = 1}{90 \div 15 = 6} \qquad \frac{15}{90} = \frac{1}{6}$$

Can you reduce $\frac{1}{6}$ to lower terms? No, because there is no number (except 1) that goes evenly into both 1 and 6.

Answer: $\frac{1}{6}$

Next, check to see if both numbers are even. That is, do they end with 0, 2, 4, 6, or 8? If so, they can be divided by 2.

EXAMPLE: Reduce $\frac{32}{38}$ to its lowest terms.

Are both the top and the bottom even numbers? Yes. Therefore you can divide them by 2.

$$\frac{32 \div 2 = 16}{38 \div 2 = 19} \qquad \frac{32}{38} = \frac{16}{19}$$

Can you reduce $\frac{16}{19}$ to lower terms? No, because there is no number (except 1) that goes evenly into both 16 and 19.

Answer: $\frac{16}{19}$

Then check to see if both numbers end with 5 or if one ends with 0 and the other with 5. If so, they can be divided by 5.

EXAMPLE: Reduce $\frac{10}{35}$ to its lowest terms.

Do both numbers end with 5? No. Does one number end with 0 and the other with 5? Yes. Therefore, divide both the top and the bottom by 5.

$$\frac{10 \div 5 = 2}{35 \div 5 = 7} \qquad \frac{10}{35} = \frac{2}{7}$$

Can you reduce $\frac{2}{7}$ to lower terms? No, because there is no number (except 1) that goes evenly into both 2 and 7.

Answer: $\frac{2}{7}$

Sometimes nothing works. There are some fractions that cannot be reduced to lower terms.

EXAMPLE. Reduce $\frac{9}{22}$ to lower terms.

Will 9 go evenly into 22? No.
Are both 9 and 22 even numbers? No, only 22 is.
Do both 9 and 22 end with 5, or one with 5 and the other with 0? No.
Is there *any* number that goes evenly into 9? Yes, 3. Will 3 go evenly into 22? No. Is there any number that goes evenly into 22? Yes, 2 and 11. Will either 2 or 11 go evenly into 9? No.

Answer: $\frac{9}{22}$ cannot be reduced to lower terms.

Check your skill at reducing fractions to their lowest terms by doing this exercise.

Exercise for Subskill 6C

Reduce these fractions to their lowest terms.

1. $\frac{12}{16}$ **2.** $\frac{15}{25}$ **3.** $\frac{7}{35}$ **4.** $\frac{8}{12}$

5. $\frac{20}{24}$ **6.** $\frac{9}{54}$ **7.** $\frac{20}{50}$ **8.** $\frac{21}{48}$

9. $\frac{4}{40}$ **10.** $\frac{9}{36}$ **11.** $\frac{18}{45}$ **12.** $\frac{12}{20}$

13. $\frac{9}{12}$ **14.** $\frac{4}{12}$ **15.** $\frac{60}{64}$ **16.** $\frac{11}{110}$

17. $\frac{22}{48}$ **18.** $\frac{10}{24}$ **19.** $\frac{40}{48}$ **20.** $\frac{45}{100}$

Check your answers on page 8 in the Answer Key for Book One. If you correctly answered sixteen of the twenty problems, go to the next subskill. If not, do the following Supplemental Exercise.

Supplemental Exercise for Subskill 6C

Read Subskill 6C again. Work through the examples as you read them. Then do this exercise.

1. $\frac{18}{21}$ **2.** $\frac{14}{28}$ **3.** $\frac{28}{35}$ **4.** $\frac{24}{28}$

5. $\frac{10}{15}$ **6.** $\frac{12}{16}$ **7.** $\frac{16}{20}$ **8.** $\frac{24}{30}$

9. $\frac{24}{36}$ **10.** $\frac{18}{24}$ **11.** $\frac{20}{30}$ **12.** $\frac{8}{20}$

13. $\frac{14}{21}$ **14.** $\frac{36}{42}$ **15.** $\frac{15}{20}$ **16.** $\frac{9}{12}$

17. $\frac{18}{30}$ **18.** $\frac{12}{20}$ **19.** $\frac{24}{60}$ **20.** $\frac{25}{50}$

Check your answers on page 8 in the Answer Key for Book One. If you correctly answered sixteen of the twenty problems, go to the next subskill. If not, ask your instructor for help.

Subskill 6D: Finding the Least Common Denominator

After studying this subskill, you will be able to find the least common denominator of two fractions.

You may have noticed already that it is often hard to tell a larger fraction from a smaller one. You know that $\frac{3}{4}$ is larger than $\frac{1}{4}$, but is $\frac{3}{4}$ larger than $\frac{2}{3}$? You can't tell, unless both fractions have the same bottom number.

The bottom number of a fraction is called the **denominator.** The top number is called the **numerator.**

$$\frac{2}{3}\ \begin{matrix}\text{Numerator}\\ \text{Denominator}\end{matrix}$$

When two fractions have the same bottom number, they have a **common denominator.**

You can find a common denominator for any two fractions by multiplying their denominators together.

EXAMPLE:

What is a common denominator of $\frac{2}{3}$ and $\frac{3}{4}$?

$\frac{2}{3}$ and $\frac{3}{4}$ $\quad$ $3 \times 4 = 12$

Answer: A common denominator of $\frac{2}{3}$ and $\frac{3}{4}$ is 12.

Now you can change both fractions to equivalent fractions that have a denominator of 12.

First, change $\frac{2}{3}$ to an equivalent fraction that has a denominator of 12. You just found the common denominator, 12, by multiplying 3 by 4. Therefore, you can change $\frac{2}{3}$ to an equivalent fraction by multiplying both the numerator and the denominator by 4.

$$\frac{2 \times 4 = 8}{3 \times 4 = 12} \qquad \frac{2}{3} = \frac{8}{12}$$

Then change $\frac{3}{4}$ to an equivalent fraction that has a denominator of 12. You found the common denominator, 12, by multiplying the 4 by 3. Therefore, you can change $\frac{3}{4}$ to an equivalent fraction by multiplying both the numerator and the denominator by 3.

$$\frac{3 \times 3 = 9}{4 \times 3 = 12} \qquad \frac{3}{4} = \frac{9}{12}$$

Now you can look at the two equivalents side by side.

$\frac{2}{3}$ and $\frac{3}{4}$

Equivalent fractions with a common denominator

$\frac{8}{12}$ and $\frac{9}{12}$

Try another example. What is a common denominator of $\frac{7}{8}$ and $\frac{5}{12}$?

Multiply the denominators together.

$\frac{7}{8}$ and $\frac{5}{12}$ $\qquad 8 \times 12 = 96$

A common denominator of $\frac{7}{8}$ and $\frac{5}{12}$ is 96.

Now change both fractions to equivalent fractions that have a denominator of 96.

First change $\frac{7}{8}$ to an equivalent fraction that has a denominator of 96. Multiply both the numerator and the denominator by 12.

$$\frac{7 \times 12 = 84}{8 \times 12 = 96} \qquad \frac{7}{8} = \frac{84}{96}$$

Then change $\frac{5}{12}$ to an equivalent fraction that has a denominator of 96. Multiply both the numerator and the denominator by 8.

$$\frac{5 \times 8 = 40}{12 \times 8 = 96} \qquad \frac{5}{12} = \frac{40}{96}$$

Now look at the two equivalents side by side.

$\frac{7}{8}$ and $\frac{5}{12}$

Equivalent fractions with a common denominator

$\frac{84}{96}$ and $\frac{40}{96}$

Finding the Least Common Denominator

The two fractions in the previous example, $\frac{7}{8}$ and $\frac{5}{12}$, have many common denominators. You just found one of them, 96. Here are some larger denominators.

$$\frac{7}{8} = \frac{105}{120} = \frac{126}{144} = \frac{147}{168}$$

$$\frac{5}{12} = \frac{50}{120} = \frac{60}{144} = \frac{70}{168}$$

There are also some smaller ones.

$$\frac{7}{8} = \frac{63}{72} = \frac{42}{48} = \frac{21}{24}$$

$$\frac{5}{12} = \frac{30}{72} = \frac{20}{48} = \frac{10}{24}$$

The smallest common denominator of $\frac{7}{8}$ and $\frac{5}{12}$ is 24. This is called the **least common denominator.** When you are working with fractions that must have a common denominator, you will find it is easier to use the least common denominator than a larger one.

Unfortunately, finding a common denominator by multiplying the two denominators together does not always give you the *least* common denominator. The previous example shows this. When you multiplied the denominators of $\frac{7}{8}$ and $\frac{5}{12}$ together, you got a common denominator of 96. But the *least* common denominator is 24. It would be easier to work with 24 than 96.

How can you find the least common denominator? First, check to see if the smaller denominator of two fractions will go evenly into the larger one. If it does, the larger denominator is the least common denominator.

EXAMPLE: Find the least common denominator of $\frac{3}{4}$ and $\frac{5}{8}$.

$\frac{3}{4}$ $\frac{5}{8}$

Will 4 go evenly into 8? Yes. Therefore, 8 is the least common denominator.

Answer: 8

Now change $\frac{3}{4}$ to an equivalent fraction that has a denominator of 8.

$$\frac{3 \times 2 = 6}{4 \times 2 = 8} \qquad \frac{3}{4} = \frac{6}{8}$$

The other fraction, $\frac{5}{8}$, already has a denominator of 8, so you do not have to change it.

The two fractions in terms of their least common denominator are $\frac{6}{8}$ and $\frac{5}{8}$.

If the smaller denominator will not go evenly into the larger one, try multiplying the larger denominator by 2. Let's return to our earlier example, $\frac{7}{8}$ and $\frac{5}{12}$.

EXAMPLE: What are $\frac{7}{8}$ and $\frac{5}{12}$ in terms of their least common denominator?

$\frac{7}{8} \qquad \frac{5}{12}$

Will 8 go evenly into 12? No. Try multiplying 12 by 2.

$12 \times 2 = 24$

Will 8 go evenly into 24? Yes. Therefore, 24 is the least common denominator.

Now change $\frac{7}{8}$ and $\frac{5}{12}$ to equivalent fractions that have a denominator of 24.

$$\frac{7 \times 3 = 21}{8 \times 3 = 24} \qquad \frac{7}{8} = \frac{21}{24}$$

$$\frac{5 \times 2 = 10}{12 \times 2 = 24} \qquad \frac{5}{12} = \frac{10}{24}$$

Answer: The two fractions in terms of their least common denominator are $\frac{21}{24}$ and $\frac{10}{24}$.

Sometimes there is no common denominator smaller than what you get by multiplying the two denominators together.

EXAMPLE: What are $\frac{4}{7}$ and $\frac{8}{11}$ in terms of their least common denominator?

$\frac{4}{7} \qquad \frac{8}{11}$

Will 7 go evenly into 11? No. Try multiplying 11 by 2.

$11 \times 2 = 22$

Will 7 go evenly into 22? No. At this point, you can try multiplying the larger denominator by 3, 4, and 5.

$11 \times 3 = 33$

$11 \times 4 = 44$

$11 \times 5 = 55$

Will 7 go evenly into 33, 44, or 55?

No. Since no smaller number works, the least common denominator must be found by multiplying the two denominators together.

$7 \times 11 = 77$

The least common denominator of $\frac{4}{7}$ and $\frac{8}{11}$ is 77.

Now change $\frac{4}{7}$ and $\frac{8}{11}$ to equivalent fractions that have a denominator of 77.

$$\frac{4 \times 11 = 44}{7 \times 11 = 77} \qquad \frac{4}{7} = \frac{44}{77}$$

$$\frac{8 \times 7 = 56}{11 \times 7 = 77} \qquad \frac{8}{11} = \frac{56}{77}$$

Answer: The two fractions in terms of their least common denominator are $\frac{44}{77}$ and $\frac{56}{77}$.

Check your skill at finding the least common denominator by doing this exercise.

Exercise for Subskill 6D

Fill in the numerator to make each of the following pairs of fractions equivalent.

1. $\frac{5}{8} = \frac{\quad}{16}$ **2.** $\frac{3}{4} = \frac{\quad}{16}$

3. $\frac{3}{4} = \frac{}{20}$ **4.** $\frac{1}{2} = \frac{}{8}$

5. $\frac{2}{5} = \frac{}{10}$ **6.** $\frac{3}{5} = \frac{}{20}$

7. $\frac{3}{10} = \frac{}{20}$ **8.** $\frac{2}{3} = \frac{}{12}$

9. $\frac{2}{5} = \frac{}{20}$ **10.** $\frac{18}{24} = \frac{}{48}$

Find the least common denominator for each of the following pairs of fractions.

11. $\frac{3}{4}$ $\frac{6}{8}$ **12.** $\frac{1}{2}$ $\frac{7}{14}$

13. $\frac{5}{6}$ $\frac{3}{8}$ **14.** $\frac{1}{12}$ $\frac{1}{9}$

15. $\frac{7}{16}$ $\frac{5}{24}$ **16.** $\frac{3}{7}$ $\frac{1}{14}$

17. $\frac{3}{10}$ $\frac{11}{12}$ **18.** $\frac{3}{14}$ $\frac{8}{35}$

19. $\frac{3}{8}$ $\frac{2}{9}$ **20.** $\frac{2}{21}$ $\frac{8}{35}$

For each of the following pairs, write the fractions in terms of their least common denominator.

21. $\frac{1}{4}$ $\frac{6}{8}$

22. $\frac{1}{2}$ $\frac{8}{14}$

23. $\frac{5}{6}$ $\frac{3}{8}$

24. $\frac{1}{12}$ $\frac{1}{9}$

25. $\frac{7}{16}$ $\frac{5}{24}$

26. $\frac{3}{7}$ $\frac{1}{14}$

27. $\frac{3}{10}$ $\frac{11}{12}$

28. $\frac{3}{14}$ $\frac{8}{35}$

29. $\frac{1}{2}$ $\frac{3}{8}$

30. $\frac{3}{14}$ $\frac{2}{21}$

Check your answers on pages 8 and 9 in the Answer Key for Book One. If you correctly answered twenty four of the thirty problems, go to the next subskill. If not, do the following Supplemental Exercise.

Supplemental Exercise for Subskill 6D

Read Subskill 6D again. Work through the examples as you read them. Then do this exercise.

Fill in the numerator to make each of the following pairs of fractions equivalent.

1. $\frac{4}{5} = \frac{}{20}$

2. $\frac{7}{8} = \frac{}{56}$

3. $\frac{3}{10} = \frac{}{100}$

4. $\frac{5}{12} = \frac{}{60}$

5. $\frac{2}{11} = \frac{}{33}$

6. $\frac{9}{10} = \frac{}{60}$

7. $\frac{2}{7} = \frac{}{21}$

8. $\frac{5}{9} = \frac{}{45}$

9. $\frac{1}{15} = \frac{}{30}$

10. $\frac{2}{3} = \frac{}{99}$

Find the least common denominator for each of the following pairs of fractions.

11. $\frac{3}{8}$ $\frac{1}{2}$

12. $\frac{5}{6}$ $\frac{7}{18}$

13. $\frac{3}{10}$ $\frac{70}{100}$

14. $\frac{15}{16}$ $\frac{11}{32}$

15. $\frac{5}{8}$ $\frac{7}{12}$

16. $\frac{12}{45}$ $\frac{7}{10}$

17. $\frac{3}{4}$ $\frac{2}{5}$

18. $\frac{21}{49}$ $\frac{18}{28}$

19. $\frac{5}{6}$ $\frac{1}{4}$

20. $\frac{11}{12}$ $\frac{7}{16}$

For each of the following pairs, write the fractions in terms of their least common denominator.

21. $\frac{3}{8}$ $\frac{1}{2}$

22. $\frac{5}{6}$ $\frac{7}{18}$

23. $\frac{3}{10}$ $\frac{70}{100}$

24. $\frac{15}{16}$ $\frac{11}{32}$

25. $\frac{5}{8}$ $\frac{7}{12}$

26. $\frac{12}{45}$ $\frac{7}{10}$

27. $\frac{3}{4}$ $\frac{2}{5}$

28. $\frac{21}{49}$ $\frac{18}{28}$

29. $\frac{1}{2}$ $\frac{5}{6}$

30. $\frac{7}{8}$ $\frac{11}{12}$

Check your answers on page 9 in the Answer Key for Book One. If you correctly answered twenty-four of the thirty problems, go to the next subskill. If not, ask your instructor for help.

Subskill 6E: Telling Larger Fractions from Smaller Ones

After studying this subskill you will be able to tell larger fractions from smaller ones.

To tell larger fractions from smaller ones, first find their least common denominator. Then write them all in terms of their least common denominator. Finally, compare their numerators.

EXAMPLE: Which is larger, $\frac{5}{6}$ or $\frac{3}{4}$?

First, find the least common denominator.

$\frac{5}{6}$ $\frac{3}{4}$

Will 4 go evenly into 6? No. Try multiplying 6 by 2.

$6 \times 2 = 12$

Will 4 go evenly into 12? Yes. Therefore, 12 is the least common denominator.

Then write both fractions in terms of their least common denominator. In other words, change $\frac{5}{6}$ and $\frac{3}{4}$ to equivalent fractions that have a denominator of 12.

$$\frac{5 \times 2 = 10}{6 \times 2 = 12} \qquad \frac{5}{6} = \frac{10}{12}$$

$$\frac{3 \times 3 = 9}{4 \times 3 = 12} \qquad \frac{3}{4} = \frac{9}{12}$$

The two fractions in terms of their least common denominator are $\frac{10}{12}$ and $\frac{9}{12}$.

Finally, compare the numerators.

$\frac{10}{12}$ $\frac{9}{12}$ 10 is larger.

Since 10 is larger than 9, $\frac{10}{12}$ is larger than $\frac{9}{12}$

Answer: Putting the fractions back into their original terms, $\frac{5}{6}$ is larger than $\frac{3}{4}$.

You can also use this method to arrange three or more fractions in order from largest to smallest.

EXAMPLE: Arrange these fractions from largest to smallest: $\frac{1}{4}$, $\frac{1}{5}$, and $\frac{3}{20}$.

First, find the least common denominator of *all three* fractions.

$\frac{1}{4}$ $\frac{1}{5}$ $\frac{3}{20}$

Will 4 go evenly into 20? Yes. But will 5 *also* go evenly into 20? Yes. Therefore, 20 is the least common denominator.

Then write all three fractions in terms of their least common denominator.

$\frac{1 \times 5 = 5}{4 \times 5 = 20}$ $\frac{1}{4} = \frac{5}{20}$

$\frac{1 \times 4 = 4}{5 \times 4 = 20}$ $\frac{1}{5} = \frac{4}{20}$

$\frac{3}{20}$ is already in terms of the least common denominator, so you do not have to change it. The three fractions in terms of their least common denominator are $\frac{5}{20}$, $\frac{4}{20}$, and $\frac{3}{20}$.

Finally, compare the numerators.

$\frac{5}{20}$ $\frac{4}{20}$ $\frac{3}{20}$

Since 5 is larger than 4 and 4 is larger than 3, the fractions in order from largest to smallest are: $\frac{5}{20}$, $\frac{4}{20}$, and $\frac{3}{20}$.

Answer: Putting them back into their original terms, their order is: $\frac{1}{4}$, $\frac{1}{5}$, and $\frac{3}{20}$.

Sometimes you can only get the least common denominator of three or more fractions by multiplying *all* their denominators together.

EXAMPLE: Arrange these fractions from largest to smallest: $\frac{2}{3}$, $\frac{3}{5}$, and $\frac{5}{7}$.

First, find the least common denominator of all three fractions.

$\frac{2}{3}$ $\quad$ $\frac{3}{5}$ $\quad$ $\frac{5}{7}$

Will 3 go evenly into 7? No. Try multiplying 7 by 2.

$7 \times 2 - 14$

Will 3 go evenly into 14? No. At this point, try multiplying the two largest denominators together.

$5 \times 7 = 35$

Will 3 go evenly into 35? No. Since no smaller number works, the least common denominator must be found by multiplying *all three* denominators together.

$3 \times 5 = 15$

$15 \times 7 = 105$

The least common denominator is 105.

Then write all three fractions in terms of their least common denominator.

$$\frac{2 \times 35 = 70}{3 \times 35 = 105} \qquad \frac{2}{3} = \frac{70}{105}$$

$$\frac{3 \times 21 = 63}{5 \times 21 = 105} \qquad \frac{3}{5} = \frac{63}{105}$$

$$\frac{5 \times 15 = 75}{7 \times 15 = 105} \qquad \frac{5}{7} = \frac{75}{105}$$

Finally, compare the numerators.

$\frac{70}{105}$ $\frac{63}{105}$ $\frac{75}{105}$ 75 is larger than 70 and 70 is larger than 63.

In order from largest to smallest:

$\frac{75}{105}$ $\frac{70}{105}$ $\frac{63}{105}$

Answer: In their original terms:

$\frac{5}{7}$ $\frac{2}{3}$ $\frac{3}{5}$

Check your skill at telling larger fractions from smaller ones by doing this exercise.

Exercise for Subskill 6E

Arrange the fractions in each of the following sets in order from largest to smallest. In your answers, write the fractions in their original terms.

1. $\frac{5}{8}$ $\frac{9}{16}$

2. $\frac{4}{9}$ $\frac{8}{18}$

3. $\frac{5}{8}$ $\frac{3}{16}$ $\frac{7}{12}$

4. $\frac{8}{15}$ $\frac{13}{20}$

Arrange the fractions in each of the following sets in order from smallest to largest. In your answers, write the fractions in their original terms.

5. $\frac{3}{8}$ $\frac{1}{4}$

6. $\frac{7}{8}$ $\frac{3}{4}$ $\frac{11}{16}$

7. $\frac{3}{4}$ $\frac{2}{3}$ $\frac{5}{6}$

8. $\frac{11}{12}$ $\frac{8}{9}$

9. Sam wants to unscrew a bolt with a socket wrench. He tries a $\frac{3}{4}$-inch socket, but it is just a little too big. He also has an $\frac{11}{16}$-inch socket and a $\frac{7}{8}$-inch socket. Which one should he try next?

10. Now Sam wants to arrange his sockets in order from smallest to largest. He has asked you to help him. These are the sizes:

$\frac{1}{2}''$, $\frac{5}{8}''$, $\frac{3}{4}''$, $\frac{9}{16}''$, $\frac{11}{16}''$, $\frac{7}{8}''$

Check your answers on page 9 in the Answer Key for Book One. If you correctly answered eight of the ten problems, go to the next subskill. If not, do the following Supplemental Exercise.

Supplemental Exercise for Subskill 6E

Read Subskill 6E again. Work through the examples as you read them. Then do this exercise.

Arrange the fractions in each of the following sets in order from smallest to largest. In your answers, write the fractions in their original terms.

1. $\frac{1}{4}$ $\frac{1}{6}$ **2.** $\frac{7}{8}$ $\frac{3}{4}$

3. $\frac{7}{8}$ $\frac{13}{16}$ $\frac{3}{4}$ **4.** $\frac{2}{15}$ $\frac{3}{25}$

Arrange the fractions in each of the following sets in order from largest to smallest. In your answers, write the fractions in their original terms.

5. $\frac{2}{3}$ $\frac{11}{12}$ $\frac{3}{4}$ **6.** $\frac{3}{8}$ $\frac{5}{12}$

7. $\frac{7}{12}$ $\frac{15}{24}$ **8.** $\frac{1}{2}$ $\frac{1}{6}$ $\frac{1}{4}$

9. For the backing of a bookcase you are building, you need the thinnest plywood you can buy. The lumber yard has three thicknesses of plywood: $\frac{1}{4}$-inch, $\frac{3}{16}$-inch, and $\frac{3}{8}$-inch. Which one should you buy?

10. Now you are going to drill holes for the screws in your bookcase. You drill a hole with a $\frac{3}{16}$-inch bit, but it is too small for your screws. You also have a $\frac{1}{4}$-inch bit and a $\frac{5}{32}$-inch bit. Which one should you try next?

Check your answers on page 9 in the Answer Key for Book One. If you correctly answered eight of the ten problems, go on to the next subskill. If not, ask your instructor for help.

Subskill 6F: Changing Improper Fractions to Mixed Numbers

After studying this subskill you will be able to change improper fractions to mixed numbers.

What is a mixed number? What is an improper fraction? All the fractions you have studied so far are **proper fractions.** In a proper fraction, the numerator is smaller than the denominator. Examples are $\frac{1}{3}$, $\frac{5}{8}$, and $\frac{14}{15}$.

An **improper fraction** is a fraction in which the numerator is larger than the denominator, or equal to it. Examples are $\frac{4}{3}$, $\frac{5}{2}$, and $\frac{7}{7}$.

A **mixed number** is a whole number *plus* a proper fraction. An example is $1\frac{1}{4}$, which is read "one and one fourth." Other examples are $3\frac{3}{4}$, $7\frac{1}{8}$, and $24\frac{8}{9}$.

To change an improper fraction to a mixed number, divide the numerator by the denominator. If there is a remainder, write it as a fraction.

EXAMPLE: Change $\frac{49}{6}$ to a mixed number.

First, divide the numerator by the denominator.

$$\begin{array}{r} 8 \\ 6\overline{)49} \\ \underline{48} \\ 1 \end{array}$$

8 is the whole number.

There is a remainder of 1.

Then write the remainder as a fraction. The remainder becomes the numerator of this fraction, and the divisor, which is the same as the denominator of the original improper fraction, becomes the denominator.

$\frac{1}{6}$ — 1: Remainder; 6: Denominator of the improper fraction

Finally, add the fraction to the whole number.

$8 + \frac{1}{6} = 8\frac{1}{6}$

Answer: $\frac{49}{6} = 8\frac{1}{6}$ (read "eight and one sixth")

After writing the remainder as a fraction, check to see if you can reduce it to lower terms.

EXAMPLE: Change $\frac{10}{4}$ to a mixed number.

First, divide the numerator by the denominator.

$$\begin{array}{r} 2 \\ 4\overline{)10} \\ \underline{8} \\ 2 \end{array}$$

2 is the whole number.

There is a remainder of 2.

Then write the remainder as a fraction.

$\frac{2}{4}$ — 2: Remainder; 4: Denominator of the improper fraction

Can $\frac{2}{4}$ be reduced to lower terms? Yes.

$\frac{2}{4} = \frac{1}{2}$

Finally, add the fraction to the whole number.

$2 + \frac{1}{2} = 2\frac{1}{2}$

Answer: $\frac{10}{4} = 2\frac{1}{2}$

Sometimes there is no remainder. In this case, the answer is not a mixed number but simply a whole number.

EXAMPLE: Change $\frac{36}{4}$ to a mixed number.

First, divide the numerator by the denominator.

$$\begin{array}{r} 9 \\ 4\overline{)36} \\ \underline{36} \\ 0 \end{array}$$

9 is the whole number.

There is no remainder.

Answer: $\frac{36}{4} = 9$

Check your skill at changing improper fractions to mixed numbers by doing the exercise on page 130.

Exercise for Subskill 6F

Change each of the following improper fractions to a mixed number (or whole number).

1. $\frac{11}{4}$	**2.** $\frac{16}{5}$	**3.** $\frac{22}{8}$
4. $\frac{8}{6}$	**5.** $\frac{13}{3}$	**6.** $\frac{42}{12}$
7. $\frac{14}{6}$	**8.** $\frac{12}{5}$	**9.** $\frac{36}{6}$
10. $\frac{29}{7}$	**11.** $\frac{7}{6}$	**12.** $\frac{4}{2}$
13. $\frac{16}{4}$	**14.** $\frac{3}{2}$	**15.** $\frac{17}{5}$
16. $\frac{32}{5}$	**17.** $\frac{9}{7}$	**18.** $\frac{15}{6}$
19. $\frac{24}{5}$	**20.** $\frac{12}{9}$	

Check your answers on page 10 in the Answer Key for Book One. If you correctly answered sixteen of the twenty problems, go to the next subskill. If not, do the following Supplemental Exercise.

Supplemental Exercise for Subskill 6F

Read Subskill 6F again. Work through the examples as you read them. Then do this exercise.

Change each of the following improper fractions to a mixed number (or whole number).

1. $\frac{11}{2}$	**2.** $\frac{10}{4}$	**3.** $\frac{6}{4}$
4. $\frac{8}{5}$	**5.** $\frac{25}{6}$	**6.** $\frac{12}{3}$

7. $\frac{18}{12}$ 8. $\frac{12}{9}$ 9. $\frac{12}{4}$

10. $\frac{12}{8}$ 11. $\frac{16}{3}$ 12. $\frac{4}{3}$

13. $\frac{9}{6}$ 14. $\frac{20}{3}$ 15. $\frac{18}{2}$

16. $\frac{7}{4}$ 17. $\frac{5}{2}$ 18. $\frac{24}{5}$

19. $\frac{8}{6}$ 20. $\frac{18}{6}$

Check your answers on page 10 in the Answer Key for Book One. If you correctly answered sixteen of the twenty problems, go to the next subskill. If not, ask your instructor for help.

Subskill 6G: Changing Mixed Numbers to Improper Fractions

After studying this subskill you will be able to change mixed numbers to improper fractions.

To change a mixed number to an improper fraction, multiply the whole number by the denominator of the fraction and add the numerator.

EXAMPLE: Change $3\frac{2}{7}$ to an improper fraction.

First, multiply the whole number by the denominator of the fraction.

$3 \times 7 = 21$

Then add the numerator of the fraction.

$21 + 2 = 23$

This gives you the numerator of the improper fraction. The denominator is the same as the denominator of the fraction in the original mixed number.

$\frac{23}{7}$ Numerator
Denominator—same as the denominator of $\frac{2}{7}$

Answer: $3\frac{2}{7} = \frac{23}{7}$

EXAMPLE:

Change $6\frac{2}{3}$ to an improper fraction.

First, multiply the whole number by the denominator of the fraction.

$6 \times 3 = 18$

Then add the numerator of the fraction.

$18 + 2 = 20$

This gives you the numerator of the improper fraction. The denominator is the same as the denominator of the fraction in the original mixed number.

$\frac{20}{3}$ Numerator
Denominator—same as the denominator of $\frac{2}{3}$

Answer: $6\frac{2}{3} = \frac{20}{3}$

Check your skill at changing mixed numbers to improper fractions by doing this exercise.

Exercise for Subskill 6G

Change each of the following mixed numbers to an improper fraction.

1. $1\frac{2}{3}$ **2.** $3\frac{1}{2}$ **3.** $7\frac{5}{8}$

4. $6\frac{2}{3}$ **5.** $12\frac{1}{2}$ **6.** $16\frac{3}{4}$

7. $5\frac{1}{5}$ **8.** $23\frac{1}{2}$ **9.** $100\frac{3}{4}$ **10.** $23\frac{6}{7}$

Check your answers on page 10 in the Answer Key for Book One. If you correctly answered eight of the ten problems, go to the Self-Check. If not, do the following Supplemental Exercise.

Supplemental Exercise for Subskill 6G

Read Subskill 6G again. Work through the examples as you read them. Then do this exercise.

Change each of the following mixed numbers to an improper fraction.

1. $2\frac{5}{8}$ 2. $6\frac{1}{9}$ 3. $14\frac{2}{5}$

4. $5\frac{4}{9}$ 5. $9\frac{1}{8}$ 6. $1\frac{1}{2}$

7. $3\frac{2}{5}$ 8. $11\frac{4}{7}$ 9. $6\frac{5}{9}$

10. $13\frac{2}{3}$

Check your answers on page 10 in the Answer Key for Book One. If you correctly answered eight of the ten problems, go to the Self-Check. If not, ask your instructor for help.

SELF-CHECK FOR SKILL UNIT 6

Which of the two fractions in each group is larger?

1. $\frac{12}{18}$ or $\frac{9}{18}$

2. $\frac{13}{16}$ or $\frac{7}{8}$

3. $\frac{7}{8}$ or $\frac{3}{4}$

4. $\frac{3}{4}$ or $\frac{15}{20}$

5. $\frac{2}{3}$ or $\frac{5}{8}$

Reduce each fraction to lowest terms.

6. $\frac{4}{6}$ **7.** $\frac{10}{15}$ **8.** $\frac{4}{12}$

9. $\frac{12}{18}$ **10.** $\frac{8}{24}$

Change each of the following fractions to a whole or mixed number.

11. $\frac{12}{4}$ **12.** $\frac{7}{2}$ **13.** $\frac{10}{4}$

14. $\frac{50}{16}$ **15.** $\frac{100}{35}$

Change each of the following to an improper fraction.

16. $1\frac{1}{2}$ **17.** $3\frac{2}{5}$ **18.** $11\frac{4}{7}$

19. $6\frac{5}{9}$ **20.** $13\frac{2}{3}$

Check your answers on page 10 in the Answer Key for Book One. If you correctly answered sixteen of the twenty problems, go on to Skill Unit 7. If not, ask your instructor for help.

Skill Unit 7
ADDING AND SUBTRACTING FRACTIONS

What Skills You Need to Begin: Basic skills with whole numbers and fractions (Skill Units 1 through 6).

What Skills You Will Learn: After studying this skill unit, you will be able to add and subtract fractions and solve word problems involving the addition and subtraction of fractions.

Why You Need This Skill: You often need to add and subtract fractions when you measure things and work with materials of any kind.

How You Will Show What You Have Learned: At the end of this skill unit is a Self-Check consisting of twenty problems in the addition and subtraction of fractions. You should allow yourself one hour to do the Self-Check. To prove that you have mastered these skills you must correctly answer sixteen of the twenty problems.

If you feel you have already mastered the addition and subtraction of fractions, complete the Self-Check on pages 162 and 163.

Subskill 7A: Adding Like Fractions

After studying this subskill you will be able to add like fractions.

Like fractions are fractions that have the *same* denominator. To add like fractions, simply add the numerators together and keep the same denominator.

EXAMPLE: Add $\frac{1}{5}$ and $\frac{3}{5}$.

$\frac{1}{5} + \frac{3}{5} = \frac{4}{5}$ Add the numerators together. Keep the same denominator.

Answer: $\frac{4}{5}$

When you get your answer, check to see if it can be reduced to lower terms.

EXAMPLE: Add $\frac{3}{8}$ and $\frac{3}{8}$.

$\frac{3}{8} + \frac{3}{8} = \frac{6}{8}$ Add the numerators together. Keep the same denominator.

The answer is $\frac{6}{8}$. But $\frac{6}{8}$ can be reduced to lower terms.

$\frac{6}{8} = \frac{3}{4}$ Answer: $\frac{3}{4}$

Sometimes the answer you get will be an improper fraction. When that happens, change it to a mixed number.

EXAMPLE: Add $\frac{5}{6} + \frac{1}{6} + \frac{2}{6}$.

$\frac{5}{6} + \frac{1}{6} + \frac{2}{6} = \frac{8}{6}$ Add the numerators together. Keep the same denominator.

The answer is $\frac{8}{6}$, an improper fraction. Change it to a mixed number.

$$\begin{array}{r} 1 \\ 6\overline{)8} \\ \underline{6} \\ 2 \end{array}$$

1 — Whole number

2 — Remainder

Write the remainder as a fraction.

$\frac{2}{6}$ The remainder is the numerator. The number you divided by is the denominator.

Put the whole number and the fraction together to make the mixed number.

$1 + \frac{2}{6} = 1\frac{2}{6}$

The answer as a mixed number is $1\frac{2}{6}$. But $\frac{2}{6}$, the fraction in the mixed number, can be reduced to lower terms.

$\frac{2}{6} = \frac{1}{3}$

Answer: $1\frac{1}{3}$

Sometimes the fractions add up to an improper fraction, and when you change it, you get a simple whole number.

EXAMPLE: Add $\frac{5}{7} + \frac{6}{7} + \frac{3}{7}$.

$\frac{5}{7} + \frac{6}{7} + \frac{3}{7} = \frac{14}{7}$ Add the numerators together. Keep the same denominator.

The answer is $\frac{14}{7}$, an improper fraction. Change it to a mixed number (or whole number).

$$\begin{array}{r} 2 \\ 7\overline{)14} \\ \underline{14} \\ 0 \end{array}$$

2 — Whole number

0 — There is no remainder.

Answer: 2

Adding Mixed Numbers That Have Like Fractions in Them

To add mixed numbers that have like fractions in them, first add the fractions and then the whole numbers.

EXAMPLE: Add $9\frac{1}{8} + 2\frac{5}{8} + 11\frac{3}{8} + 4\frac{3}{8}$.

First, add the fractions.

$$\frac{1}{8} + \frac{5}{8} + \frac{3}{8} + \frac{3}{8} = \frac{12}{8}$$

The answer is $\frac{12}{8}$, an improper fraction. Change it to a mixed number (or whole number).

$\frac{12}{8} = 1\frac{4}{8}$

Since $\frac{4}{8}$, the fraction in the mixed number, can be reduced to lower terms

$\frac{4}{8} = \frac{1}{2}$

the fractions add up to $1\frac{1}{2}$.

Then add the whole numbers and the mixed number you got by adding the fractions.

9 2 11 4	From the original problem
$1\frac{1}{2}$	From the addition of the fractions
$27\frac{1}{2}$	

Answer: $27\frac{1}{2}$

Sometimes the fractions add up to a simple whole number.

EXAMPLE: Add $4\frac{1}{3}$ and $6\frac{2}{3}$.

First, add the fractions.

$$\frac{1}{3} + \frac{2}{3} = \frac{3}{3}$$

The answer is $\frac{3}{3}$, an improper fraction. Change it to a mixed number (or whole number).

$$\frac{3}{3} = 1$$

Then add the whole numbers, including the number you got by adding the fractions.

4 6	From the original problem
1	From the addition of the fractions
11	

Answer: 11

Sometimes the fractions add up to a proper fraction, so there is no whole number to add from the addition of the fractions.

EXAMPLE: Add $10\frac{1}{8} + 6\frac{3}{8} + 15\frac{3}{8}$.

First, add the fractions.

$$\frac{1}{8} + \frac{3}{8} + \frac{3}{8} = \frac{7}{8}$$

The answer is $\frac{7}{8}$, a proper fraction. You cannot change it to a mixed number or whole number.

But can you reduce it to lower terms? No, $\frac{7}{8}$ is already in its lowest terms.

Then add the whole numbers, including the number you got by adding the fractions.

$$\left.\begin{array}{r}10\\6\\15\end{array}\right\}\quad \text{From the original problem}$$

$$\begin{array}{r}\frac{7}{8}\\ \hline 31\frac{7}{8}\end{array}\quad \text{From the addition of the fractions}$$

Answer: $31\frac{7}{8}$

Check your skill at adding like fractions by doing this exercise.

Exercise for Subskill 7A

1. $\frac{5}{7} + \frac{1}{7} =$ **2.** $\frac{1}{4} + \frac{1}{4} =$ **3.** $\frac{4}{9} + \frac{7}{9} =$

4. $\frac{7}{12} + \frac{11}{12} =$ **5.** $\frac{3}{10} + \frac{3}{10} =$ **6.** $6\frac{1}{3} + 7\frac{2}{3} =$

7. $8\frac{5}{8} + 4\frac{1}{8} =$ **8.** $8\frac{9}{11} + \frac{5}{11} =$ **9.** $\frac{7}{18} + \frac{5}{18} =$

10. $9\frac{4}{15} + 8\frac{5}{15} + \frac{3}{15} =$ **11.** $\frac{8}{13} + \frac{4}{13} + \frac{9}{13} =$ **12.** $3\frac{4}{12} + \frac{6}{12} + 9\frac{11}{12} =$

13. $\frac{1}{2} + \frac{1}{2} =$ **14.** $5\frac{3}{4} + 6\frac{3}{4} =$ **15.** $14\frac{4}{14} + 5\frac{3}{14} =$

Check your answers on pages 10 and 11 in the Answer Key for Book I. If you correctly answered twelve of the fifteen problems, go to the next subskill. If not, complete the following Supplemental Exercise.

Supplemental Exercise for Subskill 7A

Read Subskill 7A again. Work through the examples as you read them. Then do the exercise on page 140.

1. $\frac{6}{11} + \frac{4}{11} =$

2. $\frac{1}{6} + \frac{2}{6} =$

3. $\frac{7}{10} + \frac{9}{10} =$

4. $\frac{1}{2} + \frac{1}{2} =$

5. $\frac{6}{8} + \frac{6}{8} =$

6. $5\frac{4}{5} + 1\frac{1}{5} =$

7. $7\frac{2}{9} + 4\frac{1}{9} =$

8. $15\frac{8}{12} + 8\frac{5}{12} =$

9. $17\frac{13}{16} + \frac{7}{16} =$

10. $13\frac{3}{4} + 9\frac{2}{4} + 5\frac{1}{4} =$

11. $6\frac{5}{8} + 7\frac{3}{8} + 8\frac{6}{8} =$

12. $\frac{11}{18} + \frac{5}{18} + \frac{6}{18} =$

13. $\frac{4}{9} + \frac{7}{9} =$

14. $9\frac{5}{6} + 7\frac{5}{6} =$

15. $\frac{7}{15} + \frac{5}{15} =$

Check your answers on page 11 in the Answer Key for Book I. If you correctly answered twelve of the fifteen problems, go to the next subskill. If not, ask your instructor for help.

Subskill 7B: Adding Unlike Fractions

After studying this subskill you will be able to add unlike fractions.

Unlike fractions are fractions that have *different* denominators. To add unlike fractions, you must first change them to like fractions. To do this, find their least common denominator and change them to equivalent fractions that have this denominator. Then you can add them as like fractions.

EXAMPLE: Add $\frac{3}{8}$ and $\frac{5}{6}$.

First, find the least common denominator of $\frac{3}{8}$ and $\frac{5}{6}$. (You may need to review Subskill 6D.)

Will 6 go evenly into 8? No. Try 2×8.

$2 \times 8 = 16$

Will 6 go evenly into 16? No. Try 3×8.

$3 \times 8 = 24$

Will 6 go evenly into 24? Yes. The least common denominator is 24.

Then change the fractions to their equivalents that have the least common denominator.

$$\frac{3 \times 3}{8 \times 3} = \frac{9}{24}$$

$$\frac{5 \times 4}{6 \times 4} = \frac{20}{24}$$

The fractions in terms of their least common denominator are $\frac{9}{24}$ and $\frac{20}{24}$.

Now add the fractions as like fractions.

$$\frac{9}{24} + \frac{20}{24} = \frac{29}{24}$$ Add the numerators together. Keep the same denominator.

The answer is $\frac{29}{24}$, an improper fraction. Change it to a mixed number (or whole number).

$$\frac{29}{24} = 1\frac{5}{24}$$

The answer as a mixed number is $1\frac{5}{24}$. But can $\frac{5}{24}$ be reduced to lower terms? No.

Answer: $1\frac{5}{24}$

EXAMPLE: Add $\frac{2}{3} + \frac{3}{4} + \frac{1}{2}$.

First, find the least common denominator of $\frac{2}{3}$, $\frac{3}{4}$, and $\frac{1}{2}$.

Will 2 go evenly into 4? Yes. But will 3? No. Try 2×4.

$2 \times 4 = 8$

Yes, 2 will go evenly into 8, but will 3? No. Try 3×4.

$3 \times 4 = 12$

Yes, 3 will go evenly into 12, but will 2? Yes. The least common denominator is 12.

Then change the fractions to their equivalents that have the least common denominator.

$$\frac{2 \times 4}{3 \times 4} = \frac{8}{12}$$

$$\frac{3 \times 3}{4 \times 3} = \frac{9}{12}$$

$$\frac{1 \times 6}{2 \times 6} = \frac{6}{12}$$

The fractions in terms of their least common denominator are $\frac{8}{12}$, $\frac{9}{12}$, and $\frac{6}{12}$.

Now add the fractions.

$\frac{8}{12} + \frac{9}{12} + \frac{6}{12} = \frac{23}{12}$ Add the numerators together. Keep the same denominator.

The answer is $\frac{23}{12}$, an improper fraction. Change it to a mixed number (or whole number).

$\frac{23}{12} = 1\frac{11}{12}$

The answer as a mixed number is $1\frac{11}{12}$. But can $\frac{11}{12}$ be reduced to lower terms? No.

Answer: $1\frac{11}{12}$

Adding Mixed Numbers That Have Unlike Fractions in Them

To add mixed numbers that have unlike fractions in them, first add the fractions and then the whole numbers.

EXAMPLE: Add $8\frac{1}{2} + 4\frac{2}{5} + 5\frac{3}{5}$.

First, find the least common denominator of $\frac{1}{2}$, $\frac{2}{5}$, and $\frac{3}{5}$.

The least common denominator is 10. Do you see why? (If you need to review least common denominator, turn to Subskill 6D on page 114.)

What are $\frac{1}{2}$, $\frac{2}{5}$, and $\frac{3}{5}$ in terms of their least common denominator?

$\frac{1}{2} = \frac{5}{10}$

$\frac{2}{5} = \frac{4}{10}$

$\frac{3}{5} = \frac{6}{10}$

Add the fractions.

$$\frac{5}{10} + \frac{4}{10} + \frac{6}{10} = \frac{15}{10}$$

Change $\frac{15}{10}$, an improper fraction, to a mixed number.

$\frac{15}{10} = 1\frac{5}{10}$

Can $\frac{5}{10}$ be reduced to lower terms? Yes.

$\frac{5}{10} = \frac{1}{2}$

The fractions add up to $1\frac{1}{2}$.

Then add the whole numbers, including the number you got by adding the fractions.

8	
4	From the original problem
5	
$1\frac{1}{2}$	From the addition of the fractions
$18\frac{1}{2}$	

Answer: $18\frac{1}{2}$

EXAMPLE: Add $15\frac{1}{8} + 6\frac{1}{2} + 22\frac{1}{4}$.

First, find the least common denominator of $\frac{1}{8}$, $\frac{1}{2}$, and $\frac{1}{4}$.

Their least common denominator is 8.

What are $\frac{1}{8}$, $\frac{1}{2}$, and $\frac{1}{4}$ in terms of their least common denominator?

$\frac{1}{8} = \frac{1}{8}$

$\frac{1}{2} = \frac{4}{8}$

$\frac{1}{4} = \frac{2}{8}$

Add the fractions.

$$\frac{1}{8} + \frac{4}{8} + \frac{2}{8} = \frac{7}{8}$$

Do you need to change the answer, $\frac{7}{8}$, to a mixed number or whole number? No, because $\frac{7}{8}$ is already a proper fraction. Can $\frac{7}{8}$ be reduced to lower terms? No. The fractions add up to $\frac{7}{8}$.

Then add the whole numbers, including the number you got by adding the fractions.

$$\begin{array}{r} 15 \\ 6 \\ 22 \\ \frac{7}{8} \\ \hline 43\frac{7}{8} \end{array}$$

Answer: $43\frac{7}{8}$

Check your skill at adding unlike fractions by doing this exercise.

Exercise for Subskill 7B

1. $\frac{1}{3} + \frac{1}{6} =$
2. $\frac{5}{8} + \frac{1}{4} =$
3. $\frac{2}{3} + \frac{4}{9} =$
4. $\frac{1}{2} + \frac{3}{10} =$
5. $\frac{3}{4} + \frac{3}{8} =$
6. $\frac{1}{3} + \frac{4}{5} =$
7. $\frac{5}{6} + \frac{1}{4} =$
8. $\frac{4}{7} + \frac{1}{2} =$
9. $6\frac{3}{4} + 9\frac{2}{3} =$
10. $\frac{1}{6} + \frac{2}{9} =$
11. $8\frac{3}{8} + 7\frac{5}{6} =$
12. $\frac{1}{2} + \frac{1}{6} + \frac{2}{3} =$

13. $24\frac{3}{4} + 18\frac{2}{7} =$ 14. $16\frac{7}{9} + \frac{2}{3} + 8\frac{2}{6} =$ 15. $7\frac{7}{8} + 5\frac{3}{4} + 9\frac{5}{6} =$

16. $\frac{2}{5} + \frac{3}{10} =$ 17. $\frac{2}{3} + \frac{6}{7} =$ 18. $17\frac{9}{16} + 6\frac{5}{8} =$

Check your answers on page 11 in the Answer Key for Book I. If you correctly answered fifteen of the eighteen problems, go to the next subskill. If not, do the following Supplemental Exercise.

Supplemental Exercise for Subskill 7B

Read Subskill 7B again. Work through the examples as you read them. Then do this exercise.

1. $\frac{3}{4} + \frac{1}{8} =$ 2. $\frac{1}{3} + \frac{2}{9} =$ 3. $\frac{7}{10} + \frac{1}{2} =$

4. $\frac{1}{4} + \frac{7}{8} =$ 5. $\frac{2}{3} + \frac{5}{6} =$ 6. $\frac{2}{7} + \frac{1}{2} =$

7. $\frac{1}{9} + \frac{5}{6} =$ 8. $\frac{2}{5} + \frac{2}{3} =$ 9. $\frac{3}{4} + \frac{1}{6} =$

10. $8\frac{3}{8} + 7\frac{7}{16} =$ 11. $19\frac{4}{7} + 8\frac{3}{4} =$ 12. $36\frac{1}{6} + 27\frac{5}{8} =$

13. $\frac{1}{2} + \frac{2}{3} + \frac{5}{6} =$ 14. $16\frac{2}{5} + 29\frac{1}{10} + \frac{3}{4} =$ 15. $28\frac{7}{12} + 8\frac{2}{9} + 15\frac{1}{4} =$

16. $\frac{3}{5} + \frac{7}{10} =$ 17. $\frac{5}{7} + \frac{1}{3} =$ 18. $17\frac{2}{3} + 25\frac{1}{4} =$

Check your answers on page 11 in the Answer Key for Book I. If you correctly answered fifteen of the eighteen problems, go to the next subskill. If not, ask your instructor for help.

Subskill 7C: Subtracting Like Fractions

After studying this subskill you will be able to subtract like fractions.

To subtract like fractions, simply subtract the numerators and keep the same denominator.

EXAMPLE: Subtract: $\frac{7}{9} - \frac{4}{9}$.

$\frac{7}{9} - \frac{4}{9} = \frac{3}{9}$ Subtract the numerators. Keep the same denominator.

When you get your answer, check to see if it can be reduced to lower terms.

$\frac{3}{9} = \frac{1}{3}$

Answer: $\frac{1}{3}$

EXAMPLE: Subtract: $\frac{9}{16} - \frac{5}{16}$.

$$\frac{9}{16} - \frac{5}{16} = \frac{4}{16}$$

Can $\frac{4}{16}$ be reduced to lower terms?

$\frac{4}{16} = \frac{1}{4}$

Answer: $\frac{1}{4}$

Subtracting Mixed Numbers That Have Like Fractions in Them

To subtract mixed numbers that have like fractions in them, first subtract the fractions and then the whole numbers.

EXAMPLE: Subtract: $12\frac{7}{12} - 4\frac{5}{12}$.

First, subtract the fractions.

$$\frac{7}{12} - \frac{5}{12} = \frac{2}{12}$$

Can $\frac{2}{12}$ be reduced to lower terms?

$\frac{2}{12} = \frac{1}{6}$

Subtracting the fractions gives you $\frac{1}{6}$.

Then subtract the whole numbers.

$$\begin{array}{r} 12 \\ -\ 4 \\ \hline 8 \end{array}$$

Put the answer you got from subtracting the fractions together with the answer from subtracting the whole numbers. Usually this makes a mixed number.

$8 + \frac{1}{6} = 8\frac{1}{6}$

Answer: $8\frac{1}{6}$

Check your skill at subtracting like fractions by doing this exercise.

Exercise for Subskill 7C

1. $\frac{5}{7} - \frac{2}{7} =$ 2. $\frac{4}{6} - \frac{1}{6} =$ 3. $\frac{11}{12} - \frac{5}{12} =$

4. $\frac{2}{3} - \frac{1}{3} =$ 5. $17\frac{9}{10} - 8\frac{7}{10} =$ 6. $21\frac{10}{11} - 17\frac{4}{11} =$

7. $14\frac{8}{9} - 6\frac{2}{9} =$ 8. $32\frac{13}{16} - 5\frac{3}{16} =$ 9. $11\frac{15}{18} - 8\frac{7}{18} =$

10. $\frac{7}{8} - \frac{5}{8} =$ 11. $\frac{12}{15} - \frac{9}{15} =$ 12. $25\frac{5}{5} - 9\frac{3}{5} =$

Check your answers on page 11 in the Answer Key for Book I. If you correctly answered ten of the twelve problems, go to the next subskill. If not, do the following Supplemental Exercise.

Supplemental Exercise for Subskill 7C

Read Subskill 7C again. Work through the examples as you read them. Then do this exercise.

1. $\frac{7}{10} - \frac{2}{10} =$ 2. $\frac{9}{11} - \frac{4}{11} =$ 3. $\frac{8}{13} - \frac{4}{13} =$

4. $\frac{5}{8} - \frac{3}{8} =$ 5. $16\frac{5}{6} - 9\frac{3}{6} =$ 6. $23\frac{6}{7} - 18\frac{2}{7} =$

7. $15\frac{11}{12} - 7\frac{1}{12} =$ 8. $27\frac{8}{15} - 9\frac{2}{15} =$ 9. $35\frac{9}{14} - 7\frac{1}{14} =$

10. $\frac{3}{5} - \frac{1}{5} =$ 11. $\frac{17}{18} - \frac{9}{18} =$ 12. $31\frac{9}{9} - 7\frac{4}{9} =$

Check your answers on page 11 in the Answer Key for Book I. If you correctly answered ten of the twelve problems, go to the next subskill. If not, ask your instructor for help.

Subskill 7D: Subtracting Unlike Fractions

After studying this subskill you will be able to subtract unlike fractions.

To subtract unlike fractions, you must first change them to like fractions. That is, you must find their least common denominator and change them to equivalent fractions that have this denominator. Then you can subtract them as like fractions.

EXAMPLE: Subtract $\frac{2}{9} - \frac{1}{6}$.

First, find the least common denominator of $\frac{2}{9}$ and $\frac{1}{6}$.

Their least common denominator is 18.

Then change $\frac{2}{9}$ and $\frac{1}{6}$ to their equivalents that have the least common denominator.

$\frac{2}{9} = \frac{4}{18}$

$\frac{1}{6} = \frac{3}{18}$

Now subtract the fractions as like fractions.

$$\frac{4}{18} - \frac{3}{18} = \frac{1}{18}$$

Can $\frac{1}{18}$ be reduced to lower terms? No. Answer: $\frac{1}{18}$

Subtracting Mixed Numbers That Have Unlike Fractions in Them

To subtract mixed numbers that have unlike fractions in them, first subtract the fractions and then subtract the whole numbers.

EXAMPLE: Subtract $7\frac{7}{8} - 3\frac{1}{4}$.

First, what is the least common denominator of $\frac{7}{8}$ and $\frac{1}{4}$? Their least common denominator is 8. What are the fractions in terms of their least common denominator?

$$\frac{7}{8} = \frac{7}{8}$$

$$\frac{1}{4} = \frac{2}{8}$$

Subtract the fractions.

$$\frac{7}{8} - \frac{2}{8} = \frac{5}{8}$$

Can $\frac{5}{8}$ be reduced to lower terms? No. Therefore, subtracting the fractions gives you $\frac{5}{8}$.

Then subtract the whole numbers.

$7 - 3 = 4$

Put the answer from subtracting the fractions together with the answer from subtracting the whole numbers.

$4 + \frac{5}{8} = 4\frac{5}{8}$

Answer: $4\frac{5}{8}$

Check your skill at subtracting unlike fractions by doing this exercise.

Exercise for Subskill 7D

1. $\frac{1}{2} - \frac{1}{4} =$
2. $\frac{5}{6} - \frac{2}{3} =$
3. $\frac{3}{4} - \frac{1}{8} =$

4. $\frac{3}{5} - \frac{1}{2} =$ 5. $\frac{4}{7} - \frac{1}{2} =$ 6. $17\frac{4}{6} - \frac{1}{9} =$

7. $28\frac{2}{3} - 19\frac{2}{7} =$ 8. $\frac{1}{3} - \frac{1}{6} =$ 9. $41\frac{4}{9} - 27\frac{1}{3} =$

10. $36\frac{7}{10} - 8\frac{2}{5} =$ 11. $\frac{11}{12} - \frac{4}{9} =$ 12. $15\frac{3}{7} - 8\frac{1}{4} =$

13. $\frac{7}{8} - \frac{1}{4} =$ 14. $\frac{7}{8} - \frac{5}{6} =$ 15. $56\frac{3}{4} - 29\frac{2}{3} =$

Check your answers on page 12 in the Answer Key for Book I. If you correctly answered twelve of the fifteen problems, go to the next subskill. If not, do the following Supplemental Exercise.

Supplemental Exercise for Subskill 7D

Read Subskill 7D again. Work through the examples as you read them. Then do this exercise.

1. $\frac{3}{4} - \frac{1}{2} =$ 2. $\frac{2}{3} - \frac{1}{6} =$ 3. $\frac{5}{9} - \frac{1}{3} =$

4. $\frac{5}{6} - \frac{7}{12} =$ 5. $\frac{5}{7} - \frac{1}{2} =$ 6. $\frac{7}{8} - \frac{1}{4} =$

7. $15\frac{7}{10} - \frac{2}{5} =$ 8. $41\frac{6}{7} - 9\frac{2}{3} =$ 9. $\frac{2}{3} - \frac{2}{9} =$

10. $24\frac{5}{6} - 18\frac{3}{8} =$ 11. $21\frac{5}{8} - 7\frac{1}{3} =$ 12. $30\frac{3}{5} - \frac{1}{4} =$

13. $\frac{11}{15} - \frac{2}{5} =$ 14. $\frac{7}{9} - \frac{3}{4} =$ 15. $36\frac{2}{3} - 17\frac{2}{4} =$

Check your answers on page 12 in the Answer Key for Book I. If you correctly answered twelve of the fifteen problems, go to the next subskill. If not, ask your instructor for help.

Subskill 7E: Borrowing

After studying this subskill you will be able to borrow to solve problems in subtracting fractions.

Borrowing to Subtract a Fraction from a Whole Number

You cannot subtract something from nothing. How then can you solve this problem?

$$\begin{array}{r} 4 \\ -\frac{2}{5} \\ \hline \end{array}$$

There is no fraction to subtract the $\frac{2}{5}$ from. But you can make a fraction by borrowing from the 4. You can borrow a whole number 1 from the 4 and make the 1 into any fraction that has the same numerator and denominator.

EXAMPLE: $1 = \frac{2}{2} = \frac{3}{3} = \frac{4}{4} = \frac{5}{5} = \frac{6}{6}$, etc.

What fraction should you make to subtract $\frac{2}{5}$ from? Make a like fraction—that is, one that has the same denominator as $\frac{2}{5}$.

$1 = \frac{5}{5}$

When you borrowed 1 from 4, you changed the 4 to 3. Thus, you have changed the 4 to $3\frac{5}{5}$.

$4 = 3\frac{5}{5}$

To show the borrowing, write the problem like this:

$$\begin{array}{r} \overset{3}{\cancel{4}}\frac{5}{5} \\ -\ \frac{2}{5} \\ \hline \end{array}$$

and solve it by subtracting the fractions.

$$\frac{5}{5} - \frac{2}{5} = \frac{3}{5}$$

Then subtract the whole numbers.

$$\begin{array}{r} 3 \\ -0 \\ \hline 3 \end{array}$$

And put the whole number and the fraction together.

$3 + \frac{3}{5} = 3\frac{3}{5}$

Answer: $3\frac{3}{5}$

EXAMPLE: Subtract: $9 - 2\frac{1}{2}$.

First, borrow a whole number 1 from 9 to make a like fraction you can subtract from. To show the borrowing, write the problem like this:

$$\begin{array}{r} \overset{8}{\not 9}\frac{2}{2} \\ -2\frac{1}{2} \\ \hline \end{array}$$

The problem is now set up in a form that allows you to proceed.

$\frac{2}{2} - \frac{1}{2} = \frac{1}{2}$ Subtract the fractions.

$8 - 2 = 6$ Subtract the whole numbers.

$6 + \frac{1}{2} = 6\frac{1}{2}$ Put them together.

Answer: $6\frac{1}{2}$

Borrowing to Subtract a Larger Fraction from a Smaller One

You cannot subtract something larger from something smaller. How then can you solve the problem on the top of page 153?

$$\begin{array}{r} 25\frac{2}{7} \\ -\ 9\frac{5}{7} \\ \hline \end{array}$$

Since $\frac{2}{7}$ is smaller than $\frac{5}{7}$, you cannot subtract. But you can *make* $\frac{2}{7}$ *larger* by borrowing from the 25. You can borrow a whole number 1, make it into $\frac{7}{7}$, and add the $\frac{7}{7}$ to the $\frac{2}{7}$.

$$\frac{2}{7} + \frac{7}{7} = \frac{9}{7}$$

Therefore,

$$25\frac{2}{7} = 24\frac{9}{7}$$

Rewrite the problem like this:

$25\frac{2}{7}$	*becomes*	$24\frac{9}{7}$	You borrowed to make the fraction larger.
$-9\frac{5}{7}$		$-\ 9\frac{5}{7}$	Leave this as it is.

The problem is now set up in a form that allows you to proceed.

$\frac{9}{7} - \frac{5}{7} = \frac{4}{7}$	Subtract the fractions.
$24 - 9 \quad 15$	Subtract the whole numbers.
$15 + \frac{4}{7} = 15\frac{4}{7}$	Put them together.

Answer: $15\frac{4}{7}$

When you are subtracting unlike fractions, you don't know you need to borrow until you see the fractions in terms of their least common denominator.

EXAMPLE: Subtract: $17\frac{2}{3} - 8\frac{3}{4}$.

Since $\frac{2}{3}$ and $\frac{3}{4}$ are unlike fractions, you must find their least common denominator and change them to their equivalents that have this denominator.

Their least common denominator is 12. What are $\frac{2}{3}$ and $\frac{3}{4}$ in terms of their least common denominator?

$\frac{2}{3} = \frac{8}{12}$

$\frac{3}{4} = \frac{9}{12}$

Now you should be ready to subtract the fractions. However, since $\frac{9}{12}$ is larger than $\frac{8}{12}$, you will have to borrow. Rewrite the problem to show the fractions in terms of their least common denominator.

$17\frac{2}{3}$	*becomes*	$17\frac{8}{12}$
$-\ 8\frac{3}{4}$		$-\ 8\frac{9}{12}$

You must make $\frac{8}{12}$ larger by borrowing a whole number 1 from the 17. Make the 1 into $\frac{12}{12}$ and add the $\frac{12}{12}$ to the $\frac{8}{12}$.

$$\frac{8}{12} + \frac{12}{12} = \frac{20}{12}$$

Therefore,

$$17\frac{8}{12} = 16\frac{20}{12}$$

Show the borrowing by rewriting the problem once more.

$17\frac{8}{12}$	*becomes*	$16\frac{20}{12}$	You borrowed to make the fraction larger.
$-\ 8\frac{9}{12}$		$-\ 8\frac{9}{12}$	Leave this as it is.

Finally, you can solve it in the usual way.

$\frac{20}{12} - \frac{9}{12} = \frac{11}{12}$ Subtract the fractions.

$16 - 8 \quad 8$

Subtract the whole numbers.

$8 + \frac{11}{12} = 8\frac{11}{12}$ Put them together.

Answer: $8\frac{11}{12}$

EXAMPLE: Subtract: $8\frac{1}{6} - 5\frac{2}{3}$

The fractions are unlike. Find their least common denominator and change them to their equivalents that have this denominator.

The least common denominator of $\frac{1}{6}$ and $\frac{2}{3}$ is 6. What are $\frac{1}{6}$ and $\frac{2}{3}$ in terms of their least common denominator?

$\frac{1}{6} = \frac{1}{6}$

$\frac{2}{3} = \frac{4}{6}$

Now, can you subtract without borrowing?

$$\frac{1}{6} - \frac{4}{6}$$

No. Since $\frac{4}{6}$ is larger than $\frac{1}{6}$, you will have to borrow. Rewrite the problem to show the fractions in terms of their least common denominator.

$$\begin{array}{r} 8\frac{1}{6} \\ -5\frac{2}{3} \\ \hline \end{array} \quad \textit{becomes} \quad \begin{array}{r} 8\frac{1}{6} \\ -5\frac{4}{6} \\ \hline \end{array}$$

Make $\frac{1}{6}$ larger by borrowing a whole number 1 from the 8. Make the 1 into $\frac{6}{6}$ and add the $\frac{6}{6}$ to the $\frac{1}{6}$.

$$\frac{1}{6} + \frac{6}{6} = \frac{7}{6}$$

Therefore,

$8\frac{1}{6} = 7\frac{7}{6}$

Show the borrowing by rewriting the problem once more.

$8\frac{1}{6}$	*becomes*	$7\frac{7}{6}$	You borrowed to make the fraction larger.
$-5\frac{4}{6}$		$-5\frac{4}{6}$	Leave this as it is.

Solve it in the usual way.

$$\frac{7}{6} - \frac{4}{6} = \frac{3}{6}$$

Can $\frac{3}{6}$ be reduced to lower terms? Yes.

$$\frac{3}{6} = \frac{1}{2}$$

Now subtract the whole numbers.

$$\begin{array}{r} 7 \\ -5 \\ \hline 2 \end{array}$$

And put the whole number and the reduced fraction together.

$2 + \frac{1}{2} = 2\frac{1}{2}$ Answer: $2\frac{1}{2}$

Now check your skill at borrowing by doing this exercise.

Exercise for Subskill 7E

1. $\begin{array}{r} 17 \\ -\ \frac{1}{2} \\ \hline \end{array}$

2. $\begin{array}{r} 5 \\ -\ \frac{3}{8} \\ \hline \end{array}$

3. $\begin{array}{r} 9 \\ -\ \frac{5}{12} \\ \hline \end{array}$

4. $\begin{array}{r} 25 \\ -\ \frac{2}{7} \\ \hline \end{array}$

5. $\begin{array}{r} 15 \\ -\ 3\frac{2}{9} \\ \hline \end{array}$

6. $\begin{array}{r} 9\frac{1}{4} \\ -6\frac{3}{4} \\ \hline \end{array}$

7. $\begin{array}{r} 7\frac{2}{5} \\ -\ \frac{4}{5} \\ \hline \end{array}$

8. $\begin{array}{r} 15\frac{3}{7} \\ -\ 7\frac{5}{7} \\ \hline \end{array}$

9. $\begin{array}{r} 4\frac{1}{11} \\ -\ \frac{7}{11} \\ \hline \end{array}$

10. $18\frac{4}{9} - 7\frac{7}{9}$

11. $23\frac{9}{13} - 8\frac{11}{13}$

12. $17\frac{1}{6} - 9\frac{2}{3}$

13. $29\frac{1}{4} - 17\frac{1}{2}$

14. $25\frac{5}{8} - 9\frac{3}{4}$

15. $46\frac{2}{7} - 28\frac{9}{14}$

16. $37\frac{3}{8} - 19\frac{5}{6}$

17. $34\frac{2}{5} - 8\frac{3}{4}$

18. $16\frac{5}{12} - 9\frac{11}{12}$

19. $11\frac{1}{10} - 7\frac{2}{5}$

20. $52\frac{1}{4} - 17\frac{2}{3}$

Check your answers on page 12 in the Answer Key for Book I. If you correctly answered sixteen of the twenty problems, go to the next subskill. If not, complete the following Supplemental Exercise.

Supplemental Exercise for Subskill 7E

Read Subskill 7E again. Work through the examples as you read them. Then do this exercise.

1. $4 - \frac{8}{13}$

2. $9 - \frac{1}{3}$

3. $11 - \frac{5}{8}$

4. $3 - \frac{1}{2}$

5. $18 - 7\frac{1}{4}$

6. $7\frac{2}{7} - 3\frac{3}{7}$

7. $9\frac{1}{4} - \frac{3}{4}$

8. $18\frac{2}{11} - 9\frac{6}{11}$

9. $12\frac{3}{8} - \frac{7}{8}$

10. $14\frac{1}{12} - 8\frac{7}{12}$

11. $26\frac{1}{5} - 7\frac{3}{5}$

12. $35\frac{1}{4} - 18\frac{3}{8}$

13. $47\frac{1}{2} - 28\frac{3}{4}$

14. $19\frac{2}{7} - 3\frac{1}{2}$

15. $20\frac{2}{5} - 7\frac{2}{3}$

16. $32\frac{7}{10} - 5\frac{3}{4}$

17. $44\frac{2}{9} - 6\frac{5}{6}$

18. $21\frac{9}{12} - 9\frac{11}{12}$

19. $33\frac{4}{9} - 6\frac{2}{3}$

20. $45\frac{2}{3} - 19\frac{7}{8}$

Check your answers on page 12 in the Answer Key for Book I. If you correctly answered sixteen of the twenty problems, go to the next subskill. If not, ask your instructor for help.

Subskill 7F: Solving Word Problems

After studying this subskill you will be able to solve word problems involving fractions.

Many of the problems you must solve are in the form of word problems. These are the steps you should follow in solving word problems that involve fractions.

Read and Reread the Problem

Read the entire problem carefully. Read the problem again to make sure you understand what you are being asked to do.

EXAMPLE: Phillip has already used $36\frac{1}{2}$ feet of baseboard on the new room he is building. He needs $9\frac{3}{4}$ feet more to finish the job. How much baseboard will he use in all?

Now that you have read the problem, go to the next step.

Determine What You Are to Find

What does the problem ask you to do? In other words, what will you need to do to find the answer?

In the previous example, you are asked to find how much baseboard Phillip will use in his new room.

Determine What You Are Given

What facts do you know? Also, what facts are not needed to solve the problem?

You know that Phillip has used $36\frac{1}{2}$ feet of baseboard and needs $9\frac{3}{4}$ feet more.

Decide What Operation(s) to Use

This is an addition problem because your answer will be more than the amounts you started with. Also, the phrase "in all" is a clue. It usually calls for addition.

Solve the Problem

Add $\begin{array}{r} 36\frac{1}{2} \\ +\ 9\frac{3}{4} \\ \hline \end{array}$

Since the fractions $\frac{1}{2}$ and $\frac{3}{4}$ are unlike, you must find their least common denominator and change them to their equivalents that have this denominator.

Their least common denominator is 4. What are $\frac{1}{2}$ and $\frac{3}{4}$ in terms of their least common denominator?

$\frac{1}{2} \quad \frac{2}{4}$

$\frac{3}{4} = \frac{3}{4}$

Add the fractions.

$$\frac{2}{4} + \frac{3}{4} = \frac{5}{4}$$

Since $\frac{5}{4}$ is an improper fraction, change it to a mixed number.

$\frac{5}{4} = 1\frac{1}{4}$

Can $\frac{1}{4}$ be reduced to lower terms? No. The fractions add up to $1\frac{1}{4}$.

Now add the whole numbers, including the number you got by adding the fractions.

$$\begin{array}{r} 36 \\ 9 \\ 1\frac{1}{4} \\ \hline 46\frac{1}{4} \end{array}$$

Answer: Phillip will use $46\frac{1}{4}$ feet of baseboard in all.

Check Your Answer

Check your addition by adding again.

Here is another example.

EXAMPLE: James Jenkins bought a 50-foot roll of canvas. He cut off $6\frac{3}{4}$ feet to make a cover for the bed of his pickup truck. How much canvas does he have left on the roll?

To find how much canvas is left on the roll, subtract what was used from the whole roll.

$$\begin{array}{r} 50 \\ -\ 6\frac{3}{4} \\ \hline \end{array}$$

Since there is no fraction to subtract the $\frac{3}{4}$ from, make one by borrowing a whole number one, or $\frac{4}{4}$, from the 50. By borrowing to make the fraction, you have changed the 50 to $49\frac{4}{4}$.

To show the borrowing, rewrite the problem like this:

$$\begin{array}{r} 50 \\ -\ 6\frac{3}{4} \\ \hline \end{array} \quad \textit{becomes} \quad \begin{array}{r} 49\frac{4}{4} \\ -\ 6\frac{3}{4} \\ \hline \end{array}$$

$\frac{4}{4} - \frac{3}{4} = \frac{1}{4}$ Subtract the fractions.

$$\begin{array}{r} 49 \\ -\ 6 \\ \hline 43 \end{array}$$ Then subtract the whole numbers.

$43 + \frac{1}{4} = 43\frac{1}{4}$ And put them together.

Answer: James Jenkins has $43\frac{1}{4}$ feet of canvas left on the roll.

Check your skill at solving word problems by doing this exercise.

Exercise for Subskill 7F

1. Luis Lopez and Bobby Evans want to see how far they can throw a softball. Luis throws the ball $402\frac{1}{2}$ feet. Bobby throws it 349 feet. How much farther did Luis throw the ball?

2. Maria put $\frac{1}{8}$ teaspoon of oregano and $1\frac{1}{2}$ teaspoons of salt in a casserole. Then she added $\frac{1}{2}$ teaspoon of basil and $\frac{3}{4}$ teaspoon of pepper. What is the total amount of seasoning she put in the casserole?

3. Lee Stearns bought a hindquarter of beef that weighed $125\frac{9}{16}$ pounds. After the meat was trimmed of fat, it weighed $106\frac{1}{2}$ pounds. How much of the meat was fat?

4. Rob ran $\frac{7}{16}$ of a mile yesterday. He ran $1\frac{1}{8}$ miles today. How much farther did he run today?

5. A bank pays $5\frac{1}{4}$% interest on savings accounts. It pays 11% interest on certificates of deposit (CDs). How much more does the bank pay on certificates of deposit?

Check your answers on page 12 in the Answer Key for Book I. If you correctly answered four of the five problems, go to the Self-Check. If not, complete the following Supplemental Exercise.

Supplemental Exercise for Subskill 7F

Read Subskill 7F again. Work through the examples as you read them. Then do this exercise.

1. Franco has a suitcase that weighs $31\frac{1}{2}$ pounds and a garment bag that weighs $12\frac{3}{4}$ pounds. What is the total weight of his luggage?

2. Franco is flying on an airline that has a weight limit of 44 pounds of luggage per passenger. How much is his luggage over or under the limit?

3. You need a bolt to go through a piece of wood $\frac{3}{4}$ inch thick, another piece of wood $1\frac{1}{8}$ inch thick, a washer $\frac{1}{16}$ inch thick, and a nut $\frac{1}{8}$ inch thick. How long does the bolt have to be?

4. The cooling system of Leroy's car holds $18\frac{3}{5}$ quarts. He drained the system and then added $14\frac{4}{5}$ quarts of water. How much antifreeze must he add to fill the cooling system to the top?

5. Estelle worked $\frac{3}{4}$ of an hour overtime on Monday, $1\frac{1}{3}$ hours overtime on Wednesday, and $4\frac{1}{2}$ hours overtime on Saturday. How many hours of overtime did she work this week?

Check your answers on page 12 in the Answer Key for Book I. If you correctly answered four of the five problems, go to the Self-Check. If not, ask your instructor for help.

SELF-CHECK FOR SKILL UNIT 7

1. $\frac{3}{7} + \frac{5}{7} + \frac{4}{7} + \frac{1}{7} =$

2. $\frac{2}{5} + \frac{1}{3} =$

3. $\begin{array}{r} 6\frac{5}{8} \\ +9\frac{7}{8} \\ \hline \end{array}$

4. $\begin{array}{r} 12\frac{3}{4} \\ +25\frac{5}{6} \\ \hline \end{array}$

5. $\begin{array}{r} 52\frac{1}{3} \\ +13\frac{3}{4} \\ \hline \end{array}$

6. $\begin{array}{r} 15\frac{7}{10} \\ 2\frac{5}{6} \\ +\ 9\frac{1}{4} \\ \hline \end{array}$

7. $\frac{11}{12} - \frac{8}{12} =$

8. $\begin{array}{r} 23 \\ -\ 9\frac{4}{9} \\ \hline \end{array}$

9. $6 - 3\frac{7}{8}$

10. $15\frac{1}{4} - 3\frac{1}{2}$

11. $45 - 13\frac{1}{3}$

12. $13\frac{5}{12} - 8\frac{7}{8}$

13. $35\frac{3}{8} - 14\frac{3}{4}$

14. $8\frac{9}{15} - 8\frac{6}{15}$

15. $70\frac{3}{4} - 10\frac{4}{5}$

16. Mannie bought a $125\frac{3}{8}$-pound hindquarter of beef. After the meat was trimmed of fat, it weighed $107\frac{9}{16}$ pounds. How much did the fat weigh?

17. Carmen worked $7\frac{3}{4}$ hours on Monday, $8\frac{1}{4}$ hours on Tuesday, 9 hours on Wednesday, $7\frac{5}{6}$ hours on Thursday, and $7\frac{2}{3}$ hours on Friday. How many hours did she work this week in all?

18. Erin measured $20\frac{1}{2}$ inches when she was born. She was $31\frac{3}{4}$ inches tall on her first birthday. How many inches did she grow?

19. Mrs. Sims ran $1\frac{5}{8}$ of a mile on Monday, 2 miles on Tuesday, and $2\frac{1}{4}$ miles on Wednesday. How far did she run on all three days?

20. A stream is usually $36\frac{9}{16}$ inches deep. During a drought, the stream was only $19\frac{1}{2}$ inches deep. How much had the water gone down?

Check your answers on page 13 in the Answer Key for Book I. If you correctly answered sixteen of the twenty problems, go on to Skill Unit 8. If not, ask your instructor for help.

Skill Unit 8
MULTIPLYING AND DIVIDING FRACTIONS

What Skills You Need to Begin: Basic skills with whole numbers and fractions (Skill Units 1 through 7).

What Skills You Will Learn: After studying this skill unit, you will be able to multiply and divide fractions and solve word problems requiring the multiplication and division of fractions.

Why You Need This Skill: If you work a full day of 7 hours on weekdays and a half day on Saturdays, how many hours do you work on Saturdays? If you have $3\frac{1}{2}$ pounds of hamburger for a barbeque, how many quarter-pound hamburgers can you make? These are only two of the everyday problems you can solve by multiplying and dividing fractions.

How You Will Show What You Have Learned: At the end of this skill unit is a Self-Check consisting of fifteen problems in the multiplication and division of fractions. You should allow yourself one hour to complete the Self-Check. To prove that you have mastered this skill, you must correctly answer twelve of the fifteen problems.

If you feel you have already mastered the multiplication and division of fractions, complete the Self-Check on pages 189 and 190.

Subskill 8A: Multiplying a Fraction by a Fraction

After studying this subskill you will be able to multiply a fraction by another fraction.

To multiply a fraction by another fraction, first multiply the numerators and then multiply the denominators. Reduce your answer to its lowest terms.

EXAMPLE: Multiply $\frac{4}{9} \times \frac{3}{8}$.

First, multiply the numerators.

$$\frac{4}{9} \times \frac{3}{8} = \frac{12}{}$$

Then multiply the denominators.

$$\frac{4}{9} \times \frac{3}{8} = \frac{12}{72}$$

Reduce your answer to its lowest terms.

$$\frac{12 \div 12}{72 \div 12} = \frac{1}{6}$$

Answer: $\frac{1}{6}$

Here is an example with three fractions.

EXAMPLE: Multiply $\frac{1}{2} \times \frac{4}{9} \times \frac{4}{5}$.

First, multiply the numerators.

$$\frac{1}{2} \times \frac{4}{9} \times \frac{4}{5} = \frac{16}{} \qquad 1 \times 4 = 4 \quad \text{and} \quad 4 \times 4 = 16$$

Then multiply the denominators.

$$\frac{1}{2} \times \frac{4}{9} \times \frac{4}{5} = \frac{16}{90} \qquad 2 \times 9 = 18 \quad \text{and} \quad 18 \times 5 = 90$$

Reduce your answer to its lowest terms.

$$\frac{16 \div 2}{90 \div 2} = \frac{8}{45}$$

Answer: $\frac{8}{45}$

Sometimes the answer cannot be reduced to lower terms.

EXAMPLE: Multiply $\frac{1}{2} \times \frac{3}{4}$.

First, multiply the numerators.

$$\frac{1}{2} \times \frac{3}{4} = \frac{3}{}$$

Then multiply the denominators.

$$\frac{1}{2} \times \frac{3}{4} = \frac{3}{8}$$

Can you reduce $\frac{3}{8}$ to lower terms? No, $\frac{3}{8}$ is already in its lowest terms.

Answer: $\frac{3}{8}$

Cancelling

Cancelling is a way to make the multiplication of fractions easier. You do not have to cancel to get the right answer, but it helps by giving you smaller numbers to work with. To cancel, you divide any numerator *and* any denominator in the problem by the same number.

EXAMPLE: Multiply $\frac{7}{8} \times \frac{2}{3}$.

$\frac{7}{8} \times \frac{2}{3}$ Is there any number that will go evenly into one of the numerators *and* one of the denominators?

$\frac{7}{\textcircled{8}} \times \frac{\textcircled{2}}{3}$ Yes, 2 will go evenly into the 2 and the 8.

Divide the 2 and the 8 by 2. Show it like this:

$$\frac{7}{\underset{4}{\cancel{8}}} \times \frac{\overset{1}{\cancel{2}}}{3}$$

Now you are ready to multiply.

$\frac{7}{\underset{4}{\cancel{8}}} \times \frac{\overset{1}{\cancel{2}}}{3} = \frac{7}{12}$ Multiply the numerators. Then multiply the denominators.

Can $\frac{7}{12}$ be reduced to lower terms? No.

Answer: $\frac{7}{12}$

To show how cancelling makes the multiplication of fractions easier, let's go back to the example used on pages 164 and 165:

EXAMPLE: Multiply $\frac{4}{9} \times \frac{3}{8}$.

$\frac{4}{9} \times \frac{3}{8}$ Is there any number that will go evenly into one of the numerators *and* one of the denominators?

$\frac{\overset{1}{\cancel{4}}}{9} \times \frac{3}{\underset{2}{\cancel{8}}}$ Yes, 4 will go evenly into the 4 and the 8.

$\frac{\overset{1}{\cancel{4}}}{\underset{3}{\cancel{9}}} \times \frac{\overset{1}{\cancel{3}}}{\underset{2}{\cancel{8}}}$ Also, 3 will go evenly into the 3 and the 9.

Multiply.

$\frac{\overset{1}{\cancel{4}}}{\underset{3}{\cancel{9}}} \times \frac{\overset{1}{\cancel{3}}}{\underset{2}{\cancel{8}}} = \frac{1}{6}$ Multiply the numerators. Then multiply the denominators.

Can $\frac{1}{6}$ be reduced to lower terms? No. By cancelling, you have saved yourself the work of reducing $\frac{12}{72}$ to $\frac{1}{6}$.

Answer: $\frac{1}{6}$

Let's look again at the example with three fractions that is shown on page 165.

EXAMPLE: Multiply $\frac{1}{2} \times \frac{4}{9} \times \frac{4}{5}$.

$\frac{1}{2} \times \frac{4}{9} \times \frac{4}{5}$ Is there any number that will go evenly into one of the numerators *and* one of the denominators?

$\frac{1}{\underset{1}{\cancel{2}}} \times \frac{\overset{2}{\cancel{4}}}{9} \times \frac{4}{5}$ Yes, 2 will go evenly into the 4 and the 2.

$\frac{1}{\underset{1}{\cancel{2}}} \times \frac{\overset{2}{\cancel{4}}}{9} \times \frac{\overset{\downarrow}{4}}{5}$ What about the other 4? You must leave it as it is. You can't cancel it because there's not another denominator that you can cancel with it.

Multiply.

$$\frac{1}{\underset{1}{\cancel{2}}} \times \frac{\overset{2}{\cancel{4}}}{9} \times \frac{4}{5} = \frac{8}{45}$$

Multiply the numerators.
Then multiply the denominators.

Can $\frac{8}{45}$ be reduced to lower terms? No.

Answer: $\frac{8}{45}$

You can cancel when the cancelable numerator and denominator are both in the same fraction.

EXAMPLE: Multiply $\frac{3}{9} \times \frac{5}{7}$.

$$\frac{\overset{1}{\cancel{3}}}{\underset{3}{\cancel{9}}} \times \frac{5}{7}$$

3 will go evenly into the 3 and the 9. This is the same as reducing $\frac{3}{9}$ to its lowest terms.

$$\frac{\overset{1}{\cancel{3}}}{\underset{3}{\cancel{9}}} \times \frac{5}{7} = \frac{5}{21}$$

Multiply the numerators.
Then multiply the denominators.

Can $\frac{5}{21}$ be reduced to lower terms? No.

Answer: $\frac{5}{21}$

In the following example, you can reduce a fraction to its lowest terms by continuing to cancel.

EXAMPLE: Multiply $\frac{10}{14} \times \frac{7}{15}$.

$$\frac{\overset{2}{\cancel{10}}}{14} \times \frac{7}{\underset{3}{\cancel{15}}}$$

5 will go evenly into the 10 and the 15.

$$\frac{\overset{2}{\cancel{10}}}{\underset{2}{\cancel{14}}} \times \frac{\overset{1}{\cancel{7}}}{\underset{3}{\cancel{15}}}$$

7 will go evenly into the 7 and the 14.

$$\frac{\overset{\overset{1}{\cancel{2}}}{\cancel{10}}}{\underset{\underset{1}{\cancel{2}}}{\cancel{14}}} \times \frac{\overset{1}{\cancel{7}}}{\underset{3}{\cancel{15}}}$$

2 will go evenly into the 2 and the 2.

$$\frac{\overset{\overset{1}{\cancel{2}}}{\cancel{10}}}{\underset{\underset{1}{\cancel{2}}}{\cancel{14}}} \times \frac{\overset{1}{\cancel{7}}}{\underset{3}{\cancel{15}}} = \frac{1}{3}$$

Multiply the numerators.
Then multiply the denominators.

Can $\frac{1}{3}$ be reduced to lower terms? No.

Answer: $\frac{1}{3}$

But there are some problems in which cancelling is not possible at all.

EXAMPLE. Multiply $\frac{2}{5} \times \frac{8}{9} \times \frac{4}{7}$.

$$\frac{2}{5} \times \frac{8}{9} \times \frac{4}{7}$$

Is there any number that will go evenly into one of the numerators *and* one of the denominators?

No. This problem cannot be cancelled.

$$\frac{2}{5} \times \frac{8}{9} \times \frac{4}{7} = \frac{64}{315}$$

Multiply the numerators.
Then multiply the denominators.

Can $\frac{64}{315}$ be reduced to lower terms? No.

Answer: $\frac{64}{315}$

Exercise for Subskill 8A

Check your skill at multiplying fractions by doing this exercise. Reduce your answers to lowest terms.

1. $\frac{1}{2} \times \frac{1}{2} =$ **2.** $\frac{5}{6} \times \frac{1}{2} =$ **3.** $\frac{2}{3} \times \frac{6}{7} =$

4. $\frac{6}{8} \times \frac{8}{12} =$

5. $\frac{7}{8} \times \frac{4}{5} =$

6. $\frac{1}{2} \times \frac{3}{6} =$

7. $\frac{5}{8} \times \frac{6}{10} =$

8. $\frac{1}{5} \times \frac{6}{9} =$

9. $\frac{2}{5} \times \frac{3}{4} =$

10. $\frac{5}{8} \times \frac{2}{3} =$

11. $\frac{13}{16} \times \frac{8}{26} =$

12. $\frac{5}{8} \times \frac{8}{9} \times \frac{3}{5} =$

13. $\frac{5}{6} \times \frac{24}{25} =$

14. $\frac{12}{15} \times \frac{12}{20} \times \frac{5}{6} =$

15. $\frac{10}{14} \times \frac{2}{3} \times \frac{7}{15} =$

Check your answers on page 13 in the Answer Key for Book I. If you correctly answered twelve of the fifteen problems, go to the next subskill. If not, complete the following Supplemental Exercise.

Supplemental Exercise for Subskill 8A

Read Subskill 8A again. Work through the examples as you read them. Then do this exercise. Reduce your answers to lowest terms.

1. $\frac{1}{4} \times \frac{1}{4} =$

2. $\frac{2}{3} \times \frac{2}{3} =$

3. $\frac{3}{4} \times \frac{5}{6} =$

4. $\frac{7}{8} \times \frac{2}{14} =$

5. $\frac{5}{6} \times \frac{3}{7} =$

6. $\frac{1}{6} \times \frac{12}{13} =$

7. $\frac{4}{9} \times \frac{9}{11} =$

8. $\frac{3}{8} \times \frac{4}{5} =$

9. $\frac{6}{9} \times \frac{3}{8} =$

10. $\frac{7}{12} \times \frac{6}{11} =$

11. $\frac{3}{7} \times \frac{10}{15} =$

12. $\frac{25}{30} \times \frac{6}{10} =$

13. $\frac{7}{12} \times \frac{6}{9} \times \frac{4}{7} =$

14. $\frac{8}{12} \times \frac{2}{7} \times \frac{14}{16} =$

15. $\frac{5}{9} \times \frac{18}{21} \times \frac{7}{10} =$

Check your answers on page 13 in the Answer Key for Book I. If you correctly answered twelve of the fifteen problems, go to the next subskill. If not, ask your instructor for help.

Subskill 8B: Multiplying a Fraction by a Whole Number

After studying this subskill you will be able to multiply a fraction by a whole number.

To multiply a fraction by a whole number, first change the whole number to an improper fraction and then multiply the two fractions.

EXAMPLE: Multiply $\frac{1}{2} \times 4$.

First, change the whole number to an improper fraction. Any whole number can be changed into an improper fraction by writing the whole number as the numerator and using 1 as the denominator. For example,

$$1 = \frac{1}{1}$$

$$2 = \frac{2}{1}$$

$$3 = \frac{3}{1}$$

$$4 = \frac{4}{1}$$

$$5 = \frac{5}{1}$$

$$10 = \frac{10}{1}$$

$$15 = \frac{15}{1}$$

$$50 = \frac{50}{1}$$

$$100 = \frac{100}{1}$$

Since $4 = \frac{4}{1}$, you can write the problem with two fractions.

$\frac{1}{2} \times \frac{4}{1}$

Multiply the fractions.

$\frac{1}{\cancel{2}_1} \times \frac{\cancel{4}^2}{1}$ You can cancel.

$\frac{1}{\cancel{2}_1} \times \frac{\cancel{4}^2}{1} = \frac{2}{1}$ Multiply the numerators.
Then multiply the denominators.

Can $\frac{2}{1}$ be reduced to lower terms? No, but since the fraction $\frac{2}{1}$ equals the whole number 2, you should change it to 2.

Answer: 2

Here is another example.

EXAMPLE: Multiply $6 \times \frac{7}{8}$.

First, change the whole number to a fraction.

$6 = \frac{6}{1}$

$\frac{6}{1} \times \frac{7}{8}$ Write the problem with two fractions.

Multiply the fractions.

$\frac{\cancel{6}^3}{1} \times \frac{7}{\cancel{8}_4}$ You can cancel.

$\frac{\cancel{6}^3}{1} \times \frac{7}{\cancel{8}_4} = \frac{21}{4}$ Multiply the numerators.
Then multiply the denominators.

Can $\frac{21}{4}$ be reduced to lower terms? No, but it can be changed to a mixed number.

$$\begin{array}{r} 5 \\ 4\overline{)21} \\ \underline{20} \\ 1 \end{array}$$

Change the improper fraction to a mixed number by dividing the numerator by the denominator.

$\frac{21}{4} = 5\frac{1}{4}$

Answer: $5\frac{1}{4}$

If you forget to cancel, or if you don't do all the cancelling that's possible, you will have to reduce your answer to lower terms.

EXAMPLE: Multiply $\frac{5}{6} \times 3$.

$3 = \frac{3}{1}$ — Change the whole number to a fraction.

$\frac{5}{6} \times \frac{3}{1}$ — Write the problem with two fractions.

Now suppose you forget to cancel.

$\frac{5}{6} \times \frac{3}{1} = \frac{15}{6}$ — Multiply.

Can $\frac{15}{6}$ be reduced to lower terms? Yes, it can, even though it's an improper fraction.

$$\frac{15 \div 3}{6 \div 3} = \frac{5}{2}$$

Now, can $\frac{5}{2}$ be changed to a whole number or a mixed number? Yes.

$\frac{5}{2} = 2\frac{1}{2}$

Answer: $2\frac{1}{2}$

So far you have only multiplied one fraction by one whole number, but you can also multiply more.

EXAMPLE: Multiply $\frac{3}{8} \times 4 \times \frac{1}{2} \times 3$.

$4 = \frac{4}{1}$ *and* $3 = \frac{3}{1}$ — Change the whole numbers to fractions.

$\frac{3}{8} \times \frac{4}{1} \times \frac{1}{2} \times \frac{3}{1}$ Write the problem with all fractions.

$\frac{3}{\underset{2}{\cancel{8}}} \times \frac{\overset{1}{\cancel{4}}}{1} \times \frac{1}{2} \times \frac{3}{1}$ You can cancel.

$\frac{3}{\underset{2}{\cancel{8}}} \times \frac{\overset{1}{\cancel{4}}}{1} \times \frac{1}{2} \times \frac{3}{1} = \frac{9}{4}$ Multiply.

Can $\frac{9}{4}$ be reduced to lower terms? No. Can it be changed to a whole number or a mixed number? Yes.

$\frac{9}{4} = 2\frac{1}{4}$

Answer: $2\frac{1}{4}$

Check your skill at multiplying a fraction by a whole number by doing this exercise.

Exercise for Subskill 8B

1. $3 \times \frac{1}{2} =$
2. $\frac{2}{3} \times 6 =$
3. $\frac{7}{8} \times 12 =$
4. $9 \times \frac{2}{9} \times 4 =$
5. $11 \times \frac{3}{4} =$
6. $\frac{5}{14} \times 16 \times \frac{1}{4} =$
7. $6 \times \frac{5}{8} =$
8. $\frac{4}{5} \times 2 \times \frac{15}{16} \times 3 =$
9. $21 \times \frac{6}{7} =$
10. $\frac{5}{6} \times 9 =$

Check your answers on page 13 in the Answer Key for Book I. If you correctly answered eight of the ten problems, go to the next subskill. If not, complete the following Supplemental Exercise.

Supplemental Exercise for Subskill 8B

Read Subskill 8B again. Work through the examples as you read them. Then do this exercise.

1. $2 \times \frac{2}{3} =$

2. $\frac{3}{5} \times 5 =$

3. $\frac{7}{6} \times 10 =$

4. $9 \times \frac{1}{4} \times 2 =$

5. $14 \times \frac{3}{7} =$

6. $\frac{5}{8} \times 12 \times \frac{1}{5} =$

7. $\frac{8}{9} \times 3 =$

8. $7 \times \frac{1}{2} =$

9. $\frac{1}{5} \times 12 \times 4 \times \frac{5}{6} =$

10. $16 \times \frac{3}{4} =$

Check your answers on pages 13 and 14 in the Answer Key for Book I. If you correctly answered eight of the ten problems, go to the next subskill. If not, ask your instructor for help.

Subskill 8C: Multiplying Mixed Numbers

After studying this subskill you will be able to multiply mixed numbers.

To multiply mixed numbers, first change them to improper fractions. Then multiply the improper fractions.

EXAMPLE: Multiply $3\frac{6}{7} \times 4\frac{2}{3}$.

First, change both mixed numbers to improper fractions. As you remember, this is done by multiplying the whole number by the denominator and then adding the numerator.

Change $3\frac{6}{7}$ to an improper fraction.

$3 \times 7 = 21$ *and* $21 + 6 = 27$ — This gives you the numerator of the improper fraction.

$\frac{27}{7}$ Numerator
The denominator is the same as that of the original fraction.

Therefore,

$3\frac{6}{7} = \frac{27}{7}$

Now change $4\frac{2}{3}$ to an improper fraction.

$4 \times 3 = 12$ *and* $12 + 2 = 14$ This gives you the numerator.

$\frac{14}{3}$ Numerator / Denominator

Therefore, $4\frac{2}{3} = \frac{14}{3}$

Multiply the two improper fractions.

$\frac{\overset{9}{\cancel{27}}}{\underset{1}{\cancel{7}}} \times \frac{\overset{2}{\cancel{14}}}{\underset{1}{\cancel{3}}}$ You can cancel.

$\frac{\overset{9}{\cancel{27}}}{\underset{1}{\cancel{7}}} \times \frac{\overset{2}{\cancel{14}}}{\underset{1}{\cancel{3}}} = \frac{18}{1}$ Multiply the numerators.
Then multiply the denominators.

Can $\frac{18}{1}$ be reduced to lower terms? No. Can it be changed to a whole number or a mixed number? Yes.

$\frac{18}{1} = 18$

Answer: 18

You can also multiply a mixed number by a proper fraction.

EXAMPLE: Multiply $6\frac{3}{4} \times \frac{2}{9}$.

First, change the mixed number to an improper fraction.

Change $6\frac{3}{4}$ to an improper fraction.

$6 \times 4 = 24$ *and* $24 + 3 = 27$

Therefore, $6\frac{3}{4} = \frac{27}{4}$

Multiply the two fractions.

$$\frac{\overset{3}{\cancel{27}}}{\underset{2}{\cancel{4}}} \times \frac{\overset{1}{\cancel{2}}}{\underset{1}{\cancel{9}}}$$ You can cancel.

$$\frac{\overset{3}{\cancel{27}}}{\underset{2}{\cancel{4}}} \times \frac{\overset{1}{\cancel{2}}}{\underset{1}{\cancel{9}}} = \frac{3}{2}$$ Multiply.

Can $\frac{3}{2}$ be reduced to lower terms? No. Can it be changed to a whole number or a mixed number? Yes.

$\frac{3}{2} = 1\frac{1}{2}$

Answer: $1\frac{1}{2}$

You can also multiply a mixed number by a whole number.

EXAMPLE: Multiply $2\frac{4}{5} \times 10$.

First, change both the mixed number and the whole number to improper fractions.

Change $2\frac{4}{5}$ to an improper fraction.

$2 \times 5 = 10$ *and* $10 + 4 = 14$

Therefore, $2\frac{4}{5} = \frac{14}{5}$

Now change 10 to an improper fraction.

$10 = \frac{10}{1}$

Then multiply the two fractions together.

$$\frac{14}{\underset{1}{\cancel{5}}} \times \frac{\overset{2}{\cancel{10}}}{1} = \frac{28}{1}$$ Cancel and multiply.

Answer: 28

You can also multiply a proper fraction, a mixed number, and a whole number together.

EXAMPLE: Multiply $\frac{1}{5} \times 3\frac{1}{8} \times 4$.

First, change the mixed number and the whole number to improper fractions.

Change $3\frac{1}{8}$ to an improper fraction.

$3 \times 8 = 24$ *and* $24 + 1 = 25$

Therefore, $3\frac{1}{8} = \frac{25}{8}$

Change 4 to an improper fraction.

$4 = \frac{4}{1}$

Then multiply all the fractions together.

$$\frac{\overset{}{1}}{\underset{1}{5}} \times \frac{\overset{5}{25}}{\underset{2}{8}} \times \frac{\overset{1}{4}}{1} = \frac{5}{2}$$ Cancel and multiply.

$\frac{5}{2} = 2\frac{1}{2}$ Change the improper fraction to a mixed number.

Answer: $2\frac{1}{2}$

Check your skill at multiplying mixed numbers by doing this exercise.

Exercise for Subskill 8C

1. $2\frac{1}{2} \times 4 =$

2. $2\frac{6}{7} \times 2\frac{3}{5} =$

3. $3 \times 1\frac{5}{8} =$

4. $3\frac{2}{5} \times 1\frac{7}{8} \times \frac{1}{3} =$

5. $\frac{2}{7} \times 2\frac{1}{3} =$

6. $6\frac{1}{4} \times \frac{1}{4} =$

7. $1\frac{3}{4} \times 5 \times \frac{3}{14} =$ 8. $3\frac{1}{3} \times 1\frac{1}{5} =$

9. $6\frac{2}{3} \times 1\frac{2}{7} \times 7 =$ 10. $\frac{6}{8} \times 4\frac{2}{3} =$

Check your answers on page 14 in the Answer Key for Book I. If you correctly answered eight of the ten problems, go to the next subskill. If not, complete the following Supplemental Exercise.

Supplemental Exercise for Subskill 8C

Read Subskill 8C again. Work through the examples as you read them. Then do this exercise.

1. $5\frac{2}{3} \times 3 =$ 2. $1\frac{4}{5} \times 1\frac{5}{6} =$

3. $6\frac{2}{3} \times \frac{1}{8} =$ 4. $5\frac{1}{2} \times 3\frac{1}{3} \times 9 =$

5. $8 \times 1\frac{3}{16} =$ 6. $6\frac{2}{8} \times 3\frac{1}{5} =$

7. $\frac{8}{9} \times 4\frac{3}{4} \times 3 =$ 8. $4\frac{1}{6} \times 2\frac{8}{15} =$

9. $2\frac{2}{7} \times 2\frac{4}{5} \times \frac{1}{8} =$ 10. $\frac{3}{4} \times 3\frac{5}{6} =$

Check your answers on page 14 in the Answer Key for Book I. If you correctly answered eight of the ten problems, go to the next subskill. If not, ask your instructor for help.

Subskill 8D: Dividing Fractions

After studying this subskill you will be able to divide fractions.

To divide fractions, first turn the fraction you are dividing by upside down, and then multiply. For example, divide $\frac{5}{8}$ by $\frac{3}{4}$.

In solving a division problem, it is important to know which fraction you are dividing by. This is the fraction that goes into the other fraction. In the following division problem, the number you are dividing by is the number on the left.

$5\overline{)110}$ — 5 is going into 110. You are dividing by 5.

When the problem is written with a division sign, the number you are dividing by is the number on the right.

$110 \div 5$ — 5 is going into 110. You are dividing by 5.

In dividing fractions, always write the problem with a division sign. Then you know that the fraction you are dividing by is the fraction on the right.

EXAMPLE: $\frac{5}{8} \div \frac{3}{4}$

To solve the problem, first, turn the fraction you are dividing by upside down. The numerator becomes the denominator and the denominator becomes the numerator.

$\frac{3}{4}$ *becomes* $\frac{4}{3}$

Then multiply.

$\frac{5}{\cancel{8}_2} \times \frac{\cancel{4}^1}{3} = \frac{5}{6}$ — You can cancel after you have turned the fraction you are dividing by upside down and changed the problem to a multiplication problem.

Can $\frac{5}{6}$ be reduced to lower terms? No. Is it an improper fraction that must be changed to a mixed number or whole number? No.

Answer: $\frac{5}{6}$

Here is another problem.

EXAMPLE: $\frac{2}{7} \div \frac{5}{6}$

$\frac{2}{7} \div \frac{5}{6} = \frac{2}{7} \times \frac{6}{5}$ — Turn the fraction you are dividing by upside down and change the problem to a multiplication problem.

$\frac{2}{7} \times \frac{6}{5} = \frac{12}{35}$ — Multiply.

Can $\frac{12}{35}$ be reduced to lower terms? No. Is it an improper fraction that must be changed to a mixed number or whole number? No.

Answer: $\frac{12}{35}$

Here is one more problem.

EXAMPLE: $\frac{9}{16} \div \frac{3}{8}$

$$\frac{9}{16} \div \frac{3}{8} = \frac{9}{16} \times \frac{8}{3}$$

$$\frac{\overset{3}{\cancel{9}}}{\underset{2}{\cancel{16}}} \times \frac{\overset{1}{\cancel{8}}}{\underset{1}{\cancel{3}}} = \frac{3}{2}$$ Cancel and multiply.

Can $\frac{3}{2}$ be reduced to lower terms? No. Is it an improper fraction that must be changed to a mixed number or whole number? Yes.

$\frac{3}{2} = 1\frac{1}{2}$

Answer: $1\frac{1}{2}$

Check you skill at dividing fractions by doing this exercise.

Exercise for Subskill 8D

1. $\frac{5}{6} \div \frac{2}{3} =$
2. $\frac{7}{8} \div \frac{14}{15} =$
3. $\frac{4}{9} \div \frac{3}{4} =$
4. $\frac{2}{9} \div \frac{1}{3} =$
5. $\frac{3}{8} \div \frac{5}{6} =$
6. $\frac{2}{7} \div \frac{5}{7} =$
7. $\frac{12}{13} \div \frac{8}{11} =$
8. $\frac{2}{3} \div \frac{1}{2} =$
9. $\frac{14}{15} \div \frac{21}{10} =$
10. $\frac{3}{5} \div \frac{3}{5} =$

Check your answers on page 14 in the Answer Key for Book I. If you correctly answered eight of the ten problems, go to the next subskill. If not, complete the following Supplemental Exercise.

Supplemental Exercise for Subskill 8D

Read Subskill 8D again. Work through the examples as you read them. Then do this exercise.

1. $\frac{5}{8} \div \frac{1}{2} =$ **2.** $\frac{9}{10} \div \frac{5}{6} =$

3. $\frac{1}{4} \div \frac{1}{4} =$ **4.** $\frac{1}{2} \div \frac{1}{2} =$

5. $\frac{9}{11} \div \frac{18}{22} =$ **6.** $\frac{3}{8} \div \frac{8}{3} =$

7. $\frac{3}{4} \div \frac{1}{2} =$ **8.** $\frac{16}{21} \div \frac{12}{27} =$

9. $\frac{6}{7} \div \frac{7}{12} =$ **10.** $\frac{1}{6} \div \frac{1}{18} =$

Check your answers on page 14 in the Answer Key for Book I. If you correctly answered eight of the ten problems, go to the next subskill. If not, ask your instructor for help.

Subskill 8E: Dividing Fractions, Whole Numbers, and Mixed Numbers

After studying this subskill you will be able to divide fractions, whole numbers, and mixed numbers.

To solve any division problem that has a fraction or mixed number in it, first change any mixed number or whole number to an improper fraction. Then turn the fraction you are dividing by upside down and multiply.

EXAMPLE: $\frac{5}{6} \div 3\frac{1}{8}$

First, change the mixed number to an improper fraction.

Change $3\frac{1}{8}$ to an improper fraction.

$3 \times 8 = 24$ and $24 + 1 = 25$

Therefore,

$3\frac{1}{8} = \frac{25}{8}$

Then turn the fraction you are dividing by upside down and multiply.

$\frac{5}{6} \div \frac{25}{8} = \frac{5}{6} \times \frac{8}{25}$ Turn the fraction you are dividing by upside down and change the problem to a multiplication problem.

$\frac{\overset{1}{\cancel{5}}}{\underset{3}{\cancel{6}}} \times \frac{\overset{4}{\cancel{8}}}{\underset{5}{\cancel{25}}} = \frac{4}{15}$ Cancel and multiply.

Can $\frac{4}{15}$ be reduced to lower terms? No. Is it an improper fraction that must be changed to a mixed number or whole number? No.

Answer: $\frac{4}{15}$

Here is another problem.

EXAMPLE: $5 \div \frac{9}{10}$

First, change the whole number to an improper fraction.

$5 = \frac{5}{1}$

Then turn the fraction you are dividing by upside down and multiply.

$\frac{5}{1} \div \frac{9}{10} = \frac{5}{1} \times \frac{10}{9}$

$\frac{5}{1} \times \frac{10}{9} = \frac{50}{9}$ Multiply.

Can $\frac{50}{9}$ be reduced to lower terms? No. Is it an improper fraction that must be changed to a mixed number or whole number? Yes.

$$9\overline{)50}\quad 5,\; 45,\; 5$$

```
     5
 9) 5 0
    4 5
      5
```

Divide the numerator by the denominator.

$\frac{50}{9} = 5\frac{5}{9}$

Answer: $5\frac{5}{9}$

Here is one more problem.

EXAMPLE: $7\frac{1}{3} \div 1\frac{2}{9}$

First, change both mixed numbers to improper fractions.

$7\frac{1}{3} = \frac{22}{3}$

And

$1\frac{2}{9} = \frac{11}{9}$

Then turn the fraction you are dividing by upside down and multiply.

$$\frac{22}{3} \div \frac{11}{9} = \frac{22}{3} \times \frac{9}{11}$$

$$\frac{\overset{2}{\cancel{22}}}{3} \times \frac{9}{\underset{1}{\cancel{11}}} = \frac{18}{3}$$ Cancel and multiply.

Can $\frac{18}{3}$ be reduced to lower terms? Yes (because you could have done more cancelling when you multiplied).

$$\frac{18 \div 3}{3 \div 3} = \frac{6}{1}$$

Is $\frac{6}{1}$ an improper fraction that must be changed to a mixed number or whole number? Yes.

$\frac{6}{1} = 6$

Answer: 6

Check your skill at dividing fractions, whole numbers, and mixed numbers by doing this exercise.

Exercise for Subskill 8E

1. $2\frac{1}{8} \div 1\frac{1}{2} =$ **2.** $5 \div 2\frac{2}{7} =$

3. $3\frac{1}{2} \div 1\frac{3}{4} =$ **4.** $5\frac{1}{5} \div \frac{13}{14} =$

5. $8 \div 5\frac{1}{4} =$ **6.** $9 \div \frac{3}{8} =$

7. $3\frac{1}{5} \div 2\frac{2}{3} =$ **8.** $\frac{6}{7} \div 5 =$

9. $2\frac{1}{4} \div 1\frac{1}{5} =$ **10.** $7\frac{1}{3} \div \frac{11}{13} =$

11. $7 \div \frac{7}{9} =$ **12.** $2\frac{4}{5} \div 7 =$

Check your answers on page 14 in the Answer Key for Book I. If you correctly answered ten of the twelve problems, go to the next subskill. If not, complete the following Supplemental Exercise.

Supplemental Exercise for Subskill 8E

Read Subskill 8E again. Work through the examples as you read them. Then do this exercise.

1. $3\frac{1}{6} \div 2\frac{1}{3} =$ **2.** $\frac{4}{7} \div 8 =$

3. $9 \div 3\frac{2}{5} =$ **4.** $1\frac{1}{5} \div 2\frac{1}{4} =$

5. $6\frac{2}{8} \div \frac{1}{4} =$ **6.** $13 \div 7\frac{4}{5} =$

7. $4 \div \frac{7}{12} =$ **8.** $1\frac{3}{4} \div 3\frac{1}{2} =$

9. $\frac{10}{11} \div 5 =$ **10.** $3\frac{2}{9} \div 1\frac{2}{3} =$

11. $21 \div \frac{7}{8}$ **12.** $3\frac{1}{7} \div 10 =$

Check your answers on page 14 in the Answer Key for Book I. If you correctly answered ten of the twelve problems, go to the next subskill. If not, ask your instructor for help.

Subskill 8F: Solving Word Problems

After studying this subskill, you will be able to solve word problems involving the multiplication and division of fractions.

Many of the problems you must solve are in the form of word problems. These are the steps you should follow in solving word problems that require the multiplication or division of fractions.

Read and Reread the Problem

Read the *entire* problem carefully. Read the problem again to make sure you understand what you are being asked to do.

EXAMPLE: A candy recipe calls for $1\frac{1}{2}$ cups of sugar. How much sugar will you need to make $\frac{2}{3}$ of a batch of candy?

Now that you have read the problem, go to the next step.

Determine What You Are to Find

What does the problem ask you to do? In other words, what will you have to do to find the answer?

In the example above you are asked to cut a recipe by one third.

Determine What You Are Given

What facts do you know. Also, what facts are not needed to solve the problem?

You know that a whole batch of candy takes $1\frac{1}{2}$ cups of sugar.

Decide What Operation(s) to Use

Here are some hints to help you to decide whether to multiply or to divide.

If you are given facts about one item and you want to know something about more than one, *multiply*.

If you are given facts about more than one item and you want to know something about only one, *divide*.

If you are asked to share, split, or cut something into equal parts, *divide*.

If you want to know how much a fraction of something is, multiply by that fraction.

In this problem, you are finding $\frac{2}{3}$ of $1\frac{1}{2}$ cups. Two thirds of something means two thirds times something, so you should multiply.

Solve the Problem

Write the problem like this:

$\frac{2}{3} \times 1\frac{1}{2}$

And you are ready to solve it.

Change $1\frac{1}{2}$ to an improper fraction.

$1\frac{1}{2} = \frac{3}{2}$

Multiply the fractions.

$$\frac{\overset{1}{\cancel{2}}}{\underset{1}{\cancel{3}}} \times \frac{\overset{1}{\cancel{3}}}{\underset{1}{\cancel{2}}} = \frac{1}{1} \qquad \frac{1}{1} = 1$$

Answer: 1 cup of sugar.

Check Your Answer

Check your answer by multiplying again.
Here is another word problem.

EXAMPLE: Rodney bought two tons of topsoil for his garden, but he must haul it himself. His pickup truck will carry half a ton. How many trips must he make to bring the topsoil to his garden?

To find out how many trips Rodney must make, you must divide by the amount of one load.

$2 \div \frac{1}{2}$

Change 2 to an improper fraction.

$2 = \frac{2}{1}$

Divide.

$\frac{2}{1} \div \frac{1}{2} = \frac{2}{1} \times \frac{2}{1}$ Turn the fraction you are dividing by upside down and change the problem to a multiplication problem.

$\frac{2}{1} \times \frac{2}{1} = \frac{4}{1}$ Solve the multiplication problem.

$\frac{4}{1} = 4$ Answer: 4 trips.

Check your skill at solving word problems by doing this exercise.

Exercise for Subskill 8F

1. You are cooking a $5\frac{1}{4}$-pound roast to serve to 14 people. How much meat will each person get?

2. Jenny Jackson is weatherstripping the windows of her house. Each window takes $4\frac{2}{3}$ yards of stripping. How much stripping will Jenny need for 9 windows?

3. Property tax is assessed on $\frac{2}{3}$ of a house's market value. The market value of the Levines' house is $31,500. What is the assessed value of the house?

4. Mr. James wants to tile the floor in his den. The den is $15\frac{1}{3}$ feet wide. A tile measures $\frac{2}{3}$ of a foot on each side. How many tiles will there be in one row across the width of the den?

5. The rent on Ming Lee's apartment was raised by $\frac{1}{5}$ of the amount she paid last year. If her rent was $275 a month last year, how much more is she paying now?

Check your answers on page 15 in the Answer Key for Book I. If you correctly answered four of the five problems, go to the Self-Check. If not, do the following Supplemental Exercise.

Supplemental Exercise for Subskill 8F

Read Subskill 8F again. Work through the examples as you read them. Then do this exercise.

1. Mrs. Potter's backyard is 90 feet long. She plans to build a fence along the length of the yard. Each board for the fence is $\frac{5}{6}$ of a foot wide. How many boards does she need for the fence?

2. A recipe calls for $2\frac{1}{4}$ cups of flour. How much flour will you need to double the recipe?

3. The scale on a map is $\frac{1}{4}$ inch = 1 mile. How many miles are represented by $2\frac{1}{2}$ inches?

4. A large box of detergent contains 20 cups of detergent. If each load of laundry takes $1\frac{1}{4}$ cups of detergent, how many loads can be washed with the detergent in this box?

5. A dress is on sale for $\frac{1}{3}$ off the regular price. If the regular price is $45, how much do you save by buying the dress on sale?

Check your answers on page 15 in the Answer Key for Book I. If you answered four of the five problems right, go to the Self-Check. If not, ask your instructor for help.

SELF-CHECK FOR SKILL UNIT 8

Solve each of the following problems. Show your work.

1. $\frac{7}{8} \times \frac{20}{21} =$

2. $\frac{5}{6} \times 9 =$

3. $4\frac{1}{2} \times 3\frac{3}{4} =$

4. $\frac{5}{12} \div \frac{5}{6} =$

5. $\frac{4}{9} \div 9 =$

6. $4\frac{1}{2} \div 1\frac{7}{8} =$

7. $\frac{25}{42} \times \frac{7}{10} \times \frac{2}{5} =$

8. $7\frac{1}{2} \times 4 \times \frac{1}{3} =$

9. $2\frac{3}{4} \times 5\frac{1}{3} \times 3 =$

10. $\frac{3}{5} \div \frac{10}{21} =$

11. $10 \div \frac{5}{8} =$

12. A 5-gallon gas can is $\frac{2}{3}$ full. How much gas is in the can?

13. Eric is building a stave fence. The fence will be 150 feet long, and each board is $1\frac{1}{4}$ feet wide. How many boards will he need?

14. Truman needs four shelves in his garage. He has a board $12\frac{1}{2}$ feet long and wants the shelves to be of equal length. How long will each shelf be?

15. A first-class airline ticket to Chicago costs $600. A coach ticket costs $\frac{3}{4}$ as much as a first-class ticket. How much does a coach ticket cost?

Check your answers on page 15 in the Answer Key for Book I. If you correctly answered twelve of the fifteen problems, go on to Skill Unit 9. If not, ask your instructor for help.

Skill Unit 9
ADDING AND SUBTRACTING DECIMALS

What Skills You Need to Begin: Basic operations with whole numbers and fractions (Skill Units 1 through 8).

What Skills You Will Learn: After studying this skill unit, you will be able to read and write decimals, to tell higher decimals from lower ones, to round decimals off, to add and subtract decimals, and to solve word problems involving decimals.

Why You Need These Skills: When you balance your checkbook and when you count your change after buying something, you must add and subtract decimals. Also, many items you buy are sized according to the metric system, and to understand the metric system, you must understand decimals.

How You Will Show What You Have Learned: At the end of this skill unit is a Self-Check consisting of twenty-five problems involving decimals. You should allow yourself one hour to do the Self-Check. To prove that you have mastered these skills you must correctly answer twenty of the twenty-five problems.

If you feel you have already mastered the addition and subtraction of decimals, complete the Self-Check on pages 212 and 213.

Subskill 9A: Reading and Writing Decimals

After studying this subskill you will be able to read and write decimals.

What Are Decimals?

In Skill Units 1–5 you studied whole numbers, and in Skill Units 6–8 you studied fractions. In this skill unit you will learn how to use **decimals.** Decimals, like fractions, enable you to work with parts of numbers.

You have already been using decimals for a long time. In our money, any amount less than a dollar is a decimal. A penny is one cent, or one hundredth ($\frac{1}{100}$) of a dollar. There are 100 cents in a dollar. One cent can be written in several different ways:

Cents		Decimal Part of a Dollar	Fractional Part of a Dollar	Name of Coin	
one cent	1¢	\$.01	$\frac{1}{100}$	cent	penny

Other amounts of money less than a dollar can also be written in these ways:

5 cents	5¢	\$.05	$\frac{5}{100}$	$\frac{1}{20}$	nickel
10 cents	10¢	\$.10	$\frac{10}{100}$	$\frac{1}{10}$	dime
25 cents	25¢	\$.25	$\frac{25}{100}$	$\frac{1}{4}$	quarter
50 cents	50¢	\$.50	$\frac{50}{100}$	$\frac{1}{2}$	half dollar

A nickel is worth 5 pennies, or five hundredths ($\frac{5}{100}$) of a dollar. A dime is worth 10 pennies, or 2 nickels, or ten hundredths ($\frac{10}{100}$) of a dollar. A quarter is worth 25 pennies, or 5 nickels, or two dimes and a nickel, or twenty-five hundredths ($\frac{25}{100}$) of a dollar—in other words, one fourth, or a quarter, of a dollar.

Reading Decimals

Each place in a decimal number has a different value. In Skill Unit 1 you studied the place values of whole numbers. These are the places to the left of the **decimal point,** though in most whole numbers the decimal point is not shown.

Here is a number that has both a whole number and a decimal:

79,103.54

↗ comma ↖ decimal point

As you remember from Skill Unit 1, the comma helps you read the whole number by marking off the periods (thousands, millions, billions). The decimal point is different. It shows you where the whole number ends and the decimal number begins.

whole number decimal

79,103 . 54

When there is only a whole number and no decimals, we do not need to write the decimal point.

79,103

Study these place values:

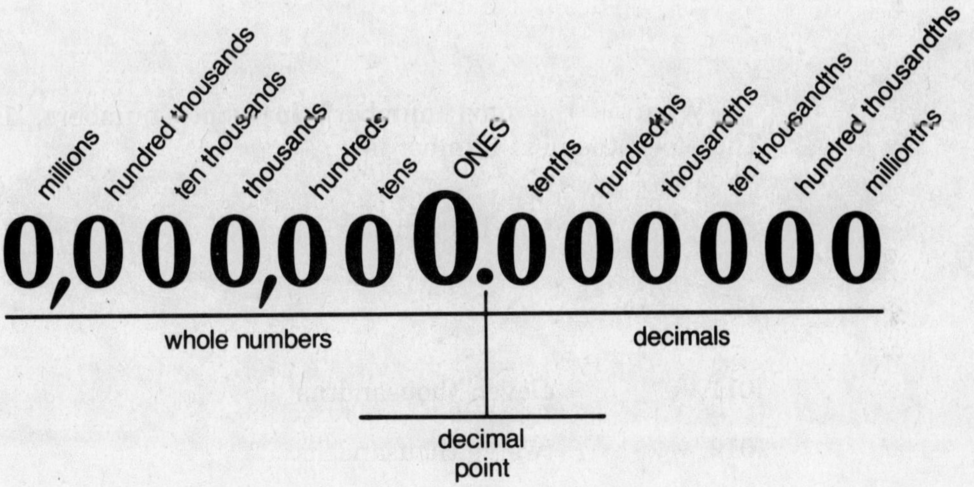

The decimal point does not take up a place. Only a number can take up a place. The decimal point simply shows where the whole number ends and the decimal begins. The place to the left of the decimal is the ones place. The next place to the left is the tens place. Two places to the left of the ones place is the hundreds place. The place to the right of the decimal is the tenths place. Two places to the right of the ones place is the hundredths place.

When written in words, the place values to the right of the decimal point all end with "th." Reading from left to right, they are tenths, hundredths, thousandths, and so on.

Knowing the place values, you know that .1 is one tenth because the 1 is in the tenths place. In the same way, .01 is one hundredth because the 1 is in the hundredths place. On page 193 are several decimals written in numerals, in words, and as fractions.

Numerals	Words	Fraction
.1	one tenth	$\frac{1}{10}$
.01	one hundredth	$\frac{1}{100}$
.001	one thousandth	$\frac{1}{1,000}$
.002	two thousandths	$\frac{2}{1,000}$
.003	three thousandths	$\frac{3}{1,000}$
.004	four thousandths	$\frac{4}{1,000}$
.005	five thousandths	$\frac{5}{1,000}$
.006	six thousandths	$\frac{6}{1,000}$
.007	seven thousandths	$\frac{7}{1,000}$
.008	eight thousandths	$\frac{8}{1,000}$
.009	nine thousandths	$\frac{9}{1,000}$

What is the next number? In whole numbers, 10 follows 9. Therefore, the next number is

.010	ten thousandths	$\frac{10}{1,000}$

Then come

.011	eleven thousandths	$\frac{11}{1,000}$
.012	twelve thousandths	$\frac{12}{1,000}$
.013	thirteen thousandths	$\frac{13}{1,000}$
.014	fourteen thousandths	$\frac{14}{1,000}$
.015	fifteen thousandths	$\frac{15}{1,000}$

Eventually you reach

.099	ninety-nine thousandths	$\frac{99}{1,000}$

The next number is

.100	one hundred thousandths	$\frac{100}{1,000}$

followed by

.101	one hundred one thousandths	$\frac{101}{1{,}000}$
.102	one hundred two thousandths	$\frac{102}{1{,}000}$
.103	one hundred three thousandths	$\frac{103}{1{,}000}$
.104	one hundred four thousandths	$\frac{104}{1{,}000}$
.105	one hundred five thousandths	$\frac{105}{1{,}000}$

The number after

.999	nine hundred ninety-nine thousandths	$\frac{999}{1{,}000}$

is

1.000	one thousand thousandths	$\frac{1{,}000}{1{,}000}$

You can leave off the zeros at the right end of a decimal and it will still equal the same amount.

$$1.\emptyset\emptyset\emptyset \text{ equals } 1 \text{ because } \frac{1{,}000}{1{,}000} = 1$$

In the same way,

$$.01\emptyset \text{ equals } .01 \text{ because } \frac{10}{1{,}000} = \frac{1}{100}$$

Here is another example. The following decimals all equal the same amount.

.800	eight hundred thousandths	$\frac{800}{1{,}000}$
.80	eighty hundredths	$\frac{80}{100}$
.8	eight tenths	$\frac{8}{10}$

However, you cannot take out zeros to the <u>left</u> of another number. If you did, the decimal would become a different amount. For example,

$$.07 \neq .7$$

Seven hundredths does not equal seven tenths.

$$\frac{7}{100} \neq \frac{7}{10}$$

The 0 in .07 is called a **placeholder.** It takes up the tenths place to keep the 7 in the hundredths place.

To read a number that has both a whole number and a decimal such as 304.52, first read the whole number—that is, the numbers to the left of the decimal point.

304.52 three hundred four

Read the decimal point as "and."

304.52 and

Then read the numbers to the right of the decimal point.

304.**52** fifty-two

Finally, read the place value of the decimal.

304.**52** The decimal ends in the hundredths place, so read "hundredths."

Put them together.

304.52 three hundred four and fifty-two hundredths.

Here are more examples.

26.084 twenty-six and eighty-four thousandths

1,891.645 one thousand eight hundred ninety-one and six hundred forty-five thousandths

Writing Decimals

If you read or hear a decimal in words, how do you write it in numerals?

EXAMPLE: Forty-eight and three tenths

First, write the whole number—that is, the number before the decimal point.

forty-eight 48

Then put a decimal point where the "and" is.

and 48.

Finally, write the decimal—that is, the number after the decimal point.

three tenths 48.3

Put them all together.

forty-eight and three tenths 48.3

EXAMPLE: Ninety-seven hundredths

In this case there are no whole numbers, and therefore no "and."

First, write the decimal number.

ninety-seven 97

Now, where does the decimal point go? The last number of the decimal must be in the hundredths place.

hundredths 97

Therefore, put the decimal point where it will show that the 7 is in the hundredths place.

ninety-seven hundredths .97

Here is a tricky one.

EXAMPLE: Eighteen thousandths

There are no whole numbers, so first, write the decimal number.

eighteen 18

Where does the decimal point go? Since the last number of the decimal is in the thousandths place,

thousandths **18**

you must put in a 0 as a placeholder to keep the 8 in the thousandths place

018

and put the decimal point before the 0.

eighteen thousandths .018

More examples:

Ninety-three hundredths	.93
Six thousandths	.006
Two and five tenths	2.5

Check your skill at reading and writing decimals by doing this exercise.

Exercise for Subskill 9A

In the number 542.1084, which number has the following place value?

1. Ten thousandths
2. Thousandths
3. Hundredths
4. Tenths

In the number 61.342

5. the 3 is in the __________ place
6. the 2 is in the __________ place
7. the 4 is in the __________ place

Write these numbers in words.

8. .781
9. 98.6
10. 10.05
11. 736.42

Write these numbers in numerals.

12. Seventy-five hundredths
13. Forty and nine tenths
14. Two hundred fifty-three and twenty-eight hundredths
15. Three thousand four and six thousandths

Check your answers on page 15 in the Answer Key for Book One. If you correctly answered twelve of the fifteen problems, go to the next subskill. If not, complete the following Supplemental Exercise.

Supplemental Exercise for Subskill 9A

Read Subskill 9A again. Work through the examples as you read them. Then try the exercise on page 199.

Name the place value of each highlighted number.

1. 53.8**2**
2. 12.**1**31
3. 7.0000**6**

What is the place value of the 1 in each of the following numbers?

4. 41.32
5. .217
6. .00315
7. 12.3

Write these numbers in words.

8. .038
9. 1.4
10. 55.55
11. 970.017

Write these numbers in numerals.

12. Two hundredths
13. Ninety-eight and six tenths
14. Five hundred eighty-seven and sixty-two thousandths
15. Nineteen thousand, fifty-two and eighty-nine hundredths

Check your answers on page 15 in the Answer Key for Book One. If you correctly answered twelve of the fifteen problems right, go to the next subskill. If not, ask your instructor for help.

Subskill 9B: Telling Higher Decimals from Lower Ones

After studying this subskill you will be able to tell higher decimals from lower ones.

Numbers That Have Both Whole Numbers and Decimals

Any decimal, no matter how large, is less than the whole number 1. Therefore, any number that has both a whole number and a decimal in it is larger than a number that has a decimal only.

1.02 is larger than .9999

For the same reason, the number with the larger whole number is always the larger number, regardless of the decimal.

$6.01 > 5.978$ The sign $>$ means "is greater than."

The sign $<$ means "is less than."

Again, the number with the largest whole number is always the largest.

EXAMPLE: Put these numbers in order from largest to smallest:

2.796 5.969 11.103 7.546

Answer:

11.103 **7**.546 **5**.969 **2**.796 You only need to look at the whole numbers. The decimals do not matter.

But what if the whole numbers are the same?

42.84 **42**.06

Now the decimals do matter. The number with the larger decimal will be the larger number.

Comparing Decimals

If there are no whole numbers, or if the whole numbers are the same, look at the number in the tenths place first. The decimal with the larger number here is the larger decimal.

.671 ↑ tenths .82 ↑ tenths

$8 > 6$

Therefore $.82 > .671$

If the numbers in the tenths place are the same, look at the numbers in the hundredths place.

.02 ↑ hundredths .018 ↑ hundredths

$$2 > 1$$

Therefore $1.02 > .018$

You may have to go even farther to the right before you come to a place where the numbers are different. For example, which is larger, 1.427 or 1.425?

1.427	1.425	1 = 1
1.427	1.425	4 = 4
1.427	1.425	2 = 2
1.427	1.425	7 > 5

Therefore $1.427 > 1.425$

Now let's compare several numbers. Write these numbers from largest to smallest:

4 4.4 .4 .44

Two of these numbers have whole numbers, so they are larger than the numbers with decimals only.

4 and 4.4 $>$ .4 and .44

But which is larger, 4 or 4.4? To find the answer, add a decimal point and a 0 after the number that has no decimal. It will still equal the same amount.

$$4.0 = 4$$

Then compare the two decimals.

4.0 4.4

$$4 > 0$$

Therefore, $4.4 > 4.0$

Now look at the numbers that have decimals only. The number in the "tenths" place is the same.

.4 .44

Go on to the "hundredths" place. Put a 0 after .4 to give it a "hundredths" place.

.40 .44

$$4 > 0$$

Therefore, .44 > .40

The numbers from largest to smallest are

4.4   4.0   .44   .40

or, dropping the zeros,

4.4   4   .44   .4

Check your skill in comparing decimals by doing this exercise.

Exercise for Subskill 9B

Which number is smaller?

1. .34 or .39
2. .463 or .513
3. 1.04 or .98
4. 54.5 or 5.451
5. .348 or .319

Which number is larger?

6. .75 or .8
7. 1.03 or 1.3
8. .666 or .665
9. .804 or .725
10. 1.987 or .999

Write these numbers from smallest to largest:

11.	.12	.1	.11	
12.	1.01	.98	1.11	
13.	4.56	4.53	4.55	
14.	.997	.991	.983	.989
15.	10.53	9.84	11.01	7.68

Write these numbers from largest to smallest:

16.	.2	.19	.29	
17.	.88	.99	.77	
18.	.1111	.111	.11	
19.	10.03	10.09	10.1	10.13
20.	.98	.989	.1053	.1051

Check your answers on pages 15 and 16 in the Answer Key for Book One. If you correctly answered sixteen of the twenty problems, go to the next subskill. If not, complete the following Supplemental Exercise.

Supplemental Exercise for Subskill 9B

Read Subskill 9B again. Work through the examples as you read them. Then do this exercise.

Which number is smaller?

1. .9 or .18
2. .74 or .7
3. 6.9 or 9.6
4. 10.98 or 9.99
5. 48.3 or 38.03

Which number is larger?

6. 1.03 or 1.3
7. 9.99 or 9.9
8. 77.7 or 77.8
9. .513 or .514
10. .2011 or .983

Write these numbers from smallest to largest:

11.	.9	1.1	1	
12.	10.01	9.98	10.1	
13.	.701	.703	.702	
14.	3.63	3.66	3.74	3.75
15.	2.22	2.2	2.02	2.022

Write these numbers from largest to smallest:

16.	.89	.91	.9	
17.	.68	.86	.66	
18.	.97	.908	.98	
19.	9.001	9.01	9.011	9.1
20.	5.61	14.72	24.72	7.33

Check your answers on page 16 in the Answer Key for Book One. If you correctly answered sixteen of the twenty problems, go to the next subskill. If not, ask your instructor for help.

Subskill 9C: Rounding Decimals Off

After studying this subskill you will be able to round decimals off.

Rounding decimals is the same as rounding whole numbers. For example, round 38.637 to the nearest tenth.

First, underline the number in the place you are rounding to.

38.$\underline{6}$37	The 6 is in the tenths place.

Next, look at the number to the right of the underlined number. Is it less than 5? If so, leave the underlined number as it is. If not, increase the underlined number by 1.

↓ 38.$\underline{6}$37	The number to the right of the 6 is 3, and 3 is less than 5. Leave the 6 as it is.
38.600	Change the numbers to the right of the underlined number to 0.
38.6	Drop the zeros after the 6. The value of the decimal does not change when you drop off the zero or zeros that appear at the end of a decimal. (38.600 = 38.6)

EXAMPLE: Round 986.389 to the nearest hundredth.

986.3$\underline{8}$9	The 8 is in the hundredths place.
↓ 986.3$\underline{8}$9	The number to the right of the 8 is 9, and 9 is not less than 5.
986.3$\underline{9}$9	Increase the underlined number by 1.
986.39	Drop the number to the right of the underlined number.

Answer: 986.39

Remember, nines can be tricky. Here are two examples.

EXAMPLE: Round 42.98 to the nearest tenth.

42.$\underline{9}$8	The 9 is in the tenths place.
↓ 42.$\underline{9}$8	The number to the right of the 9 is 8, and 8 is not less than 5.
$\begin{array}{r} 42.98 \\ +\ \ 1\ \ \\ \hline 43.08 \end{array}$	Increase the underlined number by 1. Drop the numbers to the right of the underlined number.

Answer: 43.0 or 43

EXAMPLE: Round 1.995 to the nearest hundredth.

```
 1.995
    ↓
 1.995        5 is not less than 5.

  1.995       Increase the underlined number by 1.
+    1
 ------
  2.005
```

Answer: 2.00 or 2

Check your skill at rounding decimals by doing this exercise.

Exercise for Subskill 9C

Round to the nearest tenth.

1. 7.464
2. 89.935

Round to the nearest hundredth.

3. .485
4. 4.0059

Round to the nearest thousandth.

5. 4.3675
6. 9.3095

Round these numbers to the nearest tenth, hundredth, and thousandth.

7. .2572 _____ _____ _____
8. .6936 _____ _____ _____
9. 6.0656 _____ _____ _____
10. .4381 _____ _____ _____

Check your answers on page 16 in the Answer Key for Book One. If you correctly answered eight of the ten problems, go to the next subskill. If not, complete the following Supplemental Exercise.

Supplemental Exercise for Subskill 9C

Read Subskill 9C again. Work through the examples as you read them. Then do this exercise.

1. Round 7.464 to the nearest tenth.
2. Round .485 to the nearest hundredth.

3. Round 4.3675 to the nearest thousandth.
4. Round .50191 to the nearest thousandth.
5. Round 89.985 to the nearest tenth.
6. Round 4.0059 to the nearest hundredth.
7. Round 23.6 to the nearest whole number (one).
8. Round 485.6 to the nearest hundred.
9. Round .0973 to the nearest hundredth.
10. Round 5.051 to the nearest tenth.

Check your answers on page 16 in the Answer Key for Book One. If you correctly answered eight of the ten problems, go to the next Subskill. If not, ask your instructor for help.

Subskill 9D: Adding Decimals

After studying this subskill you will be able to add decimals.

Adding decimals is similar to adding whole numbers. First, write the numbers in a column with all the decimal points lined up. If you wish, you may put in zeros at the right end of a decimal so that all the decimals have the same number of places. For example, add 2.56 + .387.

```
  2.56
+  .387
```

Write the numbers under each other with the decimal points lined up.

```
  2.560
+  .387
```

You may put in a 0 so that all the decimals have the same number of places.

Then add the numbers as if they were whole numbers.

```
  2.560
+  .387
      7
```

Start at the right. Add the thousandths: 0 + 7 = 7. Write the 7 in the thousandths column.

```
     1
  2.560
+  .387
     47
```

Add the hundredths: 6 + 8 = 14. Write the 4 in the hundredths column. Carry the 1 to the tenths column.

```
     1
  2.560
+  .387
    947
```

Add the tenths: 1 + 5 + 3 = 9. Write the 9 in the tenths column.

```
     1
  2.560
+  .387
  2 947
```

Add the ones: 2 + 0 = 2. Write the 2 in the ones column.

Finally, put the decimal point in the answer directly below the decimal points in the problem above.

```
  2.560    Line up the decimal point in the answer
+  .387    with the decimal points in the numbers
  2.947    being added.
```

EXAMPLE: Add .7 and .8

```
   .7      Write the numbers under each other with the decimal
+  .8      points lined up.

  1
   .7      Add the tenths column. Carry the 1 to the ones column.
+  .8
    5

  1
   .7      Since there are no other numbers in the ones column,
+  .8      simply bring the 1 down to the answer.
  1 5

   .7      Line up the decimal point in the answer with the
+  .8      decimal point in the numbers being added.
  1.5
```

Answer: 1.5

EXAMPLE: Add $3.50, $6, and $.87

```
   $3.50   Write the numbers to be added in a column with
    6.     all the decimal points lined up. Since 6 is a
+    .87   whole number, the decimal point is just to the
           right of it.

   $3.50   You may add 00 to the right of the decimal point
    6.00   after the 6 so that all the decimals have two
+    .87   places.

    1
    3.50   Add the numbers. Put the decimal point in the
    6.00   answer directly below the decimal points in the
+    .87   column.
  $10.37
```

Answer: $10.37

Check your skill at adding decimals by doing this exercise.

Exercise for Subskill 9D

1. $\begin{array}{r} 73.8 \\ +\ 4.1 \\ \hline \end{array}$

2. $\begin{array}{r} 78.3 \\ +21.6 \\ \hline \end{array}$

3. .9 + .3 =

4. .178 + .1624 + 5 + .07 =

5. 1.325 + 13.25 + 132.5 + .1325 =

6. $\begin{array}{r} 786.2 \\ +\ 12.99 \\ \hline \end{array}$

7. $\begin{array}{r} \$15.65 \\ +\ \ \ 3.95 \\ \hline \end{array}$

8. $35.16 + $3.07 + $7.95 =

9. $87.50 + $15.76 + $9 =

10. 3.5 + 7.065 + 3.057 =

Check your answers on page 16 in the Answer Key for Book One. If you correctly answered eight of the ten problems, go to the next subskill. If not, complete the following Supplemental Exercise.

Supplemental Exercise for Subskill 9D

Read Subskill 9D again. Work through the examples as you read them. Then do this exercise.

1. 31.9 + 42.8 + 61.3 =

2. 32.91 + .47 + 1.6 =

3. $\begin{array}{r} 43.22 \\ 19.72 \\ +\ 8.51 \\ \hline \end{array}$

4. $\begin{array}{r} 8.3 \\ 12.04 \\ +\ 6.55 \\ \hline \end{array}$

5. $\begin{array}{r} \$13.26 \\ +\ \ \ 9.75 \\ \hline \end{array}$

6. $\begin{array}{r} \$7.95 \\ +\ 3.77 \\ \hline \end{array}$

7. 8 + 6.1 + .9 =

8. 4.0076 + .035 + .4 + .05 =

9. .5 + .9 + .6 = **10.** \$4.10 + \$.32 + \$17 =

Check your answers on page 16 in the Answer Key for Book One. If you correctly answered eight of the ten problems, go to the next subskill. If not, ask your instructor for help.

Subskill 9E: Subtracting Decimals

After studying this subskill you will be able to subtract decimals.

Subtracting decimals is similar to subtracting whole numbers. First, write the two numbers, one below the other, with the decimal points lined up. For example, to subtract .48 from 5.3, write the problem like this:

```
  5. 3 0
-   . 4 8
---------
```

Put a 0 to the right end of 5.3 so that both decimals have the same number of places.

Next, subtract the same way you would with whole numbers.

```
 4 12 10
  5. 3 0
 -  . 4 8
---------
  4  8 2
```

In this problem you must borrow.

Then put the decimal point in the answer directly below the decimal points in the problem.

```
  5. 3 0
-   . 4 8
---------
  4. 8 2
```

Finally, check your subtraction by adding the difference to the smaller of the two numbers—the number with the minus sign. The sum should be the larger number in the subtraction problem.

```
    . 4 8
+ 4. 8 2
---------
  5. 3 0
```

The smaller number (with the minus sign) plus the difference equals the larger number in the subtraction problem.

Here are more examples for you to study.

EXAMPLE: Subtract \$1.25 from \$5.

```
  $ 5.
-   1. 2 5
----------
```

\$5 means five dollars even, no cents. The decimal point comes right after the 5.

$$\begin{array}{r} \$5.00 \\ -\ \ 1.25 \\ \hline \end{array}$$

Put 00 after 5 and the decimal point. It is still five dollars and no cents.

$$\begin{array}{r} \scriptstyle 9 \\ \scriptstyle 4\ \ \not{1}\not{0}\ \not{1}\not{0} \\ \$\not{5}.\not{0}\not{0} \\ -\ \ 1.25 \\ \hline \$3.75 \end{array}$$

Borrow as you do in subtracting whole numbers. Bring the decimal point straight down.

Answer: $3.75

EXAMPLE: Subtract $1.25 from $6.28

$$\begin{array}{r} \$6.28 \\ -\ \ 1.25 \\ \hline \$5.03 \end{array}$$

The 0 in the answer shows that there are no tenths—no dimes. In words, the answer is five dollars and three cents.

Answer: $5.03

EXAMPLE: Subtract $4.33 from $4.43

$$\begin{array}{r} \$4.43 \\ -\ \ 4.33 \\ \hline \$\ \ .10 \end{array}$$

The answer is $.10—that is, 10 cents. If this were not a money problem, you could have dropped the 0.

Answer: $.10

EXAMPLE: Subtract 2.91 from 4.857

$$\begin{array}{r} \scriptstyle 3\ \ 18\ \ \ \ \ \\ \not{4}.\not{8}57 \\ -\ 2.910 \\ \hline 1.947 \end{array}$$

Since you cannot subtract 9 tenths from 8 tenths, you must borrow.

Answer: 1.947

Check your skill at subtracting decimals by doing this exercise.

Exercise for Subskill 9E

1. 3.72 − 1.4 =

2. 6.04 − 2.3276 =

3. 372 − 135.006 =

4.
$$\begin{array}{r} 117.7 \\ -\ \ \ 3.5 \\ \hline \end{array}$$

5.
$$\begin{array}{r} \$75.95 \\ -\ \ 34.23 \\ \hline \end{array}$$

6. 3.7 − 1.156 =

7. 123.98 − 24.99 =

8. \$35.16 − \$3.07 =

9.
$$\begin{array}{r} 17.041 \\ -12.156 \\ \hline \end{array}$$

10.
$$\begin{array}{r} 36.222 \\ -\ 2.455 \\ \hline \end{array}$$

Check your answers on page 16 in the Answer Key for Book One. If you correctly answered eight of the ten problems, go to the next subskill. If not, complete the following Supplemental Exercise.

Supplemental Exercise for Subskill 9E

Read Subskill 9E again. Work through the examples as you read them. Then do this exercise.

1.
$$\begin{array}{r} 63 \\ -\ 1.04 \\ \hline \end{array}$$

2.
$$\begin{array}{r} 7.096 \\ -\ .704 \\ \hline \end{array}$$

3. \$7.71 − \$4.24 =

4. \$64 − \$.96 =

5.
$$\begin{array}{r} .033 \\ -.00165 \\ \hline \end{array}$$

6.
$$\begin{array}{r} 5.41 \\ -2.45 \\ \hline \end{array}$$

7. 41 − .57 =

8. 3 − 1.8712 =

9.
$$\begin{array}{r} \$17.25 \\ -\ 2.13 \\ \hline \end{array}$$

10.
$$\begin{array}{r} 12.177 \\ -\ 3.42 \\ \hline \end{array}$$

Check your answers on page 16 in the Answer Key for Book One. If you correctly answered eight of the ten problems, go to the next subskill. If not, ask your instructor for help.

Subskill 9F: Solving Word Problems

After studying this subskill you will be able to solve word problems involving the addition and subtraction of decimals.

When solving a word problem, read the problem carefully. Decide whether you will have to add or subtract. Look for any hidden questions. When you get the answer, ask yourself if it sounds reasonable. Read the problem again to see if your answer makes sense. Be sure to check your work.

Remember, when you are asked to find out how much you have when two or more things are put together, you add. When you are asked to find out how much you have left when something is taken away, you subtract.

EXAMPLE: Jason bought the following items:

Shirt	$12.98
Slacks	$28.95
Necktie	$ 6
Sweater	$35.20

Sales tax was $4.16. What was the total cost of his purchases?

The problem asks for total cost. This means you must add.

$12.98	items
28.95	
6.00	
35.20	
4.16	tax
$87.29	total

Answer: $87.29

EXAMPLE: At the beginning of a trip, Marlene checked the odometer of her car and recorded the reading of 23,984.8 miles. At the end of the trip, the odometer reading was 24,321.3 miles. How many miles did she travel?

Marlene's trip mileage is the difference between the odometer reading at the start of the trip and the reading at the end of the trip. To find a difference, you subtract.

24,321.3	miles at end
− 23.984.8	miles at start
336.5	miles on trip

Answer: 336.5 miles

EXAMPLE: Emanuel bought a set of tires on sale for $232.35. The original price of the tires was $250. How much did he save by buying them on sale?

To find how much Emanuel saved, you must subtract the sale price from the original price.

$250.00	original price
− 232.35	sale price
$ 17.65	savings

Answer: $17.65 saved

Check your skill at solving word problems by doing this exercise.

Exercise for Subskill 9F

1. Myra's car gets 28.7 miles per gallon in town and 35 miles per gallon on the highway. What is the difference between the two?

2. Normal body temperature is 98.6 degrees. How many degrees above normal is a temperature of 101 degrees.

3. Dave received a $210.65 paycheck for the week. He took $75 cash for his out-of-pocket expenses and deposited the rest in his checking account. Before the deposit, the balance in his checking account was $56.47. What was the balance after the deposit?

4. Jan bought gas three times during a trip. She bought 13.7 gallons, 15 gallons, and 14.8 gallons. How many gallons of gasoline did she buy on the trip?

5. Your grocery bill at the checkout counter is $48.07. You give the clerk three $20 bills. How much change will you receive?

Check your answers on page 16 in the Answer Key for Book One. If you correctly answered four of the five problems, go to the Self-Check. If not, complete the following Supplemental Exercise.

Supplemental Exercise for Subskill 9F

Read Subskill 9F again. Work through the examples as you read them. Then do this exercise.

1. Matti bought a hamburger for $1.25, french fries for 49 cents, a drink for 59 cents, and hot apple pie for 65 cents. Sales tax was 15 cents. How much did the whole meal cost?

2. Your purchases at a store total $22.17. You give the clerk $25. How much change should you get?

3. Anne kept a record of the gas she bought on her trip. At stations along the way, she bought 11.7 gallons, 13.2 gallons, 12.5 gallons, 9.6 gallons, and 10.1 gallons. How much did she buy on the trip?

4. Hamburger is on sale for $1.49 a pound today. Regular price is $1.98 a pound. How much do you save on a pound of hamburger by buying it today?

5. A large bottle of olive oil contains .75 liters. A small bottle contains .42 liters. How much more olive oil do you get by buying the large bottle?

Check your answers on page 17 in the Answer Key for Book One. If you correctly answered four of the five problems, go to the Self-Check. If not, ask your instructor for help.

SELF-CHECK FOR SKILL UNIT 9

Compare these decimals. Fill in each blank with the correct symbol: = if the two numbers are the same, > if the first number is larger than the second, or < if the first number is smaller than the second.

1. 3.82 _____ 3.816
2. .04 _____ .40
3. .67 _____ .607
4. 9 _____ 9.00

5. Arrange these numbers from smallest to largest:
   .54 .59 .583 .6

Round 35.6845 to the nearest:

6. ten
7. one
8. tenth
9. hundredth
10. thousandth

Solve these problems.

11. .8 + .8
12. 5.4 + .85 =
13. 33.4 + .005 + 4.83 =
14. .1 + .7 + .8 + .5 =
15. 8.7 + .53 + 12 + 9.04 =
16. 25.8 − 1.64 =
17. 7.27 − 3.8 =
18. 25 − 19.84 =
19. 17.003 − 15.852 =
20. 12.12 − 12 =

Solve these word problems. Show your work.

21. Last year Don's best time for running a mile was 4.586 minutes. This year his best time is 4.173 minutes. How much faster did he run the mile this year?

22. Yesterday at noon the temperature was 63.4 degrees. At noon today it was 48.6 degrees. How much warmer was it yesterday?

23. Jim spent 63 cents for a ball-point pen, $1.05 for a looseleaf binder, and 52 cents for filler paper.

a. How much did he spend in all?

b. If Jim gave the clerk a $5 bill, how much change should he get?

24. Normal body temperature is 98.6 degrees. Linda's temperature is 2.5 degrees above normal. What is Linda's temperature?

25. One tablet of a pain reliever contains .325 grams of the drug acetaminophen. How many grams of acetaminophen do two tablets contain?

Check your answers on page 17 in the Answer Key for Book One. If you correctly answered twenty of the twenty-five problems, go on to Skill Unit 10. If not, ask your instructor for help.

Skill Unit 10
MULTIPLYING AND DIVIDING DECIMALS

What Skills You Need to Begin: Basic operations with whole numbers, fractions, and decimals (Skill Units 1–9).

What Skills You Will Learn: After studying this skill unit, you will be able to multiply decimals, divide decimals, and solve word problems involving decimals.

Why You Need This Skill: Suppose the sales tax in your state is 5 cents on the dollar. To figure out how much sales tax you must pay on two tires that sell for $97.89, you must multiply decimals. Or suppose you and a friend go out for pizza. The total bill is $12.99. To find out how much each of you should pay, you must divide decimals. As these examples show, decimals are a part of our daily life. You need to be able to multiply and divide decimals just as easily as whole numbers.

How You Will Show What You Have Learned: At the end of this skill unit is a Self-Check consisting of fifteen problems involving decimals. You should allow yourself one hour to do the Self-Check. To prove that you have mastered these skills you must correctly answer twelve of the fifteen problems.

If you feel you have already mastered the multiplication and division of decimals, complete the Self-Check on page 228.

Subskill 10A: Multiplying Decimals

After studying this subskill you will be able to multiply decimals.

Multiplying decimals is like multiplying whole numbers. The only difference is that you must decide where to put the decimal point in the answer. For example, multiply 40.2 by 3.

First, multiply.

40.2	Factor
× 3	Factor
1206	Product

Then find out how many decimal places there should be in the answer by counting the decimal places in both factors.

40.2	One decimal place.
× 3	No decimal places.
120 6	Total—one decimal place. Thus, there should be one decimal place in the answer.

Finally, put the decimal point in the product. Count from right to left. Go over the same number of places you counted in both factors and mark a decimal point in the product.

40.2	
× 3	
120.6 ↑	The decimal point in the product should be one place from the right.

EXAMPLE: Multiply 3.47 by .15.

3.47	First, multiply the two factors. Where should you put the decimal point in the answer?
× .15	
1735	
347	
5205	

Count the decimal places in both factors. There are two decimal places in 3.47 and two in .15—four in all. Thus, there should be four decimal places in the product.

.5205 ↑	Count four places from the right and put in the decimal point.

Answer: .5205

Now look at this problem.

EXAMPLE: Multiply 1.62 by .04.

1.62	There are four decimal places in both factors. Where should you put the decimal point in the answer?
× .04	
648	

Since there must be four decimal places in the product, put a 0 to the left of the answer. The 0 is a placeholder. Put the decimal point to the left of the 0.

.0648 Now the answer has four decimal places.

Answer: .0648

Sometimes you must put more than one 0 to the left of the answer to get all the places you need.

EXAMPLE: Multiply .004 by .02.

.004 × .02 8	There are five decimal places in both factors. So the answer must also have five decimal places.
.00008	Put in all the zeros necessary to give the answer five decimal places. Then put in the decimal point.

Answer: .00008

The answer to a money problem should always be rounded off to the nearest cent.

EXAMPLE: Multiply $96.18 by .4.

$96.17 × .4 38472	There are three decimal places in both factors. So the answer must also have three decimal places.
$38.472	Count three decimal places to the left and put in the decimal point. Write the dollar sign.
$38.472 ↓	Round off the answer to the nearest cent. A cent is a hundredth of a dollar.
$38.472	Since 2 is less than 5, leave the 7 as it is.
$38.47	And drop the 2.

Answer: $38.47

Check your skill at multiplying decimals by doing this exercise.

Exercise for Subskill 10A

1. .041 × .03

2. .384 × .302

3. .79 × 8.6 =

4. .786 × 11 =

5. $76 × .732 =

6. 21.37 × .85

7. $\begin{array}{r} .67 \\ \times .22 \\ \hline \end{array}$ 8. $2.463 \times 8.4 =$ 9. $\$108.30 \times 5.7 =$

10. $6.9 \times .048 =$

Check your answers on page 17 in the Answer Key for Book One. If you correctly answered eight of the ten problems, go to the next subskill. If not, complete the following Supplemental Exercise.

Supplemental Exercise for Subskill 10A

Read Subskill 10A again. Work through the examples as you read them. Then do this exercise.

1. $3.48 \times .821 =$ 2. $34.2 \times .07 =$ 3. $2.75 \times 3.13 =$

4. $\begin{array}{r} 33.008 \\ \times \quad 1.2 \\ \hline \end{array}$ 5. $\begin{array}{r} \$2.40 \\ \times \quad .45 \\ \hline \end{array}$

6. $6.307 \times 6.91 =$ 7. $.907 \times 6.19 =$ 8. $22.1 \times 1.92 =$

9. $\begin{array}{r} \$13.04 \\ \times \quad 10 \\ \hline \end{array}$ 10. $\begin{array}{r} 56.13 \\ \times \quad .4 \\ \hline \end{array}$

Check your answers on page 17 in the Answer Key for Book One. If you correctly answered eight of the ten problems, go to the next subskill. If not, ask your instructor for help.

Subskill 10B: Dividing Decimals

After studying this subskill you will be able to divide decimals.

Dividing decimals is like dividing whole numbers. The only difference is that you must decide where to put the decimal point in the answer. For example, divide 3.75 by 12.5.

First, look for a decimal point in the divisor (the number you are dividing by).

$12.5\overline{)3.75}$ The number you are dividing by is 12.5. It has a decimal point.

12.5) 3.75 — Move the decimal point in the divisor to the right.

Then move the decimal point to the right in the dividend (the number you are dividing). Move it the same number of places.

125.) 3.75 — In the divisor you moved the decimal point one place. Therefore, you must move the decimal point one place to the right in the dividend.

Now do the division.

```
        3
125. ) 37.5
       37 5
```

Write the answer, 3, directly above the 5 in the number you are dividing.

Put the decimal point in the quotient directly above the decimal point in the dividend.

```
       .3
125. ) 37.5
       37 5
```

The decimal point in .3 is directly above the decimal point in 37.5

Finally, check your answer. Put the decimal points back where they were before you moved them. Multiply the divisor and the quotient. You should get the dividend. If you don't, you have made a mistake.

12.5	Divisor
× .3	Quotient
3.75	Dividend

EXAMPLE: Divide 9.76 by 244.

244) 9.76 — There is no decimal point in 244, so you do not need to move it. And because you did not move it in the divisor, you do not need to move it in the dividend.

```
          4
244 ) 9.76
    − 9 76
         0
```

Do the division. Write the 4 directly above the 6 in the number you are dividing. Now, where should you put the decimal point in the quotient?

```
         04
244 ) 9.76
```

Put a 0 to the left of the 4 as a placeholder.

```
        .04
244 ) 9.76
```

Put the decimal point in the answer directly above the decimal point in the dividend.

Answer: .04

Here is another problem in which you must add zeros, but not to the answer.

EXAMPLE: Divide 156 by .05.

$.05\overline{)156}$ There is a decimal point in .05, so you must move it to the right end of the number.

$.05_{\curvearrowright}\overline{)156}$ The decimal point was moved two places.

$05.\overline{)156}$ Therefore, you must move the decimal point two places to the right in 156. But 156 doesn't have a decimal point. What should you do?

A whole number such as 156 needs no decimal point. But you can put a decimal point at the right end of it and put as many zeros as you want, and it will still equal the same number. 156.0000 equals 156. This will help you solve the problem:

$05.\overline{)156.00}$ Put a decimal point at the right end of 156. Add two zeros because you need two places.

$05.\overline{)156.00}$ Move the decimal point two places to the right.

Now you are ready to do the division.

$$
\begin{array}{r}
3120 \\
05.\overline{)15600.} \\
-15 \\
\hline
06 \\
-5 \\
\hline
10 \\
-10 \\
\hline
\end{array}
$$

Put the decimal point in the quotient directly above the decimal point in the dividend.

$$
\begin{array}{r}
3120. \\
05.\overline{)15600.}
\end{array}
$$

The decimal point is at the right end of the answer, so you can drop it.

3120. = 3120

Answer: 3120

Using Decimals to Divide a Remainder

As you learned in Skill Unit 5, some division problems do not come out even. For example, 9 divided by 2 equals 4 with 1 left over—that is, with a remainder of 1.

```
   4 R1
2 ) 9
  -8
   1        Remainder
```

In many problems you can use decimals to divide the remainder and come out even. For example, since 9.0 equals 9, you can solve the problem like this:

```
   4.5
2 ) 9.0     Put a decimal point to the right
  -8        of the 9 and add a 0.
   1 0
  -1 0
     0
            No remainder
```

Thus, 9 divided by 2 equals 4.5 exactly.

Some problems do not come out even until they are carried out to several decimal places. For example, divide $3,495 by 96.

```
      $  36.40625
96 ) $3495.00000
     -288
       615
      -576
        39 0
       -38 4
           600
          -576
            240
           -192
             480
            -480
               0  No remainder.
```

This is a money problem, so you should round the answer off to the nearest cent.

$36.4<u>0</u>625 (↓)	6 is not less than 5.
$36.4<u>1</u>625	So change the 0 to 1,
$36.41	and drop all the decimals to the right of it.

If you know you are going to round off the answer, you do not need to keep dividing until it comes out even. In a money problem, for example, you know you are going to round the answer off to the nearest cent. Therefore, you only need to carry the division to the thousandths place.

EXAMPLE: Divide $19.61 by 3

```
     $ 6.536
3 ) $19.610
    -18
      1 6
     -1 5
        11
        -9
        20
       -18
         2  There is still a remainder.
```

There is still a remainder, but it doesn't matter. You have worked the answer out to the thousandths place, and that is all you need to round it to the nearest cent. Round $6.536 to $6.54.

Answer: $6.54

Some problems will never come out even no matter how far you carry them out.

EXAMPLE: Divide 11 by 3.

```
      3.6666666
3 ) 11.0000000
    -9
     2 0
    -1 8
       20
      -18
       20
```

Round off the quotient, depending on how many decimal places you need.

Answer: 3.6666666

You can also use decimals to divide a smaller whole number by a larger one.

EXAMPLE: Divide 7 by 8.

8) 7.0 Put a decimal point to the right of the 7 and put in zeros as needed. Divide.

$$
\begin{array}{r}
.875 \\
8\overline{)7.000} \\
-\underline{6\,4} \\
60 \\
\underline{56} \\
40 \\
\underline{40}
\end{array}
$$

Answer: .875

Check your skill at dividing decimals by doing this exercise.

Exercise for Subskill 10B

1. $.0816 \div 34 =$

2. $7 \div 9 =$ (Round off your answer to the nearest hundredth.)

3. $11.76 \div 21 =$

4. $54\overline{)40.5}$

5. $.89\overline{)1,335}$

6. $4.54 \div .2 =$

7. $735 \div .21 =$

8. $\$705.65 \div 23 =$

9. $1.3\overline{).5044}$

10. $.07\overline{)5.472}$ (Round off your answer to the nearest thousandth.)

Check your answers on page 17 in the Answer Key for Book One. If you correctly answered eight of the ten problems, go to the next subskill. If not, complete the following Supplemental Exercise.

Supplemental Exercise for Subskill 10B

Read Subskill 10B again. Work through the examples as you read them. Then do this exercise.

1. $\$170.50 \div 62 =$

2. $\$31,378.62 \div 1,642 =$

3. $.6724 \div 82 =$

4. $13\overline{)7}$ (Round off your answer to the nearest hundredth.)

5. $15\overline{)1.23}$

6. $.007\overline{)3.28}$ (Round off your answer to the nearest thousandth.)

7. $2.25\overline{)2475}$ **8.** \$242.76 ÷ 2.3 =

9. \$73.50 ÷ .25 = **10.** .9063 ÷ 3.18 =

Check your answers on page 17 in the Answer Key for Book One. If you correctly answered eight of the ten problems, go to the next subskill. If not, ask your instructor for help.

Subskill 10C: Solving Word Problems

After studying this subskill you will be able to solve word problems involving the multiplication and division of decimals.

The best way to learn how to solve word problems is to work through several examples and then try some problems yourself. Be sure to read each problem carefully, at least twice. Underline the key words. When you get an answer, check to see if it makes sense. Then check your work to make sure you made no errors in arithmetic.

EXAMPLE: Sales tax is 5 cents on the dollar. How much sales tax must you pay on a \$25.75 purchase?

To find the tax on the purchase, you must multiply.

\$25.75	Purchase amount
× .05	Tax rate—5 cents is 5 hundredths
\$1.2875	Amount of tax on purchase

Round \$1.2875 to \$1.29.

EXAMPLE: The bill for a pizza and drinks totaled \$12.75. If Marlene and Fred want to split the cost, how much should each pay?

There are two people, so to find the cost per person, divide by 2.

```
     $ 6.375
2 ) $12.750
    -12
       7
      -6
      15
     -14
      10
     -10
       0
```

Round \$6.375 to \$6.38.

Answer: \$6.38

EXAMPLE: A case of 24 cans of motor oil costs $25.20. How much does one can cost?

To find the cost of one can, you must divide.

```
      $ 1.05
24 ) $24.20
      24
       1 20
       1 20
```

Answer: $1.05

EXAMPLE: Elaine earns $4.75 an hour. If she works overtime, she is paid time and a half. That means she makes 1.5 times her regular pay. How much does Elaine earn on overtime?

To find Elaine's overtime pay, you must multiply.

```
   $4.75    Regular pay
 ×   1.5    Overtime rate
    2375
    475
  $7.125    Overtime pay
```

Round $7.125 to $7.13. Answer: $7.13

EXAMPLE: Gene's car gets 23.4 miles per gallon of gas. He is going on a 300-mile trip tomorrow. How much gas should he expect to use?

To find the amount of gas, you must divide.

```
23.4 ) 300

234. ) 3000.
```

Move both decimal points one place to the right.

```
         12.82
234. ) 3000.00
      - 234
         66 0
        -46 8
         19 20
        -18 72
            580
           -468
            112
```

The answer could be carried out even further because there is still a remainder.

There is no need to carry the answer out any further, however, because gas is measured in tenths of gallons. Round 12.82 to 12.8.

Answer: 12.8 gallons

Check your skill at solving word problems by doing this exercise.

Exercise for Subskill 10C

1. Gretchen earns $6.75 an hour. If she worked 40 hours last week, how much did she earn?

2. Donuts cost $1.89 a dozen. There are 12 donuts in a dozen. How much does one donut cost?

3. Gas costs $1.259 a gallon. How much will 15 gallons cost? (Be sure to round your answer to the nearest cent.)

4. Paul has driven 245.6 miles on 8.9 gallons of gasoline. What was his gas mileage? Round your answer off to the nearest tenth.

5. The charge for a telephone call between two cities is 52 cents for the first minute and 32 cents for each additional minute. How much will a five-minute call cost?

Check your answers on page 17 in the Answer Key for Book One. If you correctly answered four of the five problems, go to the Self-Check. If not, complete the following Supplemental Exercise.

Supplemental Exercises for Subskill 10C

Read Subskill 10C again. Work through the examples as you read them. Then do this exercise.

1. Macaroni and cheese is on sale at 5 boxes for $1. How much do 2 boxes cost?

2. Tires are on sale at $62.49 each. Federal tax on each tire is $2.27. What is the total cost, including the tax, of 4 tires?

3. Mr. and Mrs. Voyles are buying a car. The salesman gives them a choice of two payment plans. On one plan, they will pay $135.84 a month for 36 months. On the other plan, they will pay $109.55 a month for 48 months. How much will they pay in total on the 36-month plan?

4. How much will they pay on the 48-month plan?

5. Which plan is cheaper? How much cheaper?

Check your answers on page 17 in the Answer Key for Book One. If you correctly answered four of the five problems, go to the Self-Check. If not, ask your instructor for help.

SELF-CHECK FOR SKILL UNIT 10

1. $.8 \times .3 =$
2. $.3 \times .2 =$
3. $.25 \times .4 =$
4. $3.14 \times 9 =$
5. $460 \times 4.08 =$
6. $.0474 \div 6 =$
7. $4 \div 200 =$
8. $126 \div 4.2 =$
9. $9.25 \div .5 =$
10. $452.4 \div .052 =$
11. A finance company offers two plans for repayment of a $1,000 loan. On one plan, you would make 6 monthly payments of $181.50 each. How much would you pay in total?
12. On the other plan, you would make 12 monthly payments of $97.50 each. How much would you pay in total?
13. Which plan is cheaper? How much cheaper?
14. Carlos noted that his car odometer showed 28,904.6 miles at the beginning of a trip. After the trip, the odometer showed 29,350.1 miles. Carlos bought 18.8 gallons of gasoline during the trip. How many miles did Carlos go?
15. What was Carlos's gas mileage for the trip? Round your answer to the nearest tenth of a gallon.

Check your answers on pages 17 and 18 in the Answer Key for Book One. If you correctly answered twelve of the fifteen problems, go on to Skill Unit 11. If not, ask your instructor for help.

Skill Unit 11
RATIO AND PROPORTION

What Skills You Need to Begin: Basic operations with whole numbers, fractions, and decimals (Skill Units 1–10).

What Skills You Will Learn: After studying this skill unit, you will be able to read and understand ratios, solve proportions, and use proportions to solve word problems.

Why You Need This Skill: Proportions are useful in solving many problems. Here are some examples of problems that can be solved with proportions:

Three cans of corn cost $1.05. How much will five cans cost?

On a map, 1 inch equals 50 miles. If two towns are 4 inches apart on the map, how far apart are they in miles?

To make a certain shade of blue, two parts of black paint must be mixed with nine parts of blue paint. If you have 6 gallons of blue paint, how many gallons of black paint must you mix with it to make this shade?

How You Will Show What You Have Learned. At the end of this skill unit is a Self-Check consisting of fifteen problems involving proportions. You should allow yourself one hour to do the Self-Check. To prove that you have mastered the skills you must correctly answer twelve of the fifteen problems.

If you feel you have already mastered ratio and proportion, do the Self-Check on page 242.

Subskill 11A: Reading Ratios

After studying this subskill you will be able to read and understand ratios.

What Is a Ratio?

A **ratio** shows the relationship between two numbers. The following page shows you the three ways a ratio can be written.

With the Word "to"	With a Colon	As a Fraction
6 to 10	6:10	$\frac{6}{10}$

When ratios are written as fractions, they are usually reduced to their lowest terms.

$\frac{6}{10} = \frac{3}{5}$

Here are more examples.

$\frac{5}{15} = \frac{1}{3}$

$\frac{9}{12} = \frac{3}{4}$

$\frac{21}{18} = \frac{7}{6}$

Notice that the last example, $\frac{21}{18}$, is an improper fraction—that is, its numerator is larger than its denominator. Improper fractions can often be reduced to lower terms. For example:

$\frac{12}{9} = \frac{4}{3}$

$\frac{20}{14} = \frac{10}{7}$

$\frac{16}{2} = \frac{8}{1}$

But when you are working with ratios, you should not change an improper fraction to a mixed number or a whole number. For example:

Do not change $\frac{4}{3}$ to $1\frac{1}{3}$.

Do not change $\frac{10}{7}$ to $1\frac{3}{7}$.

Do not change $\frac{8}{1}$ to 8.

Of course, some fractions cannot be reduced to lower terms. For example,

$\frac{4}{3}$

$\frac{9}{23}$

$\frac{64}{111}$

cannot be reduced because they are already in their lowest terms.

Understanding Ratios

Ratios are used to show the relationship between the number of one thing and the number of another thing. When you write a ratio, you must keep in mind which number belongs to which thing. For example, suppose you come into a room and see that there are 15 people but only 10 chairs. The ratio of people to chairs is 15 to 10.

15 (people) to 10 (chairs) 15:10 $\frac{15}{10} = \frac{3}{2}$

Thus, there are 3 people for every 2 chairs.

What is the ratio of chairs to people?

10 (chairs) to 15 (people) 10:15 $\frac{10}{15} = \frac{2}{3}$

Thus, there are only 2 chairs for every 3 people.

Here is another example. Suppose that last season a basketball team won 18 games and lost 6. The ratio of games won to games lost is 18 to 6.

18 (won) to 6 (lost) 18:6 $\frac{18}{6} = \frac{3}{1}$

Thus, the team won 3 games to every game it lost.

What is the ratio of games lost to games won?

6 (lost) to 18 (won) 6:18 $\frac{6}{18} = \frac{1}{3}$

Thus, the team lost 1 game to every 3 it won.

Although the two numbers in a ratio belong to two different things, they can often be put in the same unit. For example, suppose you are a salesperson earning 2 cents commission on every dollar's worth of merchandise you sell. Since 1 dollar equals 100 cents, you can put both numbers of the ratio in cents.

2¢ (commission) to 100¢ (sales) 2:100 $\frac{2}{100} = \frac{1}{50}$

Thus, the ratio of commission to sales is $\frac{1}{50}$.

Here is another example. Suppose you are drawing a plan for a new garage you want to build. You decide that 1 inch on your drawing will stand for 3 feet of the garage. Since 1 foot equals 12 inches, you can put both numbers of the ratio in inches.

1 inch (drawing) to 3 feet (garage)

$3 \times 12 \text{ inches} = 36 \text{ inches}$

1 inch (drawing) to 36 inches (garage) 1:36 $\frac{1}{36}$

Thus, the ratio of length on your drawing to length of the garage is $\frac{1}{36}$. Another way of saying this is that the scale of your drawing is 1:36. Scale on drawings and maps is usually written with a colon, not as a fraction.

In some ratios the two numbers cannot be put in the same unit. For example, suppose you travelled 110 miles in 2 hours. There is no unit of distance that equals an hour, and there is no unit of time that equals a mile. So you must leave the ratio in different units.

110 miles to 2 hours 110:2 $\frac{110}{2} = \frac{55}{1}$

Thus, the ratio of distance travelled to travel time is $\frac{55}{1}$. Another way of saying this is that you travelled 55 miles per hour. "Per hour" means "in one hour."

Check your skill at reading and understanding ratios by doing this exercise.

Exercise for Subskill 11A

1. A recipe calls for three cups of flour to one cup of sugar. What is the ratio of flour to sugar?

2. The flywheel in a machine turns 9,000 times in 5 minutes. Another word for "turn" is "revolve," and one turn is one revolution. What is the ratio of revolutions to minutes? Give your answer in revolutions per minute. "Per minute" means "in one minute."

3. To make a certain shade of yellow, you must mix 2 quarts of white paint with 3 quarts of yellow paint. What is the ratio of white paint to yellow paint?

4. What is the ratio of 5 inches to 1 foot?

5. What is the ratio of 400 homes to 500 television sets?

Check your answers on page 18 in the Answer Key for Book One. If you correctly answered four of the five problems, go to the next subskill. If not, complete the following Supplemental Exercise.

Supplemental Exercise for Subskill 11A

Read Subskill 11A again. Work through the examples as you read them. Then solve the following problems on page 233.

1. To make orange juice from orange juice concentrate, you add 3 cans of water to 1 can of concentrate. What is the ratio of water to concentrate?

2. It takes you 3 hours to drive 120 miles. What is the ratio of miles to hours? Give your answer in miles per hour.

3. To make the fuel for a certain motor, you must add 2 quarts of oil to every 15 gallons of gas. What is the ratio of oil to gas? (Note: 1 gallon contains 4 quarts.)

4. What is the ratio of 5 dimes to 1 dollar?

5. What is the ratio of 300 cars to 500 families?

Check your answer, on page 18 in the Answer Key for Book One. If you correctly answered four of the five problems, go to the next subskill. If not, ask your instructor for help.

Subskill 11B: Solving Proportions

After studying this subskill you will be able to solve proportions.

What Is a Proportion?

A **proportion** is a statement that two ratios are equal. Thus,

$$\frac{3}{4} = \frac{6}{8}$$

states that the ratio $\frac{3}{4}$ is equal to the ratio $\frac{6}{8}$.

Proportions can also be written with colons:

$$3:4 = 6:8$$

Regardless of whether the proportion is written as a fraction or with colons, it is read: "Three is to four as six is to eight."

EXAMPLE: How would you write the proportion "twelve is to eight as three is to two"?

Answer: $\frac{12}{8} = \frac{3}{2}$ or $12:8 = 3:2$

How can you tell if the two ratios in a proportion are really equal? By cross multiplying them. Multiply the top of one ratio by the bottom of the other ratio, and vice versa. For example:

$$\frac{3}{4} \times \frac{6}{8} \qquad \begin{matrix} 3 \times 8 \\ 4 \times 6 \end{matrix}$$

If the answers to the two multiplication problems are the same, the two ratios are equal.

$4 \times 6 = 24$

$3 \times 8 = 24$

Since 24 is the same as 24, the two ratios are equal.

If the answers to the two multiplication problems are not the same, then the two ratios are not equal. And if the two ratios are not equal, what you were given is not a true proportion.

EXAMPLE: Is $\frac{3}{4} = \frac{9}{10}$ a true proportion?

First, cross multiply.

$$\frac{3}{4} \times \frac{9}{10} \qquad \begin{matrix} 4 \times 9 \\ 3 \times 10 \end{matrix}$$

The answers are:

$4 \times 9 = 36$
$3 \times 10 = 30$

Compare the answers. Since 36 and 30 are not the same, $\frac{3}{4}$ does not equal $\frac{9}{10}$. What you were given is not a true proportion.

Answer: No, it is not.

Solving Proportions

You can also use cross multiplication to find an unknown number in a proportion if you know the other three numbers.

EXAMPLE: 5 is to 10 as 20 is to an unknown number. What is the unknown number?

First, write the proportion. Let x stand for the unknown number.

$$\frac{5}{10} = \frac{20}{x}$$

Then cross multiply.

$$\frac{5}{10} \times \frac{20}{x} \qquad \begin{matrix} 10 \times 20 \\ 5 \times x \end{matrix}$$

The answers are:

$10 \times 20 = 200$

$5 \times x = 5x$ $5x$ means 5 x's, whatever x is.

Assuming that the proportion is a true proportion, the two answers must be equal.

$200 = 5x$

If 5 x's equal 200, what does 1 x equal? To solve this problem, divide by the number of x's—in this case, by 5. Divide *both* $5x$ and 200 by 5 to keep them equal.

$$\frac{\overset{40}{\cancel{200}}}{\underset{1}{\cancel{5}}} = \frac{\overset{1}{\cancel{5}x}}{\underset{1}{\cancel{5}}}$$ You can cancel.

Since $1x$ is simply x, the answer is

$x = 40$

Finally, check your answer by changing the x to 40 in the original proportion. Is it still a true proportion?

$\frac{5}{10} = \frac{20}{40}$

Cross multiply.

$$\frac{5}{10} \times \frac{20}{40} \qquad \begin{matrix} 10 \times 20 \\ 5 \times 40 \end{matrix}$$

The answers are:

$10 \times 20 = 200$

$5 \times 40 = 200$

Since 200 is the same as 200, this is still a true proportion and the answer $x = 40$ is correct.

Answer: 40.

EXAMPLE: If 9 is to an unknown number as 3 is to 2, what is the unknown number?

$\frac{9}{x} = \frac{3}{2}$ Write the proportion. Let x stand for the unknown number.

$\frac{9}{x} \times \frac{3}{2}$ Cross multiply. $x \times 3$ / 9×2

$x \times 3 = x3$
$9 \times 2 = 18$

$x3$ means x number of 3's. It can also be written $3x$, meaning 3 x's. In multiplication, it doesn't matter which number comes first. For example, $9 \times 2 = 18$ and $2 \times 9 = 18$.

Assuming this is a true proportion, the two answers must be equal.

$3x = 18$

If $3x = 18$, what does $1x$ equal?

$\frac{\overset{1}{\cancel{3}x}}{\underset{1}{\cancel{3}}} = \frac{\overset{6}{\cancel{18}}}{\underset{1}{\cancel{3}}}$ Divide by the number of x's—in this case, by 3. You can cancel.

Check your answer by changing x to 6 in the original proportion. Is it still a true proportion?

$\frac{9}{6} = \frac{3}{2}$ Change x to 6.

$\frac{9}{6} \times \frac{3}{2}$ Cross multiply.

$6 \times 3 = 18$
$9 \times 2 = 18$

Since 18 is the same as 18, this is still a true proportion and the answer $x = 6$ is correct. Answer: 6

Check your skill at telling whether a proportion is true and at solving proportions by doing this exercise.

Exercise for Subskill 11B

In problems 1–10, use cross multiplication to tell whether each proportion is true. Write "T" in the blank if it is a true proportion. Write "F" if it is not.

1. $\frac{1}{2} = \frac{4}{10}$ ______

2. $\frac{3}{6} = \frac{4}{8}$ ______

3. $\frac{2}{3} = \frac{12}{18}$ ______

4. $\frac{90}{100} = \frac{9}{10}$ ______

5. $\frac{2}{5} = \frac{4}{6}$ ______

6. $\frac{7}{8} = \frac{21}{24}$ ______

7. $\frac{40}{45} = \frac{8}{10}$ ______

8. $\frac{6}{8} = \frac{9}{12}$ ______

9. $\frac{4}{5} = \frac{6}{7}$ ______

10. $\frac{18}{20} = \frac{16}{18}$ ______

In problems 11–20, what is x?

11. $\frac{7}{9} = \frac{21}{x}$

12. $\frac{20}{x} = \frac{5}{4}$

13. $\frac{x}{3} = \frac{10}{15}$

14. $\frac{15}{9} = \frac{5}{x}$

15. $\frac{x}{9} = \frac{1}{3}$

16. $\frac{2}{3} = \frac{x}{18}$

17. $\frac{5}{x} = \frac{20}{28}$

18. $\frac{x}{3} = \frac{24}{36}$

19. $\frac{8}{x} = \frac{1}{2}$

20. $\frac{3}{5} = \frac{x}{25}$

Check your answers on page 18 in the Answer Key for Book One. If you correctly answered sixteen of the twenty problems, go to the next subskill. If not, complete the following Supplemental Exercise.

Supplemental Exercise for Subskill 11B

Read Subskill 11B again. Work through the examples as you read them. Then do this exercise.

In problems 1–10, use cross multiplication to tell whether each proportion is true. Write "T" in the blank if it is a true proportion. Write "F" if it is not.

1. $\frac{3}{4} = \frac{75}{100}$ ______

2. $\frac{7}{10} = \frac{8}{11}$ ______

3. $\frac{4}{9} = \frac{6}{11}$ ______

4. $\frac{3}{6} = \frac{8}{16}$ ______

5. $\frac{1}{5} = \frac{1}{10}$ ______

6. $\frac{8}{12} = \frac{12}{18}$ ______

7. $\frac{70}{75} = \frac{14}{15}$ ______ **8.** $\frac{3}{5} = \frac{33}{55}$ ______

9. $\frac{12}{15} = \frac{3}{5}$ ______ **10.** $\frac{20}{35} = \frac{4}{5}$ ______

In problems 11–20, what is x?

11. $\frac{x}{4} = \frac{5}{10}$ **12.** $\frac{7}{3} = \frac{x}{6}$

13. $\frac{8}{x} = \frac{4}{5}$ **14.** $\frac{4}{x} = \frac{2}{16}$

15. $\frac{100}{x} = \frac{25}{3}$ **16.** $\frac{x}{100} = \frac{3}{25}$

17. $\frac{7.5}{x} = \frac{2}{4}$ **18.** $\frac{6}{9} = \frac{x}{3}$

19. $\frac{15}{54} = \frac{10}{x}$ **20.** $\frac{x}{8} = \frac{6}{16}$

Check your answers on page 18 in the Answer Key for Book One. If you correctly answered sixteen of the twenty problems, go to the next subskill. If not, ask your instructor for help.

Subskill 11C: Solving Word Problems

After studying this subskill you will be able to use proportions to solve word problems.

First, read the entire problem carefully. For example, a train goes 120 miles in 2 hours. At that speed, how far will it go in 3 hours?

Next, write a proportion that shows the statements and questions given in the problem. Take the first sentence:

A train goes 120 miles in 2 hours

This sentence can be written as a ratio:

$$\frac{120}{2} \quad \begin{matrix}\text{miles}\\ \text{hours}\end{matrix}$$

Then look at the second sentence:

At that speed, how far will it go in 3 hours?

With x standing for the unknown number, this sentence can also be written as a ratio:

$$\frac{x}{3} \quad \begin{matrix} \text{miles} \\ \text{hours} \end{matrix}$$

Now you have a proportion:

$$\frac{120}{2} = \frac{x}{3} \quad \begin{matrix} \text{miles} \\ \text{hours} \end{matrix}$$

Notice that in both ratios the miles are on top and the hours are on the bottom. Whatever the problem is about, the things that the numbers belong to should be in the same position, top or bottom, in both ratios. Also notice that when you read this proportion in words, it sounds like the problem:

120 miles are to 2 hours as how many miles are to 3 hours?

Now you are ready to solve the proportion.

$$\begin{matrix} 120 & & x \\ 2 & & 3 \end{matrix}$$ Cross multiply. $$\begin{matrix} 2 \times x - 2x \\ 120 \times 3 = 360 \end{matrix}$$

$2x = 360$ What does $1x$ equal?

$$\frac{\overset{1}{\cancel{2}x}}{\underset{1}{\cancel{2}}} = \frac{\overset{180}{\cancel{360}}}{\underset{1}{\cancel{2}}}$$ Divide by the number of x's—in this case, by 2.

$x = 180$

Answer: The train will go 180 miles in 3 hours.

Finally, check your answer. Change x to 180 in the original proportion. Is it still a true proportion?

$$\frac{120}{2} = \frac{180}{3}$$ Change x to 180.

$$\begin{matrix} 120 & & 180 \\ 2 & & 3 \end{matrix}$$ Cross multiply.

$2 \times 180 = 360$
$120 \times 3 = 360$

Since 360 is the same as 360, this is still a true proportion and the answer $x = 180$ is correct.

EXAMPLE: Two cans of beans cost 50 cents. How much will 5 cans cost?

Write the first sentence in the problem as a ratio.

$\frac{2}{50}$ (cans) / (cents)

Then write the second sentence in the problem as a ratio. Let x stand for the unknown number.

$\frac{5}{x}$ (cans) / (cents)

Now you have a proposition:

$\frac{2}{50} = \frac{5}{x}$ (cans) / (cents) — Cans are on top of both ratios. Cents are on the bottom of both ratios.

Read the proportion in words.

2 cans are to 50 cents as 5 cans are to how much?

This sounds like the problem. You have written the proportion correctly.

Next, solve the proportion.

$\frac{2}{50} \times \frac{5}{x}$ Cross multiply. $50 \times 5 = 250$; $2 \times x = 2x$

$2x = 250.$ What does $1x$ equal?

$\frac{\overset{1}{\cancel{2}x}}{\underset{1}{\cancel{2}}} = \frac{\overset{125}{\cancel{250}}}{\underset{1}{\cancel{2}}}$ Divide by the number of x's—in this case, by 2.

$x = 125$

Finally, check your answer. Change x to 125 in the original proportion. Is it still a true proportion?

$\frac{2}{50} = \frac{5}{125}$ Change x to 125.

$\frac{2}{50} \times \frac{5}{125}$ Cross multiply. $50 \times 5 = 250$; $2 \times 125 = 250$

Since 250 is the same as 250, this is still a true proportion and the answer $x = 125$ is correct.

Answer: 5 cans of beans will cost 125 cents, or $1.25.

Check your skill at using proportions to solve word problems by doing this exercise.

Exercises for Subskill 11C

1. Paul walked 18 miles in 6 hours. If he kept going at the same speed, how far would he go in 8 hours?

2. Ted earns $300 in 5 days. With the same pay, how much will he earn in 10 days?

3. Eight cases of tomato juice cost $60. What would 12 cases cost?

4. A telephone pole casts a shadow that is 40 feet long. At the same time of day, a fence post casts a shadow that is 5 feet long. The fence post is 3 feet high. How high is the telephone pole?

5. Mary saved $60 in 4 weeks. If she keeps saving at the same rate, how much will she save in 10 weeks?

Check your answers on page 18 in the Answer Key for Book One. If you correctly answered four of the five problems, go to the Self-Check. If not, complete the following Supplemental Exercises.

Supplemental Exercises for Subskill 11C

Read Subskill 11C again. Work through the examples as you read them. Then do this exercise.

1. Orange juice concentrate is mixed with water in a ratio of 1 to 3. How much water should be mixed with 2 cans of concentrate?

2. Darlene's car used 4 gallons of gas on a 90-mile trip. If it gets the same mileage, how much gas will it use on a 225-mile trip?

3. A copying machine makes 50 copies in 2 minutes. How long will it take to make 125 copies?

4. Bell peppers are marked 3 for 84 cents. How much would two bell peppers cost?

5. Carolyn earns $34 for an 8-hour day. Yesterday she took 3 hours off without pay. How much money did she lose?

Check your answers on page 18 in the Answer Key for Book One. If you correctly answered four of the five problems, go to the Self-Check. If not, ask your instructor for help.

SELF-CHECK FOR SKILL UNIT 11

1. What is the ratio of 3 inches to 1 foot?

2. A restaurant has 24 tables and 3 waiters. What is the ratio of tables to waiters?

Tell whether each of the following proportions is true. Write "T" in the blank if it is a true proportion. Write "F" if it is not.

3. $\frac{2}{3} = \frac{6}{9}$ ______ 4. $\frac{7}{8} = \frac{13}{16}$ ______

5. $\frac{3}{2} = \frac{18}{12}$ ______ 6. $\frac{48}{100} = \frac{9}{20}$ ______

7. $\frac{1}{3} = \frac{5}{16}$ ______

Solve each of the following proportions.

8. $\frac{x}{8} = \frac{6}{16}$ 9. $\frac{7}{9} = \frac{x}{27}$

10. $\frac{5}{x} = \frac{35}{49}$ 11. $\frac{x}{6} = \frac{6}{9}$

12. $\frac{12}{16} = \frac{18}{x}$

Use proportions to solve the following word problems.

13. A photograph 3 inches wide and 4 inches long is enlarged to 9 inches wide. How long will it be?

14. Twelve peaches cost 98 cents. How much do eight peaches cost?

15. Two gallons of paint cover 450 square feet. How much paint do you need to cover 1,350 square feet?

Check your answers on page 18 in the Answer Key for Book One. If you correctly answered twelve of the fifteen problems, go on to Skill Unit 12. If not, ask your instructor for help.

Skill Unit 12
PERCENTS

What Skills You Need to Begin: Basic operations with whole numbers, fractions, decimals, ratio, and proportion (Skill Units, 1 through 11).

What Skills You Will Learn: After studying this skill unit, you will be able to read and write percents, change percents to decimals and decimals to percents, and change percents to fractions and fractions to percents.

Why You Need This Skill: You use percents when you do your income tax return, when you figure the amount of interest you will pay on a loan or installment purchase, and on many jobs you might like to qualify for. In order to use percents, you must understand what they are and what they mean in terms of decimals and fractions.

How You Will Show What You Have Learned: At the end of this skill unit is a Self-Check consisting of twenty problems involving percents. You should allow yourself one hour to do the Self-Check. To prove that you have mastered this skill you must correctly answer sixteen of the twenty problems.

If you feel you have already mastered this skill, do the Self-Check on pages 259 and 260.

Subskill 12A: Reading and Writing Percents

After studying this subskill you will be able to read and write percents.

What Is a Percent?

The word "**percent**" means "in one hundred." Thus, 5 percent means "five in one hundred" and is equal to the fraction $\frac{5}{100}$. In the same way,

25 percent equals $\frac{25}{100}$

100 percent equals $\frac{100}{100}$, or the whole number 1

Percent is usually written with the symbol %. Read 51% as "fifty-one percent."

You can picture 100% as a block with 100 squares in it. If 6 squares are shaded, 6% of the block is shaded.

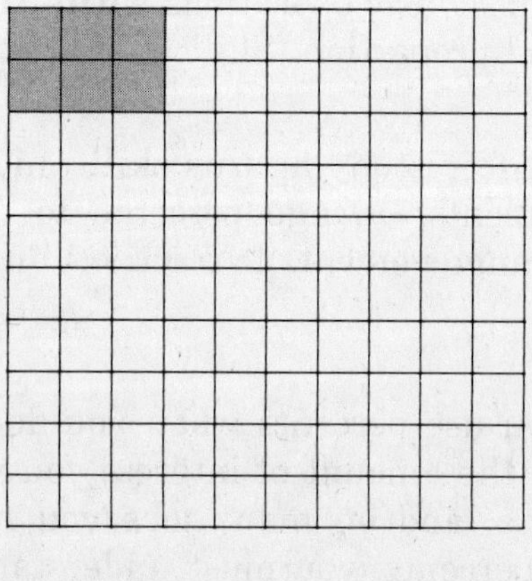

This block has 100 squares in it. Six of the squares are shaded. Therefore, 6% of the block is shaded, or $\frac{6}{100}$ of the block is shaded.

Here are more examples:

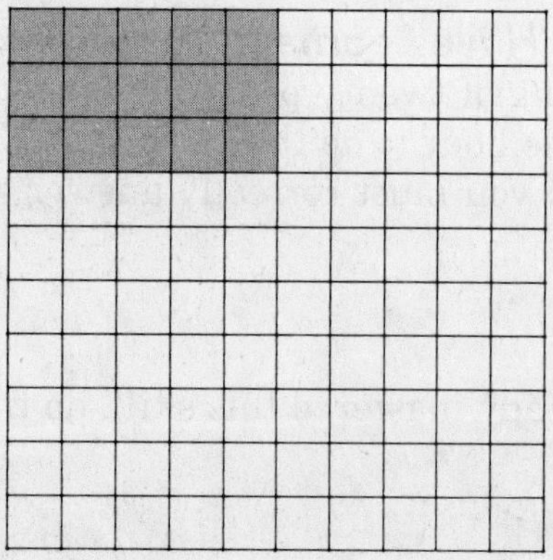

15 squares are shaded. Therefore, 15% of the block is shaded, or $\frac{15}{100}$ of the block is shaded.

50 squares are shaded. Therefore, 50% of the block is shaded, or $\frac{50}{100}$ of the block is shaded.

Percents Over 100

Even though "percent" means "in one hundred," a percent can be more than 100. A percent larger than 100 is equal to an improper fraction—that is, a fraction whose numerator is larger than its denominator. For example:

$105\% = \frac{105}{100}$

$115\% = \frac{115}{100}$

$200\% = \frac{200}{100}$, or 2

$310\% = \frac{310}{100}$

Percents Less Than 1

A percent can also be less than 1. It can be a fraction of 1% such as $\frac{1}{2}\%$. This is read "one half of one percent." Or it can be a decimal of 1% such as .2%. This is read "two tenths of one percent."

Check your skill at reading and writing percents by doing this exercise.

Exercise for Subskill 12A

What percent of each block is shaded?

1.

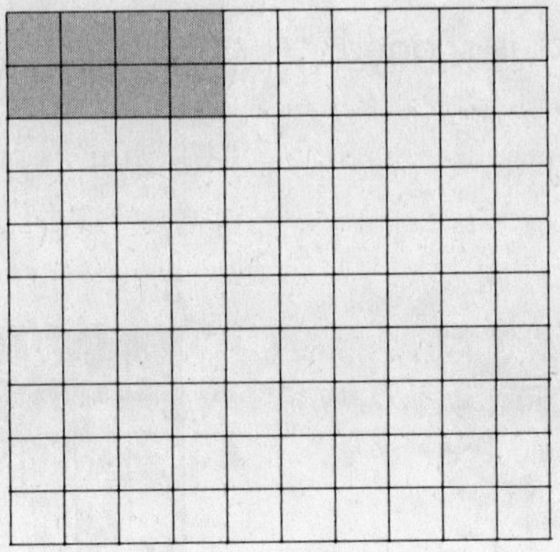

_____%

2.

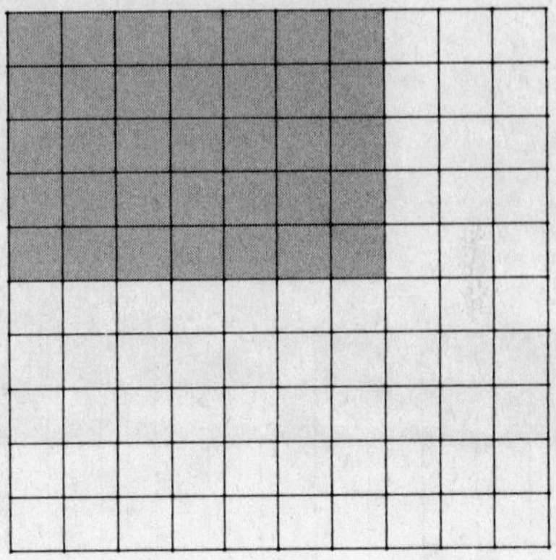

_____%

3.

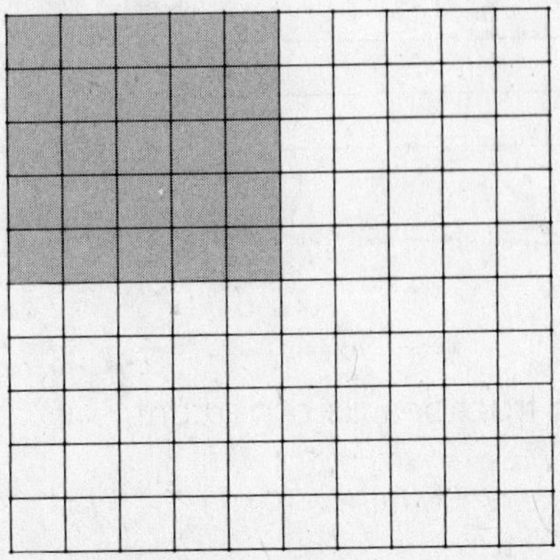

_____%

Write each of the following fractions as a percent.

4. $\frac{45}{100}$ **5.** $\frac{1}{100}$

6. $\frac{128}{100}$ **7.** $\frac{4}{100}$

Write each of the following percents as a fraction.

8. 42% **9.** 255%

10. 75%

Check your answers on page 19 in the Answer Key for Book One. If you correctly answered eight of the ten problems, go the next subskill. If not, complete the following Supplemental Exercise.

Supplemental Exercise for Subskill 12A

Read Subskill 12A again. Work through the examples as you read them. Then do this exercise.

What percent of each block is shaded?

1.

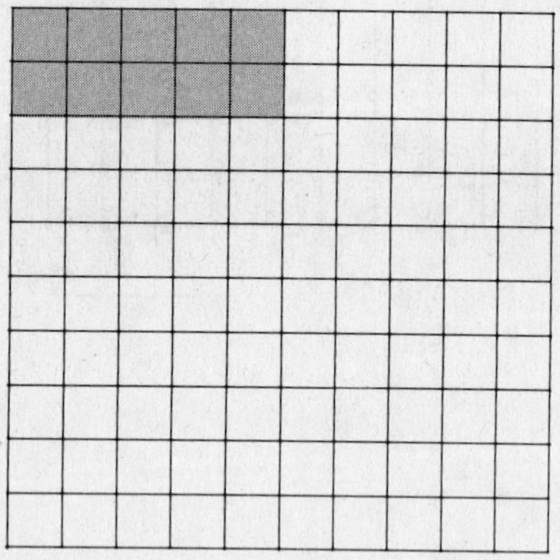

_____%

2.

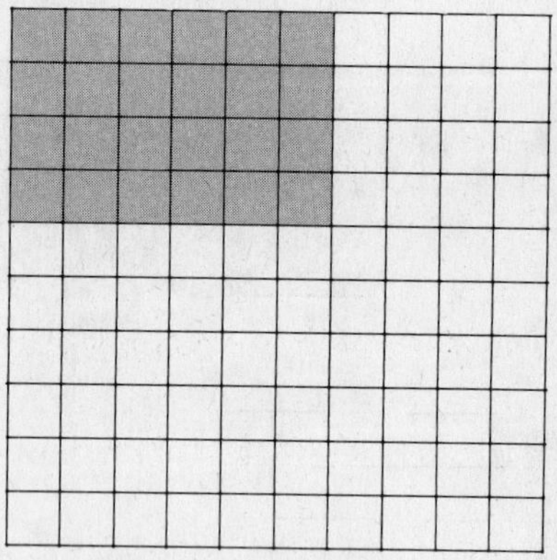

_____%

3.

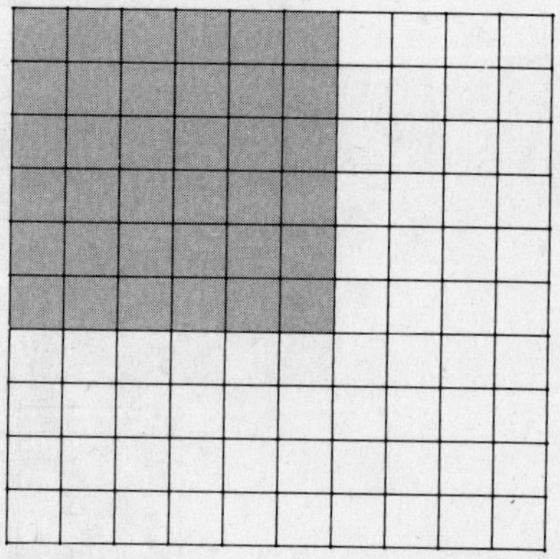

_____%

Write each of the following fractions as a percent.

4. $\frac{33}{100}$ **5.** $\frac{210}{100}$ **6.** $\frac{8}{100}$

Write each of the following percents as a fraction.

7. 6% **8.** 25%

9. 180% **10.** 15%

Check your answers on page 19 in the Answer Key for Book One. If you correctly answered eight of the ten problems, go to the next subskill. If not, ask your instructor for help.

Subskill 12B: Changing Percents to Decimals

After studying this subskill you will be able to change percents to decimals.

To change a percent to a decimal, drop the word "percent" or the symbol % and move the decimal point two places to the left.

EXAMPLE: Change 97% to a decimal.

97 First drop the symbol.

Now, where is the decimal point? In any number that has no decimal point, it is understood to be at the right end of the number.

97. Put in the decimal point.

Then move the decimal point two places to the left.

.97

Answer: 97% = .97 (97 hundredths)

EXAMPLE: Change 5% to a decimal.

5 Drop the symbol.

5. Put in the decimal point.

Although you must move the decimal point two places to the left, 5. only has one place. Therefore you must put in a 0 to the left of the 5 to serve as a placeholder.

05.

Then you can move the decimal point two places to the left.

.05

Answer: 5% = .05 (5 hundredths)

EXAMPLE: Change 375% to a decimal.

375	Drop the symbol.
375.	Put in the decimal point.
3.75	Move the decimal point two places to the left. No matter how many numbers you have, you always move the decimal point two places.

Answer: 375% = 3.75 (3 and 75 hundredths)

EXAMPLE: Change 100% to a decimal.

100	Drop the symbol.
100.	Put in the decimal point.
1.00	Move the decimal point two places to the left.
100% = 1	When a percent like 100%, 200%, or 300% is changed to a decimal, the answer is a whole number.

Here is one more example. Percents sometimes have decimals in them. You might read, for example, that 87.3% of all cars have radios.

EXAMPLE: Change 87.3% to a decimal.

87.3	Drop the symbol.
87.3	The decimal point is already there. You do not need to put it in.
.873	Move the decimal point two places to the left.

Answer: 87.3% = .873 (873 thousandths)

Check your skill at changing percents to decimals by doing the following exercise on page 249.

Exercise for Subskill 12B

Change each of the following percents to a decimal.

1. 20% **2.** 8%

3. 62.5% **4.** 400%

5. 125% **6.** 17%

7. 5% **8.** 175%

9. 3.1% **10.** 1%

Check your answers on page 19 in the Answer Key for Book One. If you correctly answered eight of the ten problems, go to the next subskill. If not, complete the following Supplemental Exercise.

Supplemental Exercise for Subskill 12B

Read Subskill 12B again. Work through the examples as you read them. Then do this exercise.

Change each of the following percents to a decimal.

1. 25% **2.** 40%

3. 7% **4.** 37.5%

5. 600% **6.** 270%

7. 75% **8.** 3%

9. 8.8% **10.** 150%

Check your answers on page 19 in the Answer Key for Book One. If you correctly answered eight of the ten problems, go to the next subskill. If not, ask your instructor for help.

Subskill 12C: Changing Decimals to Percents

After studying this subskill you will be able to change decimals to percents.

As you just learned, a percent is changed to a decimal by moving the decimal point two places to the left. Changing a decimal to a percent is just the opposite. You move the decimal point two places to the right.

EXAMPLE: Change .32 to a percent.

First, move the decimal point two places to the right.

32.

Now the decimal point is at the right end of the number, so you can drop it. Add the word "percent" or the percent symbol.

32% Drop the decimal point and put in %.

Answer: .32 = 32%

EXAMPLE: Change .09 to a percent.

.09 Move the decimal point two places to the right.

9. You can drop the 0 because it is no longer needed as a placeholder.

9% Drop the decimal point and put in %.

Answer: .09 = 9%

EXAMPLE: Change 1.19 to a percent.

119. Move the decimal point two places to the right.

119% Drop the decimal point and put in %.

Answer: 1.19 = 119%

EXAMPLE: Change .6 to a percent.

.6 There is only one decimal place. How can you move the decimal point two places to the right?

.60 Put in a 0 to the right of the 6 to serve as a placeholder.

60. Then move the decimal point two places to the right.

60% Drop the decimal point and add %.

Answer: .6 = 60%

One more example follows on page 251.

EXAMPLE: Change .417 to a percent.

41.7	Move the decimal point two places to the right.
41.7	Should you drop the decimal point? No, because it's not at the right end of the number.
41.7%	Leave the decimal point as it is and add %.

Answer: .417 = 41.7%

Note that you always move the decimal points two places to the right.

.2 = 20%	Even if you have to put in a 0 as a placeholder.
2.42 = 242%	Even if the answer is over 100%.
.861 = 86.1%	And even if the answer has a decimal in it.
.002 = .2%	
.0555 = 5.55%	

Check your skill at changing decimals to percents by doing this exercise.

Exercise for Subskill 12C

Change each of the following decimals to a percent.

1. .03 **2.** .37

3. .625 **4.** .006

5. 1.39 **6.** .8

7. .085 **8.** .015

9. .16 **10.** .5

Check your answers on page 19 in the Answer Key for Book One. If you correctly answered eight of the ten problems, go to the next subskill. If not, complete the following Supplemental Exercise.

Supplemental Exercise for Subskill 12C

Read Subskill 12C again. Work through the examples as you read them. Then do the exercise on page 252.

Change each of the following decimals to a percent.

1. .87 **2.** .1

3. 1.19 **4.** .25

5. .505 **6.** .032

7. 4.75 **8.** .09

9. .74 **10.** .3

Check your answers on page 19 in the Answer Key for Book One. If you correctly answered eight of the ten problems, go to the next subskill. If not, ask your instructor for help.

Subskill 12D: Changing Percents to Fractions

After studying this subskill you will be able to change percents to fractions.

To change a percent to a fraction, first change it to a decimal and then change the decimal to a fraction. For example, here is how to change 15% to a fraction.

First, change the percent to a decimal.

$15\% = .15$ Change the percent to a decimal by dropping the % symbol and moving the decimal point two places to the left.

Then change the decimal to a fraction.

$.15 = \frac{15}{100}$

Finally, reduce the fraction to its lowest terms.

$\frac{15}{100} \div \frac{5}{5} = \frac{3}{20}$ Answer: $15\% = \frac{3}{20}$

EXAMPLE: Change 4% to a fraction.

$4\% = .04$ First change the percent to a decimal. To move the decimal point two places to the left, you must put in a 0 as a placeholder.

$.04 = \frac{4}{100}$ Then change the decimal to a fraction.

$\frac{4}{100} \div \frac{4}{4} = \frac{1}{25}$ Finally, reduce the fraction to its lowest terms.

Answer: 4% $= \frac{1}{25}$

There are some fractions that cannot be reduced to lower terms.

EXAMPLE: Change 39% to a fraction.

39% = .39 Change the percent to a decimal.

$.39 = \frac{39}{100}$ Change the decimal to a fraction.

$\frac{39}{100}$ This fraction cannot be reduced to lower terms.

Answer: 39% $= \frac{39}{100}$

Here is a different example.

EXAMPLE: Change 325% to a fraction.

325% = 3.25 To change a percent to a decimal, you always move the decimal point two places to the left, no matter how many numbers you have. In this case, you get a whole number and a decimal—3 and 25 hundredths.

$3.25 = 3\frac{25}{100}$ Change the decimal part to a fraction.

$\frac{25}{100} \div \frac{25}{25} = \frac{1}{4}$ Reduce the fraction to its lowest terms, but don't forget the whole number in your answer.

Answer: 325% $= 3\frac{1}{4}$

Here is a percent with a decimal in it.

EXAMPLE: Change 37.5% to a fraction.

37.5% = .375 Change the entire percent to a decimal. Note that when you move the decimal point two places to the left, you get a decimal with three places—375 thousandths.

$.375 = \frac{375}{1,000}$ Change the decimal to a fraction. Since the decimal is 375 thousandths, the bottom number of the fraction must be 1,000.

$\frac{375}{1,000} \div \frac{125}{125} = \frac{3}{8}$ Reduce the fraction to its lowest terms.

Answer: $37.5\% = \frac{3}{8}$

Here is a percent with a fraction in it.

EXAMPLE: Change $6\frac{1}{4}\%$ to a fraction.

This takes an extra step. First you must change the fraction to a decimal.

$\frac{1}{4}$ means $4\overline{)1}$

$4\overline{)1.00}$ with quotient .25 — Do the division.

So

$\frac{1}{4} = .25$

And

$6\frac{1}{4} = 6.25\%$

Now change the entire percent to a decimal.

$6.25\% = .0625$ To move the decimal point two places to the left, you must add a 0 as a placeholder. You get a decimal with four places—625 ten thousandths.

$.0625 = \frac{625}{10,000}$ Change the decimal to a fraction. Since the decimal is 625 ten thousandths, the bottom number of the fraction must be 10,000.

$\frac{625}{10,000} \div \frac{625}{625} = \frac{1}{16}$ Reduce the fraction to its lowest terms.

Answer: $6\frac{1}{4}\% = \frac{1}{16}$

Check your skill at changing percents to fractions by doing this exercise.

Exercise for Subskill 12D

Change each of the following percents first to a decimal and then to a fraction.

	Decimal	Fraction		Decimal	Fraction
1. 45% =	______ =	______	**2.** 120% =	______ =	______
3. 71% =	______ =	______	**4.** $12\frac{1}{2}\%$ =	______ =	______
5. 2.5% =	______ =	______	**6.** 416% =	______ =	______
7. 8% =	______ =	______	**8.** 18.75%	______ =	______
9. 9% =	______ =	______	**10.** $31\frac{1}{4}\%$ =	______ =	______

Check your answers on page 19 in the Answer Key for Book One. If you correctly answered eight of the ten problems, go to the next subskill. If not, complete the following Supplemental Exercise.

Supplemental Exercise for Subskill 12D

Read Subskill 12D again. Work through the examples as you read them. Then do this exercise.

Change each of the following percents first to a decimal and then to a fraction.

	Decimal	Fraction		Decimal	Fraction
1. 60% =	______ =	______	**2.** 5% =	______ =	______
3. 7.5% =	______ =	______	**4.** 43% =	______ =	______

5. $62\frac{1}{2}$ = ________ = ________ **6.** 11% = ________ = ________

7. $43\frac{3}{4}\%$ = ________ = ________ **8.** 120% = ________ = ________

9. 87.5% = ________ = ________ **10.** 2% = ________ = ________

Check your answers on page 19 in the Answer Key for Book One. If you correctly answered eight of the 10 problems, go on to the next subskill. If not, ask your instructor for help.

Subskill 12E: Changing Fractions to Percents

After studying this subskill you will be able to change fractions to percents.

To change a fraction to a percent, first change the fraction to a decimal, and then change the decimal to a percent.

EXAMPLE: Change $\frac{1}{2}$ to a percent.

First, change the fraction to a decimal.

$\frac{1}{2}$ means $2\overline{)1}$

$$\begin{array}{r} .5 \\ 2\overline{)1.0} \end{array}$$ Do the division.

$\frac{1}{2} = .5$

Then change the decimal to a percent.

.5 = 50.% To move the decimal point two places to the right, you must put in a 0 after the 5 as a placeholder.

Answer: $\frac{1}{2}$ = 50%

Here is another example.

EXAMPLE: Change $\frac{7}{8}$ to a percent.

$$\begin{array}{r} .875 \\ 8\overline{)7.000} \\ -6\,4 \\ \hline 60 \\ -56 \\ \hline 40 \\ -40 \\ \hline \end{array}$$

First, change the fraction to a decimal by doing the division.

$.875 = 87.5\%$ Then change the decimal to a percent by moving the decimal point two places to the right. You get a percent with a decimal in it.

Answer: $\frac{7}{8} = 87.5\%$

Sometimes the division does not come out even.

EXAMPLE: Change $\frac{2}{3}$ to a percent.

First, change $\frac{2}{3}$ to a decimal.

$$\begin{array}{r} .6666 \\ 3\overline{)2.0000} \\ -1\,8 \\ \hline 20 \\ -18 \\ \hline 20 \\ -18 \\ \hline 20 \\ -18 \\ \hline 2 \end{array}$$

Carry the division out to four decimal places. (You can show that the same number will continue to repeat by using the sign for the repeating decimal, $.\overline{6666}$. The answer may also be rounded-off.)

Round the decimal off to the nearest thousandth.

.6666 rounds to .667

Then change the decimal to a percent.

$.667 = 66.7\%$ Move the decimal point two places to the right.

Answer: $\frac{2}{3} = 66.7\%$

Here is an example involving a mixed number.

EXAMPLE: Change $4\frac{3}{8}$ to a percent.

First, change the fractional part of the mixed number to a decimal.

$\frac{3}{8}$ means $8\overline{)3}$

$$\begin{array}{r} .375 \\ 8\overline{)3.000} \\ -2\,4 \\ \hline 60 \\ -56 \\ \hline 40 \\ -40 \\ \hline 0 \end{array}$$

Do the division.

Then add the decimal to the whole number.

$4 + .375 = 4.375$

Finally, change the entire number to a percent.

$4.375 = 437.5\%$ Move the decimal point two places to the right.

Answer: $4\frac{3}{8} = 437.5\%$

Check your skill at changing fractions to percents by doing this exercise.

Exercise for Subskill 12E

Change each of the following fractions first to a decimal and then to a percent.

	Decimal	Percent		Decimal	Percent
1. $\frac{1}{5}$ =	______ =	______	**2.** $\frac{3}{4}$ =	______ =	______
3. $\frac{1}{8}$ =	______ =	______	**4.** $\frac{1}{3}$ =	______ =	______
5. $2\frac{1}{25}$ =	______ =	______	**6.** $\frac{3}{20}$ =	______ =	______
7. $\frac{4}{5}$ =	______ =	______	**8.** $\frac{9}{10}$ =	______ =	______

9. $\frac{1}{7}$ = ______ = ______ **10.** $1\frac{3}{10}$ = ______ = ______

Check your answers on page 20 in the Answer Key for Book One. If you correctly answered eight of the ten problems, go to the Self-Check. If not, complete the following Supplemental exercise.

Supplemental Exercise for Subskill 12E

Read Subskill 12E again. Work through the examples as you read them. Then do this exercise.

Change each of the following fractions first to a decimal and then to a percent.

	Decimal	Percent		Decimal	Percent
1. $\frac{7}{10}$ =	______ =	______	**2.** $\frac{3}{5}$ =	______ =	______
3. $3\frac{3}{16}$ =	______ =	______	**4.** $\frac{1}{10}$ =	______ =	______
5. $\frac{3}{8}$ =	______ =	______	**6.** $\frac{1}{20}$ =	______ =	______
7. $\frac{7}{50}$ =	______ =	______	**8.** $\frac{1}{25}$ =	______ =	______
9. $2\frac{1}{4}$ =	______ =	______	**10.** $\frac{1}{6}$ =	______ =	______

Check your answers on page 20 in the Answer Key for Book One. If you correctly answered eight of the ten problems, go to the Self-Check. If not, ask your instructor for help.

SELF-CHECK FOR SKILL UNIT 12

Change each of the following percents to a decimal.

1. 48% **2.** 200% **3.** 3%

Change each of the following decimals to a percent.

4. .2 **.5** .05 **6.** .075

Change each of the following percents to a fraction.

7. 25% **8.** 87.5% **9.** 19%

Change each of the following fractions to a percent.

10. $\frac{1}{20}$ **11.** $\frac{3}{8}$ **12.** $\frac{1}{3}$

Fill in the blanks.

	Fraction		Decimal		Percent
13.	$\frac{1}{8}$	=	______	=	______
14.	______	=	.015	=	______
15.	______	=	______	=	30%
16.	______	=	______	=	5%

Check your answers on page 20 in the Answer Key for Book One. If you correctly answered twelve of the sixteen problems, go on to Skill Unit 13. If not, ask your instructor for help.

Skill Unit 13
SOLVING PERCENT PROBLEMS

What Skills You Need to Begin: Basic operations with whole numbers, fractions, decimals, ratio, proportion, and percents (Skill Units 1–12).

What Skills You Will Learn: After studying this skill unit, you will be able to find what number is a certain percent of another number, to find what percent one number is of another, to find an unknown number when another number is a certain percent of it, and to figure interest.

Why You Need This Skill: You need to solve percent problems in figuring discounts on purchases and sales, in figuring interest on loans and deposits, and in doing your tax return.

How You Will Show What You Have Learned: At the end of this skill unit is a Self-Check consisting of fifteen problems involving percents. You should allow yourself two hours to do the Self-Check. To prove that you have mastered this skill, you must correctly answer twelve of the fifteen problems.

If you feel you have already mastered percent problems, do the Self-Check on page 276.

Subskill 13A: Finding What Number Is a Certain Percent of Another Number

After studying this subskill you will be able to find what number is a certain percent of another number.

For example, what is 10% of 150? To solve this problem, first, write the percent as a fraction. Then use that fraction to write the problem as a proportion. And finally, solve the proportion for the unknown number.

EXAMPLE: What is 10% of 150?

First, write the percent as a fraction.

$10\% = \frac{10}{100}$ You do not need to reduce the fraction to lower terms.

Then use the fraction to write the problem as a proportion.

$\frac{10}{100} = \frac{x}{150}$ *x* stands for the unknown number.

Finally, solve the proportion for the unknown number. (You may need to review Skill Unit 11.)

$\frac{10}{100} \times \frac{x}{150}$ $\quad x = 100x$, $\quad 150 = 1500$ Cross multiply.

$100x = 1500$

$\frac{\cancel{100}^{1}x}{\cancel{100}_{1}} = \frac{\cancel{1500}^{15}}{\cancel{100}_{1}}$ Divide both numbers by 100 to keep them equal. You can cancel.

$x = 15$

Answer: 15 is 10% of 150.

The only hard step is to write the problem correctly as a proportion. Let's take another example.

EXAMPLE: What is 5% of 200?

First, write the percent as a fraction.

$5\% = \frac{5}{100}$

Then use the fraction to write the problem as a proportion. But where does the 200 go, the top or the bottom?

$\frac{5}{100} = \frac{200}{x}$ *or* $\frac{5}{100} = \frac{x}{200}$

To answer this question, note that in the percent fraction, 5 is a part of the whole, and the whole is 100. The part is on top and the whole is on the bottom.

$\frac{5 \text{ (part)}}{100 \text{ (whole)}}$ 5% or $\frac{5}{100}$ means 5 parts out of a whole of 100.

On the other side of the proportion, the part must also be on top and the whole must be on the bottom.

$$\frac{5}{100} = \frac{\text{Part}}{\text{Whole}}$$

Now which is 200, the part or the whole? Which is x? In any such problem, the *part* usually comes just before or after the word "is." The *whole* usually follows the word "of."

In this problem, "What is 5% of 200?", the unknown—"What"—comes just before the "is." This must be the part. The 200 follows "of," so it must be the whole.

$$\frac{5 \text{ (part)}}{100 \text{ (whole)}} = \frac{x \text{ (part)}}{200 \text{ (whole)}}$$

The correct proportion is

$$\frac{5}{100} = \frac{x}{200}$$

Finally you can solve the proportion for the unknown number.

$$\frac{5}{100} \times \frac{x}{200} \quad \begin{matrix} = 100x \\ = 1{,}000 \end{matrix}$$ Cross multiply.

$100x = 1{,}000$

$$\frac{\overset{1}{\cancel{100}x}}{\underset{1}{\cancel{100}}} = \frac{\overset{10}{\cancel{1{,}000}}}{\underset{1}{\cancel{100}}}$$ Divide both numbers by 100. You can cancel.

$x = 10$

Answer: 10 is 5% of 200.

Here is another example.

EXAMPLE: What is 12.5% of \$360?

First, write the percent as a fraction.

$12.5\% = \frac{12.5}{100}$ You can leave the decimal in the fraction.

Then use the fraction to write the problem as a proportion. In the percent side of the proportion, the part is on top and the whole is on the bottom. The other side of the proportion must be the same.

$$\frac{12.5}{100} = \frac{\text{Part}}{\text{Whole}}$$

Look at the problem again: What is 12.5% of $360? The unknown—"what"—comes just before the "is," so it must be the part. The $360 follows "of," so it must be the whole. The correct proportion is

$$\frac{12.5}{100} = \frac{x}{\$360}$$

Finally, solve the proportion for the unknown number.

$$\frac{12.5}{100} \times \frac{x}{\$360} \quad \begin{matrix} = 100x \\ = \$4{,}500 \end{matrix}$$ Cross multiply.

$$100x = \$4{,}500$$

$$\frac{\overset{1}{\cancel{100}x}}{\underset{1}{\cancel{100}}} = \frac{\overset{\$45}{\cancel{\$4{,}500}}}{\underset{1}{\cancel{100}}}$$ Divide each side by 100.

$$x = \$45$$

Answer: $45 is 12.5% of $360.

Check your skill at finding what number is a certain percent of another number by doing this exercise.

Exercise for Subskill 13A

1. What is 50% of 60?
2. What is 75% of 8?
3. What is 8.2% of $2,200?
4. What is 26% of 150?
5. What is 88% of 110?

6. The Hofstrands are buying a washer and dryer on time. The washer and dryer cost $640, and the Hofstrands must pay 20 percent down. How much is this down payment?

7. The Hofstrands must pay the balance in twelve equal monthly installments. How much will they pay each month?

8. A store is selling winter coats at 15% off the regular price. How much would you save on a coat that regularly sells for $115?

9. Bob's health insurance pays 80% of his family's medical expenses. The hospital bill for his wife and new baby totals $2,025. How much of the bill will the insurance pay?

10. A bank pays 5.25% interest on savings accounts. How much interest will you earn on $125?

Check your answers on page 20 in the Answer Key for Book One. If you correctly answered eight of the ten problems, go to the next subskill. If not, complete the following Supplemental Exercise.

Supplemental Exercise for Subskill 13A

Read Subskill 13A again. Work through the examples as you read them. Then do this exercise.

1. What is 40% of 25?
2. What is 7.5% of 200?
3. What is 25% of 36?
4. What is 80% of 80?
5. What is 60% of 230?

6. Advisers recommend that a family spend no more than 25% of its income for housing. If your monthly income is $975, what is the most you should spend for housing?

7. Fran wants to charge a coat on a layaway plan. The coat costs $108 and she must make a down payment of 10% to hold it. How much money does she need for the down payment?

8. Certificates of deposit (CDs) are currently paying interest of 10.5% a year. What is the annual interest on a $1,000 CD?

9. The federal government withholds 7% of your pay for Social Security. If your pay is $750, how much will be withheld for Social Security?

10. Your raise for the new year is 5.75%. If your present pay is $18,250, how much more will you earn next year?

Check your answers on page 20 in the Answer Key for Book One. If you correctly answered eight of the ten problems, go to the next subskill. If not, ask your instructor for help.

Subskill 13B: Finding What Percent One Number Is of Another

After studying this subskill you will be able to find what percent one number is of another.

What percent of 45 is 9? To solve this problem, first, write the unknown percent as a fraction. Then use that fraction to write the problem as a proportion. And finally, solve the proportion for the unknown percent.

EXAMPLE: What percent of 45 is 9?

First, write the unknown percent as a fraction, using x to stand for the unknown.

$$x\% = \frac{x}{100}$$

Even though you don't know what the percent is yet, you can write it as a fraction because any percent equals a fraction with 100 as the denominator.

Then use the fraction to write the number as a proportion. Again, the part is on top and the whole is on the bottom in the percent side of the proportion, so it must be the same on the other side.

$$\frac{x}{100} = \frac{\text{Part}}{\text{Whole}}$$

Now which is 45, the part or the whole? Which is 9? Remember, the *part* usually comes just before or after the word "is." The *whole* usually follows the word "of." Look at the problem again.

What percent of 45 is 9?

45 must be the whole. 9 must be the part. The correct proportion is

$$\frac{x}{100} = \frac{9}{45}$$

Finally, solve the proportion for the unknown percent.

$$\begin{matrix} x & \searrow\nearrow & 9 & = 900 \\ 100 & \nearrow\searrow & 45 & = 45x \end{matrix}$$

$$45x = 900$$

$x = 20$

Answer: 9 is 20% of 45.

EXAMPLE: What percent of 80 is 120?

First, write the unknown percent as a fraction.

$$x\% = \frac{x}{100}$$

Then use the fraction to write the problem as a proportion.

$$\frac{x}{100} = \frac{\text{Part}}{\text{Whole}}$$

Remember: Part *is* . . . *of* whole.

The problem again: What percent *of* 80 . . . *is* 120?

The correct proportion is

$$\frac{x}{100} = \frac{120}{80}$$

Finally, solve the proportion for the unknown percent.

$$\frac{x}{100} \times \frac{120}{80} \qquad \begin{aligned} 120 &= 12{,}000 \\ 80 &= 80x \end{aligned}$$

$80x = 12{,}000$

$x = 150$

Answer: 120 is 150% of 80.

Here is one more example.

EXAMPLE: What percent of 26 is 8?

First, write the unknown percent as a fraction.

$$x\% = \frac{x}{100}$$

Then use the fraction to write the problem as a proportion.

$$\frac{x}{100} = \frac{8}{26}$$

Finally, solve the proportion for the unknown percent.

$$\frac{x}{100} \times \frac{8}{26} \qquad 8 \times 100 = 800 \qquad 26 \times x = 26x$$

$26x = 800$

$$26\overline{)800.00} = 30.76$$

```
     30.76
26)800.00
  -78
    20 0
   -18 2
     1 80
    -1 56
       24
```

If the division does not come out evenly, carry it out to two decimal places.

30.76 rounds to 30.8 — And round off to the nearest tenth.

$x = 30.8$

Answer: 8 is 30.8% of 26.

Check your skill at finding what percent one number is of another by doing this exercise.

Exercise for Subskill 13B

1. What percent of 200 is 84?
2. What percent of 40 is 68?
3. What percent of 4 is 3?
4. What percent of 20 is 19?
5. What percent of $909 is $145?

6. Your pay voucher shows that your gross wages were $716, but $88 were withheld for federal income taxes. What percent of your gross wages was withheld for income taxes? (Round your answer to the nearest tenth.)

7. Jefferson County has 33,015 registered voters. In the last election, only 19,809 people voted. What percent of the registered voters actually voted?

8. A CB radio usually sells for $140. It is marked down $21. What is the percent of the markdown?

9. Frank was given a raise of $45.75 a month. His salary before the raise was $802. What was the percent of his raise?

10. Your old lease has run out, and the landlord is offering you a new lease. The old rent is $480. The new rent will be $518.40. What

is the percent of the increase? (Hint: First, you must find the amount of the increase.)

Check your answers on page 20 in the Answer Key for Book One. If you correctly answered eight of the ten problems, go to the next subskill. If not, complete the following Supplemental Exercise.

Supplemental Exercise for Subskill 13B

Read Subskill 13B again. Work through the examples as you read them. Then do this exercise.

1. What percent of 20 is 15?
2. What percent of 12 is 9?
3. What percent of 50 is 17?
4. What percent of 42 is 6?
5. What percent of 30 is 40?

6. A car that cost $8,000 when it was new is worth $6,800 at the end of the first year. What percent of the original cost is the value of the car after one year?

7. John earned $450 interest on an investment of $5,000. What percent of the investment was the interest?

8. Carolyn earned $2,500 more this year than last year. Last year she earned $12,500. What percent of her last year's salary is the increase?

9. Mr. and Mrs. Blickstein bought a house for $75,000. In five years the value of the house increased $12,000. What percent of the original price is the increase?

10. Jill pays $45 a week for babysitting. She earns $400 a week at her job. What percent of her salary does Jill spend on babysitting?

Check your answers on page 20 in the Answer Key for Book One. If you correctly answered eight of the ten problems, go to the next subskill. If not, ask your instructor for help.

Subskill 13C: Finding an Unknown Number When Another Number Is a Certain Percent of It

After studying this subskill you will be able to find an unknown number when another number is a certain percent of it.

48 is 16% of what number? To solve this problem, follow the same steps as you did in the previous subskills. First, write the percent as a fraction. Then use that fraction to write the problem as a proportion. And finally, solve the proportion for the unknown number.

EXAMPLE: 48 is 16% of what number?

First, write the percent as a fraction.

$$16\% = \frac{16}{100}$$

Then use the fraction to write the problem as a proportion.

$$\frac{16}{100} = \frac{\text{Part}}{\text{Whole}}$$

Remember: Part is . . . of whole.

The problem again: 48 is 16% of what number?

The correct proportion is

$$\frac{16}{100} = \frac{48}{x}$$

Finally, solve the proportion for the unknown number.

$$\begin{matrix} 16 & 48 & 4{,}800 \\ 100 & x & = 16x \end{matrix}$$

$$16x = 4{,}800$$

$$x = 300$$

Answer: 48 is 16% of 300.

EXAMPLE: 66 is 150% of what number?

First, write the percent as a fraction.

$$150\% = \frac{150}{100}$$

Then use the fraction to write the problem as a proportion.

$$\frac{150}{100} = \frac{\text{Part}}{\text{Whole}}$$

The problem again: 66 *is* 150% *of* what number?

The correct proportion is

$$\frac{150}{100} = \frac{66}{x}$$

Finally, solve the proportion for the unknown number.

$$\begin{matrix} 150 & \times & 66 & = 6{,}600 \\ 100 & & x & = 150x \end{matrix}$$

$$150x = 6{,}600$$

$$x = 44$$

Answer: 66 is 150% of 44.

Check your skill at finding an unknown number when another number is a certain percent of it by doing this exercise.

Exercise for Subskill 13C

1. 90 is 45% of what number?
2. 36 is 120% of what number?
3. 49 is 35% of what number?
4. 30 is 2% of what number?
5. 5.7 is 19% of what number?

6. A long-distance phone call that Sylvia made cost $2.36. Because she called after 11 p.m., the cost was 40% of the daytime rate. How much would the call have cost in the daytime?

7. Glenna is a real estate agent. She gets a 5% commission on all of her sales. Last year she earned $22,500 in commissions. What were her total sales?

8. You can buy day-old bread at 65% of the price of fresh bread. If a loaf of day-old bread costs 52 cents, what does a loaf of fresh bread cost?

9. A suit is on sale for $101.25. The ad says the sale price is 45% of the regular price. What is the regular price of the suit?

10. A theater subscription costs $66 for four plays. This is only 55% of the cost of tickets to all four plays if you bought them separately. How much would the tickets cost if you did buy them separately?

Check your answers on page 13 in the Answer Key for Book One. If you correctly answered eight of the ten problems, go to the next subskill. If not, complete the following Supplemental Exercise.

Supplemental Exercise for Subskill 13C

Read Subskill 13C again. Work through the examples as you read them. Then do this exercise.

1. 15 is 150% of what number?
2. 248 is 40% of what number?
3. 18 is 30% of what number?
4. 9 is 25% of what number?
5. 100 is 80% of what number?

6. Annabelle bought an iron for 75% of the regular price. She paid $27 for the iron. What was the regular price of the iron?

7. Purple Cross Insurance Company paid 80% of Gene's hospital bill. The insurance company paid $1,840. What was the total bill?

8. Leon receives a commission of 5% on his sales. Last month his commission was $680. What were his sales for the month?

9. A building contractor pays 80% of the retail price for appliances. A stove costs a contractor $350. What is the retail price?

10. The weekday rate for rental cars is 65% of the weekend rate. The weekday rate is $29.25. What is the weekend rate?

Check your answers on page 21 in the Answer Key for Book One. If you correctly answered eight of the ten problems, go to the next subskill. If not, ask your instructor for help.

Subskill 13D: Figuring Interest

After studying this subskill you will be able to figure interest.

What Is Interest?

Interest is the money you pay for borrowing money. How much interest you pay on any loan depends on three things: 1) how much you borrow, 2) how long you keep the money before paying it back, and 3) the interest rate, which is a percent.

When you deposit money in a bank, the deposit is like a loan to the bank. Therefore, the bank pays you interest on the deposit. How much interest the bank pays depends on the same three things.

1. The amount of money you borrow, or the amount you deposit, is called the **principal.** It is a dollar amount.

2. How long you keep the money you borrow, or how long you leave your deposit in the bank before taking it out, is the **time** of the loan or deposit. It is figures in years or fractional parts of a year.

3. The interest **rate** is a percent of the principal. It is based on a period of one year. For example, if you leave $100 in the bank for one year, and the interest rate on your deposit is 5%, the bank will pay you $5.

The **amount** of interest you receive on a deposit, or pay on a loan, is a dollar amount.

How to Figure Interest

To figure the amount of interest on any deposit or loan, simply multiply the principal times the rate and get the interest for one year. Then multiply by the actual time to get the answer.

EXAMPLE: What is the amount of interest on $4,200 deposited at 8% for two years?

The principal is $4,200.
The rate is 8%.
The time is two years.

First, multiply the principal by the rate. Change the percent to a decimal for your multiplication.

8% = .08 Change the percent to a decimal.

$$\begin{array}{r} \$4{,}200 \\ \times\ \ .08 \\ \hline \$336.00 \end{array}$$

Multiply the principal by this decimal.

And get the amount of interest for one year.

Then multiply the interest for one year by the actual time of the deposit.

$$\begin{array}{r} \$336 \\ \times\ \ 2 \\ \hline \$672 \end{array}$$

The answer is $672.

EXAMPLE: You want to borrow $2,000 for three years. The credit union will loan you the money at 11.5% interest. How much interest will you have to pay?

First, multiply the principal by the rate.

11.5% = .115 Change the percent to a decimal.

$2,000 × .115 = 10000 + 2000 + 2000 = $230.000	Multiply the principal by the decimal. And get the amount of interest for one year.

$$\begin{array}{r} \$2,000 \\ \times .115 \\ \hline 10000 \\ 2000 \\ 2000 \\ \hline \$230.000 \end{array}$$

Then multiply the interest for one year by the actual time you will keep the money.

$$\begin{array}{r} \$230 \\ \times\ 3 \\ \hline \$690 \end{array}$$

Answer: $690.

Here is one more example.

EXAMPLE: What is the amount of interest on $15,000 borrowed at 12% for three months?

First, multiply the principal by the rate.

12% = .12 Change the percent to a decimal.

$$\begin{array}{r} \$15,000 \\ \times\ .12 \\ \hline \$1,800.00 \end{array}$$

Multiply the principal by the decimal. And get the amount of interest for one year.

Then multiply the amount of interest for one year by the actual time of the loan. But the actual time is only three months. What number should you multiply by?

Since there are twelve months in a year, three months are $\frac{3}{12}$ of a year.

Reduce this fraction to its lowest terms

$$\frac{3}{12} = \frac{1}{4}$$

And multiply by the fraction.

$$\$1,800 \times \frac{1}{4} = \$450$$

Answer: $450.

Check your skill at figuring interest by doing the exercise on page 275.

Exercise for Subskill 13D

1. You have borrowed $2,000 at 11% for one year. How much interest will you pay?

2. You have $400 in your savings account. Your bank pays 4.75% interest. How much interest will you have earned at the end of six months?

3. Brian borrowed $4,200 to buy a used car. He pays 14% interest on the two-year loan. How much interest will he pay at the end of the two years?

4. What is the interest charge on a $5,000 loan at 8% for three years?

5. What is the interest charge on a credit card balance of $38.25 at 18% for one month?

Check your answers on page 21 in the Answer Key for Book One. If you correctly answered four of the five problems, go to the Self-Check. If not, complete the following Supplemental Exercise.

Supplemental Exercise for Subskill 13D

Read Subskill 13D again. Work through the examples as you read them. Then do this exercise.

1. Mr. and Mrs. Ross got a $1,000 home improvement loan at 12% for one year. How much interest will they pay?

2. You have $300 that you can deposit in a savings account. A bank pays 5.75% interest. How much interest would the bank pay in six months?

3. You can deposit the $300 in a savings and loan that pays 6.5% interest. How much interest would you earn in six months at the savings and loan?

4. To buy a car, you borrow $6,500 at 14.25% for three years. How much interest will you pay?

5. Bill bought new tires for his truck. The total cost was $358. He financed the purchase at 18% for three months. How much interest will he pay?

Check your answers on page 21 in the Answer Key for Book One. If you correctly answered four of the five problems, go to the Self-Check. If not, ask your instructor for help.

SELF-CHECK FOR SKILL UNIT 13

1. What percent of 5 is 2?
2. 2 is 8% of what?
3. What is 2.5% of 180?
4. What is 5% of $12?
5. 72 is 120% of what?
6. What percent of 3 is 6?
7. What is 1.8% of $150?
8. 21 is 7% of what?

9. Frank has $1,050 in his savings account. The account earns 5.25% interest. How much interest does Frank earn in six months?

10. Ivan bought a VCR for $395. The sales tax was 5%. How much tax did he pay?

11. Chico pays $225 a month rent on his apartment. He earns $750 a month. What percent of his salary goes for rent?

12. A house worth $29,900 is insured for 80% of its value. If the house burns down, how much will the owner receive?

13. You have to buy a new water heater for $580. The bank will loan you the money for one year at 14%. How much interest will you pay?

14. Corey got a $20 raise. His pay before the raise was $160 a week. What percent of his original pay was the raise?

15. You are doing your federal income tax return. The form tells you to "enter 1% of Form 1040, line 31." The amount on Form 1040, line 31 is $10,250. What amount should you enter?

Check your answers on page 21. If you correctly answered twelve of the fifteen problems, you have proved that you have mastered this skill. If not, ask your instructor for help.

POSTTEST

This test is designed to determine whether or not you have mastered the skills in this book. Try to answer all of the questions, but you should not spend a lot of time on any one question. If you encounter difficulties, skip the question and return to it later.

You may establish a time limit upon your particular schedule. However, it is recommended that no more than two hours be allowed for completion of the test. Check your answers by using the separate Answer Key for Book One.

Skill Unit 1

1. Write this number in numerals:
seven hundred thirty thousand, three hundred two

2. Write 678,002 in words.

3. Which number is larger: 1,076 or 1,706?

4. Round 5,608 to the nearest hundred.

Skill Unit 2

5. $8 + 5 =$

6. $45 + 22 =$

7. $$\begin{array}{r} 44 \\ 41 \\ +13 \\ \hline \end{array}$$

8. $$\begin{array}{r} 758 \\ +261 \\ \hline \end{array}$$

9. The three sections of a newspaper have 24 pages, 36 pages, and 16 pages. How many pages are in the newspaper?

Skill Unit 3

10. $13 - 7 =$

11. $\begin{array}{r} 548 \\ -\,301 \\ \hline \end{array}$

12. $\begin{array}{r} 2{,}144 \\ -\;\;573 \\ \hline \end{array}$

13. A restaurant has 128 tomatoes in its kitchen. During the day the chef uses 77 tomatoes. How many are left?

Skill Unit 4

14. $5 \times 9 =$

15. $\begin{array}{r} 44 \\ \times\;\;2 \\ \hline \end{array}$

16. $\begin{array}{r} 65 \\ \times 32 \\ \hline \end{array}$

17. $\begin{array}{r} 311 \\ \times 248 \\ \hline \end{array}$

18. A photo album has 52 pages. Each page has 8 photos on it. How many photos are in the album?

Skill Unit 5

19. $56 \div 7$

20. $9\overline{)\,594}$

21. $13\overline{)\,936}$

22. $120\overline{)\,36840}$

23. Willie has 532 record albums, divided evently among 28 boxes. How many albums are in each box?

Skill Unit 6

24. $\frac{3}{5} = \frac{?}{25}$

25. Reduce $\frac{6}{18}$ to its lowest terms.

26. What is the lowest common denominator of $\frac{3}{4}$ and $\frac{2}{7}$?

27. Which is bigger: $\frac{4}{5}$ or $\frac{13}{20}$?

28. Change $2\frac{1}{6}$ to an improper fraction.

29. Change $\frac{17}{4}$ to a mixed number.

Skill Unit 7

30. $\frac{14}{21} + \frac{5}{21}$

31. $\frac{1}{4} + \frac{3}{16}$

32. $\frac{11}{15} - \frac{4}{15}$

33. $\frac{4}{5} - \frac{1}{2}$

34. $3\frac{2}{7} - \frac{5}{7}$

35. To get to Hendersonville from Pine Valley, Marlene has to drive through Lucasburg. Lucasburg is $17\frac{3}{7}$ miles from Pine Valley, and Hendersonville is $11\frac{3}{4}$ miles from Lucasburg. What is the total distance from Pine Valley to Hendersonville?

Skill Unit 8

36. $\frac{1}{2} \times \frac{5}{6} =$

37. $\frac{7}{10} \times 4$

38. $2\frac{2}{3} \times 4\frac{5}{6}$

39. $\frac{7}{8} \div \frac{4}{5}$

40. $\frac{2}{5} \div 3\frac{1}{8}$

41. Bob has to drive $5\frac{4}{5}$ miles to get to work. If he drives back and forth to work four times a week, how far does he have to drive?

Skill Unit 9

42. Write fifteen hundredths in decimals.

43. Which is larger: 5.13 or 5.099?

44. Round off 5.601 to the nearest hundredth.

45. 1.263 + 4.904

46. 5.309 − 2.372

47. A box of nuts weighs 4.56 pounds. A box of bolts weighs 2.77 pounds. How much heavier is the box of nuts?

Skill Unit 10

48. 24.57 × 1.4

49. 1.56 ÷ 1.3

50. George has cycled around his block 10.4 times. The distance around the block is 1.8 miles. How far has George cycled?

Skill Unit 11

51. A kennel has 16 employees to watch over 400 dogs. What is the ratio of dogs to employees?

52. $\frac{3}{15} = \frac{?}{35}$

53. To get the color dove-white, Ken mixes black paint and white paint in a ratio of 5:3. He used 20 gallons of black paint. How much white paint did he use?

Skill Unit 12

54. $\frac{77}{100} =$ ____%

55. Write 54% as a decimal.

56. Write 6.07 as a percent.

57. Write 60% as a fraction.

58. $\frac{5}{8} =$ ____%

Skill Unit 13

59. ____ = 25% of 56

60. 15 = ____% of 50

61. 4 = 16% of ____

62. You have $700 in a bank account that pays 5.25% simple yearly interest. How much interest would you earn in one year?

Skills Correlation Chart for Posttest

After you check your answers, look at the following chart. Circle the numbers of any problems you missed. Then review the subskill in which the skills for the problem you missed are explained.

	QUESTION NO.	SUBSKILL NO.	SUBSKILL NAME	PAGE NUMBERS
Skill Unit One Reading and Writing Whole Numbers	1	1A	Writing Whole Numbers	pages 1–11
	2	1A	Writing Whole Numbers	pages 1–11
	3	1B	Comparing Numbers	pages 11–15
	4	1C	Rounding Numbers Off	pages 15–19
Skill Unit Two Adding Whole Numbers	5	2A	Adding One-Digit Numbers	pages 21–24
	6	2B	Adding Two Numbers Without Carrying	pages 24–27
	7	2C	Adding Three or More One-Digit Numbers	pages 27–29
	8	2D	Adding With Carrying	pages 30–33
	9	2E	Solving Word Problems	pages 33–36
Skill Unit Three Subtracting Whole Numbers	10	3A	Subtracting One- and Two-Digit Numbers	pages 37–41
	11	3B	Subtracting Without Borrowing	pages 42–44
	12	3C	Subtracting With Borrowing	pages 44–49
	13	3D	Solving Word Problems	pages 50–52
Skill Unit Four Multiplying Whole Numbers	14	4A	Using the Multiplication Table	pages 54–58
	15	4B	Multiplying by One-Digit Numbers	pages 58–62
	16	4C	Multiplying by Two-Digit Numbers	pages 62–66
	17	4D	Multiplying by Three-Digit Numbers	pages 66–71
	18	4E	Solving Word Problems	pages 71–73
Skill Unit Five Dividing Whole Numbers	19	5A	Understanding Division	pages 75–80
	20	5B	Dividing by One-Digit Numbers	pages 80–89
	21	5C	Dividing by Two-Digit Numbers	pages 89–93
	22	5D	Dividing Larger Numbers	pages 94–97
	23	5E	Solving Word Problems	pages 97–101
Skill Unit Six Fractions	24	6B	Equivalent Fractions	pages 107–111
	25	6C	Reducing a Fraction to Its Lowest Terms	pages 111–114
	26	6D	Finding the Least Common Denominator	pages 114–123
	27	6E	Telling Larger Fractions from Smaller Ones	pages 128–131
	28	6F	Changing Improper Fractions to Mixed Numbers	pages 128–131
	29	6G	Changing Mixed Numbers to Improper Fractions	pages 131–133
Skill Unit Seven Adding and Subtracting Fractions	30	7A	Adding Like Fractions	pages 135–140
	31	7B	Adding Unlike Fractions	pages 140–145
	32	7C	Subtracting Like Fractions	pages 145–148
	33	7D	Subtracting Unlike Fractions	pages 148–150
	34	7E	Borrowing	pages 151–158
	35	7F	Solving Word Problems	pages 158–162
Skill Unit Eight Multiplying and Dividing Fractions	36	8A	Multiplying a Fraction by a Fraction	pages 164–171
	37	8B	Multiplying a Fraction by a Whole Number	pages 171–175
	38	8C	Multiplying Mixed Numbers	pages 175–179
	39	8D	Dividing Fractions	pages 179–182
	40	8E	Dividing Fractions, Whole Numbers and Mixed Numbers	pages 182–186
	41	8F	Solving Word Problems	pages 186–189

	QUESTION NO.	SUBSKILL NO.	SUBSKILL NAME	PAGE NUMBERS
Skill Unit Nine — Adding and Subtracting Decimals	42	9A	Reading and Writing Decimals	pages 191–199
	43	9B	Telling Higher Decimals from Lower Ones	pages 199–203
	44	9C	Rounding Decimals Off	pages 203–206
	45	9D	Adding Decimals	pages 206–209
	46	9E	Subtracting Decimals	pages 209–211
	47	9F	Solving Word Problems	pages 211–214
Skill Unit Ten — Multiplying and Dividing Decimals	48	10A	Multiplying Decimals	pages 216–219
	49	10B	Dividing Decimals	pages 219–225
	50	10C	Solving Word Problems	pages 225–228
Skill Unit Eleven — Ratio and Proportion	51	11A	Reading Ratios	pages 229–233
	52	11B	Solving Proportions	pages 233–238
	53	11C	Solving Word Problems	pages 238–242
Skill Unit Twelve — Percents	54	12A	Reading and Writing Percents	pages 243–247
	55	12B	Changing Percents to Decimals	pages 247–249
	56	12C	Changing Decimals to Percents	pages 249–252
	57	12D	Changing Percents to Fractions	pages 252–256
	58	12E	Changing Fractions to Percents	pages 256–259
Skill Unit Thirteen — Solving Percent Problems	59	13A	Finding What Number Is a Certain Percent of Another Number	pages 261–265
	60	13B	Finding What Percent One Number Is of Another	pages 266–269
	61	13C	Finding an Unknown Number When Another Number is a Certain Percent of It	pages 269–272
	62	13D	Figuring Interest	pages 272–275